D0875924

# BRITAIN
# IN OUR
# CENTURY

Arthur Marwick

# BRITAIN IN OUR CENTURY

## Images and Controversies

*with 149 illustrations*

 Thames and Hudson

*'the value of the work the Association has done
would be better appreciated 100 years hence.
If a photograph of the landing of William the
Conqueror was in existence we should travel far
to see it (hear! hear!)'*

Report of Final Meeting of
National Photographic Record Association, 1910

© 1984 Arthur Marwick

First published in the USA in 1985 by Thames and Hudson Inc.,
500 Fifth Avenue, New York, New York 10110

Library of Congress Catalog Card Number 84-50339

Printed and bound in the German Democratic Republic

# Contents

# Acknowledgments

A student of mine twenty years ago, now a colleague and close friend, Dr Henry Cowper has once again read my text and commented helpfully on it. Five years ago Charles Craig made the trip to Milton Keynes specially to ask me to act as external supervisor for his thesis on 'The British Documentary Photography as a Medium of Information and Propaganda During the Second World War, 1939–1945'. Charles in his turn has now put his great knowledge of photography at my disposal in commenting constructively on this book.

A book of this sort must be a team effort. I am grateful to my publishers for providing the understanding support which made it possible for the complete work to come out in exactly the form I intended. I would wish particularly to thank Sheila Lee who indefatigably, and with flair and sensitivity, carried through the picture research. Karen Hazell once again rose magnificently to all the demands of typing and preparing for publication the often difficult text together with the photographic captions.

My grateful thanks to all of these; I need scarcely add that the imperfections are my responsibility alone.

# Introduction:
# Images and Controversies

First of all, this book is an essay in the value to the historian of visual sources. Usually, illustrated historical works fall into two rather separate parts: a straightforward piece of historical writing provided by the historian, and a series of more or less relevant photographs added by the publisher, usually with more of an eye to audience appeal than serious enhancement of historical knowledge. This book follows the model established in my *The Home Front: The British and the Second World War*, where, having first selected the photographs, I then wrote the book in such a way as to bring out the significance of the photographs as historical documents. Without being fully aware of it, we learn much from visual sources: the quotation that prefaces this book points up how impoverished our knowledge is of ages pre-dating the invention of the camera. We need to become more conscious of what it is we can learn from visual sources and also of what we cannot learn. Television programmes abound in which photographs, etchings, cartoons are dispensed like ersatz champagne at a suburban wedding while everything communicated to the viewer is in fact contained on the soundtrack.

Much of what is most important in historical study, the relationships between cause and effect, between individual initiatives and the social context, or between material circumstances and intellectual, religious and political ideas, derives little illumination from visual sources (though the detailed reconstructions upon which such discussions must depend will often be greatly enhanced by the exploitation of visual evidence). While this book deals first of all with 'images', it sets out also to explore some of the major controversies which have divided historians in discussing Britain's history in this century (the significance for social change of the First World War, for example, or the extent of social conflict in the 1930s). There is no one simple account (let alone an account to be 'illustrated' by a careful selection of photographs, tendentiously captioned).

Though the visual documents should be savoured and lingered over, the printed text of this book is quite short. My concern is with how we have got to where we are now in the 1980s, with how far previous decades were similar to our own, and how far different. In concentrating on such issues and on the basic controversies to which they give rise, I have made no attempt at comprehensive factual coverage. For those seeking such detail, there are many other longer books, including my own *Britain in the Century of Total War*, and, for the more recent period, *British Society since 1945*. By sticking to major issues, without pretending that there is agreement over the really big ones, and by exploring visual images, I hope to bring out in strong colours what it is that has been happening to us in this most exciting century, our century.

I will not delay the reader here with a disquisition on the nature of photographic evidence. My text contains critical commentaries on the individual visual documents, sufficiently, I hope, to make the point that like all other sources, photographs are fallible, and that different types of photograph are fallible in different ways. Most of the pictures by 'art' photographers such as James Jarché or Humphrey Spender originally considered I finally rejected, preferring the simple (though nothing is ever that simple) 'newspaper photograph' (to stick to the term which obtained for much of the period), 'record photo' – which is the visual analogue of a social survey – publicity photo, or, occasionally, 'campaign photo', which can itself be an agent of social change. 'Documentary' and 'propaganda' are not such obvious terms as they may seem, and are to be used with care. My captions are usually short. Unfortunately photographic archives do not always have the information on provenance, usage, etc. that one would like to have. Where it seemed useful to quote original captions these are cited within quotation marks.

## Chapter One

# Into the Twentieth Century: 1900–1914

## Geography, Technology, Economics

Edward VII was the last British monarch to have an age called after him. Edwardian society (usually taken to include not just Edward, who reigned from 1901 to 1910, but also the first years of the reign of George V up to 1914) has been variously described. Obviously, it is important to get our picture of Edwardian society right if we are to understand what has changed and what has not changed in Britain since. A concept of American political science which has enjoyed a vogue among certain social historians is that of *modernization*. It has been defined by Peter Stearns thus:

> Modernization includes industrialization and the extension of a profit-making, market mentality to shops, farms, and even individual families to some extent. It embraces political change. A modern political society has an active state (whether totalitarian or democratic) and a population that is conscious of the national political process and insistent on having at least a pro forma voice in it; hence the universality of popular elections in all modern countries. Most of all, modernization involves a change in outlook. Compared to pre-modern people, modern man is rational, believing that planning and good order are important and possible; secular, with little or no interest in traditional religion; and progressive, holding that change is desirable and that the future is likely to be better than the past.[1]

One problem with the modernization thesis is that it seems to imply a unilinear idea of progress towards some universal goal. Actually, historical processes involve much that is contingent, much that is unexpected, decline as well as progress (even if one could agree over what constituted progress), disruptions, side alleys, gains and losses. For the purposes of this study, the thesis may also seem rather general and crude. Many of the developments given in the definition go back far into British history; industrialization, certainly, was under way by the end of the eighteenth century.

One extreme view is that by the outbreak of the First World War all of the fundamental characteristics of twentieth-century British society had established themselves. According to this view the great industrial and technological innovations of the late nineteenth century had worked themselves out so that Britain was already definitively an urban, mass-consumption society, with effective inter- and intra-urban transport systems, a popular press, mass advertising and sophisticated mass-marketing techniques. Thereafter, according to this view, despite wars, depression, and much conscious striving after social reform and social engineering, very little changed. The opposite view would paint Edwardian society as backward, undemocratic, slum-ridden, and altogether too dependent upon the industrial developments and social structures of the nineteenth century. It was possible, for those who warmed to the values, and privileges, of an earlier age, to view this image of Edwardian society nostalgically, to see Edwardian society as living in a golden age of tranquillity and security, washed away for good in the deluge of the First World War.

Would, then, a time-traveller from the mid-Victorian era have found Edwardian society disconcertingly 'modern' and alien, or would he have found it largely familiar and little changed in essence from that of the heyday of Queen Victoria? If we ourselves could be transported back to Edwardian society would we be struck by its familiarity or its strangeness, would we find it amazingly 'contemporary' or quite positively a bygone era?

Without any doubt the opening of the Edwardian age marked a new stage in the growth in the size and significance of cities. In 1871 there were only 37 towns in England and Wales with a population of over 50,000; 64 per cent of the people of these two nations still lived in towns and villages with a population of less than that figure. By 1901 the number of towns with more than 50,000 inhabitants had doubled. 'By the beginning of the twentieth century,' as Professor Donald Read has written, 'Britain's towns and cities had reached novel proportions, creating an urban crisis of scale and quality of life which the Edwardians were the first people to encounter.'[2] In the decade 1891–1901 the most noteworthy expansion of population took place in those towns which formed 'satellites' round major cities: for example, Smethwick to the west of Birmingham, Wallasey across the Mersey from Liverpool, and Croydon to the south of London. Shortly after the 1911 census several of the largest cities expanded their boundaries, giving administrative recognition to the growing urban sprawl: Birmingham now had 840,202 inhabitants, Glasgow 784,496, Liverpool 746,421, Manchester 714,333, Leeds 445,550, Newcastle 266,603. It was already recognized that 'Greater London', with a population of $7\frac{1}{4}$ million inhabitants, extended well beyond the territory administered by the London County Council. As an official government report put it:

> Among the various phases of the London traffic problem, one most important feature is the daily movement of a very large section of the population from their residences with an area of thirty miles round London to places of business in Central London and back again. . . .
> Street accidents are an unfortunate phase of the traffic problem and there is no hope that they can ever be entirely eliminated. . . .[3]

But traffic problems were by no means confined to London, and the admixture of horse-drawn vehicles, trams confined inflexibly to their tracks, and the odd motor vehicle could, earlier in the period, be a chaotic one: *Plate 1* shows a great confusion of open-top corporation electric trams and commercial horse-drawn traffic in Manchester; the sense of being barely 'into the twentieth century' is reinforced by the design of the electric street lights, still in a style derived from gas lamps. Today when, quite rightly, we worry about the pall of diesel and petrol fumes poisoning our streets, we forget that heavy rain acting upon copious horse droppings could often render streets less than salubrious for pedestrians.

Manchester was perhaps pre-eminent among the great provincial centres which added a special quality to Edwardian life taken as a whole. It was the home

of the Hallé Orchestra, the great liberal daily newspaper the *Manchester Guardian*, and of a vigorous intellectual life, featuring such distinguished playwrights as Stanley Houghton (see below, page 30). Other provincial cities manifested great civic initiative and pride also. The mid-Victorians had built magnificent town halls; the late Victorians bequeathed to the Edwardians such municipal enterprises as corporation tramways.

We can learn about the nature of the urban environment in Edwardian times, and attitudes towards it, from photographs, from surviving housing, from maps, and from the way in which new words came into use at that time. 'Suburbia' is a word of the 1890s; 'town planning' came in during the mid-1900s, the first ever Housing and Town Planning Act being the rather ineffective one of 1909; 'conurbation' is a word of the very end of the period. The upper-class writer C. F. G. Masterman, brilliant radical intellectual and hopeless Liberal politician,

1 Manchester, 17 December 1902. Record photo, showing intersection of Market Street (looking south) and Cross Street. Like all the photos in this chapter, taken by the clumsy plate-camera.

wrote in his *The Condition of England*, published in 1909, of the 'suburbans', whose male population

> is sucked into the City at daybreak, and scattered again as darkness falls. It finds itself towards evening in its own territory in the miles and miles of little red houses in little silent streets, in number defying imagination. Each boasts its pleasant drawing-room, its bow-window, its little front garden, its high-sounding title – 'Acacia Villa' or 'Camperdown Lodge' – attesting unconquered human aspiration.[4]

This 'suburbia' still exists; it is now inner-city suburbia, and, in most cases, has gone up in the world socially. The houses we are speaking of almost all had a ponderous scaled-down classical appearance. The far-flung, massive, suburban estates, with houses built in a freer and sometimes more 'modernistic' style, are still in the future.

Whatever the contemporary emphasis placed on the problems of the towns, 21.9 per cent of the population of England and Wales still lived in what the 1911 census, somewhat imprecisely, referred to as 'rural districts'. Out of a total employed population (Great Britain) of 12,927,000, 1,436,000 were in agricultural occupations. British farming had suffered seriously in the late nineteenth century, though pastoral farming never as badly as crop farming.

Central to Britain's historical and social development is its remarkable geographical diversity contained within a limited space: mainland Britain is an island only 600 miles long and, at its greatest extent, 320 miles wide. This island can be roughly divided into three geographical types: lowland, upland and highland. In the lowland regions of the south lay the original agricultural wealth of England, while it was amid the mineral wealth of the upland areas of south Wales, the Pennines and central Scotland that the Industrial Revolution took place, creating in some parts an ugliness unsurpassed in Western Europe and in others a strange beauty of mingled industrial and natural landscape; the highland regions of central Wales and of Scotland remained 'unspoiled', left to decay while the rest of the land prospered, unexploited (save in the interests of a few wealthy landowners), though rich in potential hydro-electric power. While the south-east corner of the country enjoys an untypical proportion of dry and sunny weather, the rest of the island is subject to frequent mists and rain showers, heavy rain being commonest in the west, drizzle a feature of the east. The north-west coast of Scotland benefits from the benign influence of the Gulf Stream, but in general Scotland is subject to wetter, windier, and more inhospitable weather conditions than the rest of the country.

In Edwardian times regional differences still stood out very starkly: to go from London into rural Kent, or from industrial Birmingham into the heart of Worcestershire, was to move from one sub-culture into another. In farming generally there was a slight revival in the Edwardian period, and some increase in investment in 'modern' farming machinery. But the overwhelming impression one gets is of not really being that far away from the world of Thomas Hardy (*Plate* 2). Although the employment of women as farm labourers was in decline, in 1914 there were 190,000 females employed in the various branches of agriculture, and at harvest, or haymaking time, it was still very necessary in the villages and country areas to mobilize all available female labour, as also child labour. *Plate* 2, though highly composed, does bring out authentically the part of both women and children in the agricultural effort. Of the entire company, only

two small boys and one little girl (and she has a hat on the ground beside her), are not wearing some kind of headgear. The pinched faces of the children have that characteristic 'old-before-their-time' look.

As had been the pattern from the earliest days of industrialization, the population of Great Britain (40.8 million, that is to say about 10 million families, in 1911) was increasing, though less markedly so than in the nineteenth century. The other Britannic island, Ireland, in its entirety part of the United Kingdom, had never been fully affected by industrialization, and was, in contrast, declining in population (just over 4 million in 1911). The most appalling conditions of deprivation and starvation were now a thing of the past, for, thanks to the 'killing Home Rule with kindness' policies of the Edwardian Conservatives, the peasantry were establishing themselves as independent proprietors. Nevertheless, Ireland was still essentially a poverty-ridden agrarian society. Dublin had the Georgian elegance of the chosen city of the former Protestant ruling class, but there was scarcely the real wealth to support its pretensions. The heavy hand of industrialization was to be detected only amid the shipyards and engineering works of Belfast: the prospect of regular wages had sucked in both Protestants (the majority community in the surrounding area) and Catholics; urban squalor existed on a scale to match anything found amid the worst slums of mainland Britain.

Central to any concept of modernization is the increasingly potent interaction between science and technology on the one side, and economic growth and almost all other social phenomena on the other. It is a cliché of the polemics of

2 Haymakers near Bewdley, Worcestershire, 1910. This is a deliberately composed photograph, yet basically taken for record purposes.

our own day that from the mid-nineteenth century Britain's rulers had failed to give due attention to the crucial significance of scientific innovation and technological education. The cliché is no recent coinage. 'The majority of those who have received what is known as a "liberal" education', lamented the effervescent Liberal backbencher Sir Leo Chiozza Money, 'could not intelligently explain the ringing of an electric bell or the action of their own hearts. This deplorable neglect of science', he continued, 'is sadly handicapping us as a nation in every department, and it is a notable fact that the majority of recent scientific discoveries have been made in other lands.'[5] Broadly, the cliché was accurate, and any improvements in the Edwardian period were distinctly modest ones. Opening the National Physical Laboratory in 1902, the Prince of Wales described it as 'almost the first instance of the State taking part in scientific research'. In the same year the Government took over the Imperial Institute, which sponsored some scientific research related to industry, and in 1907 the Imperial College of Science and Technology was founded. In 1914 the government grant to the National Physical Laboratory was still no more than £7,000 per annum, with an additional grant for aeronautical research. A little noticed sub-section of the 1911 National Insurance Act made provision for a medical research fund, and it was out of this that, just before the war, the Medical Research Committee began to take shape.[6]

However, if we recognize expansion and innovation in communications' technology as a critical feature of twentieth-century society, then we must also recognize that, as with urbanization, the Edwardian era does mark an important stage. The telephone was the convenience of the upper-middle class, the motor car the luxury of the rich, the aeroplane the passion of the star-struck few, and radio communication only just revealing its potential. But already the motor bus was revealing its superiority to electric trams as well as to horse-drawn vehicles (though the former still had a long life ahead of them, as, indeed, had horse-drawn vehicles for private commercial purposes). In the words of the government report quoted earlier: 'the convenience of the mechanically-propelled vehicle for passenger purposes very rapidly asserted itself, and today it accounts for fully 94 per cent of the passenger vehicles met with on the roads round London.'[7] Relatively minor advances in newspaper technology hastened the progress of the cheap, mass-circulation press. The *Daily Mirror*, essentially a picture paper aimed at the relatively prosperous middle class, overtook the *Daily Mail*, essentially aimed at a lower-middle-class readership, and in 1912 became the first daily to achieve a circulation of one million.

The other area of technological and industrial development of most significance in the present context is that of chemicals, particularly with reference to domestic toiletries and food processing. These changes are in turn allied to changes in consumer advertising and in retailing techniques. It was, for example, in 1904 that a team at Cadburys, including N. P. Booth, the Chief Chemist, were able to announce that they could now emulate the Swiss in blending fresh milk (rather than milk powder) with their chocolate. The Cadburys Dairy Milk advertisements joined those for soaps and ready-prepared soups in the stations frequented by the urban multitudes. The deliberate up-market quality of the elegantly drawn dried-soup mix advertisement reproduced in *Plate 3* drives home the point that the main target was the aspiring lower-middle class. It is hard to

3 Poster advertising dried-soup mix, 1907. The poster bears the signature of the artist, Louis Weierter, and, at the bottom, the name of the Fleet Street 'Advertiser's agent'.

believe that a woman employing a living-in cook, as portrayed, would wish to see her family on pre-packed soup, though no doubt the powder had the other uses listed. Lower-middle-class families, however, would indeed have had some servant to do the cooking as required.

One rather simple way of breaking up the whole modern age of industrialization and technological innovation into separate 'periods' is by reference to the long-term movements in the trade cycle. The 'period' from 1849 to 1873 was one of rising prices and generally, though with many short-term slumps along the way, a time of prosperity and good profits; it is thus sometimes spoken of as 'the mid-Victorian boom'. From 1873 to the late 1890s, the long-term cycle was one of falling prices, so that this period is sometimes spoken of as 'the Great Depression'. From the late 1890s, and throughout the so-called 'Edwardian boom', prices were again rising. It is useful to look at some of the detailed implications of the behaviour of the trade cycle, though great care should be exercised in too readily attributing, for example, moods of optimism to rising prices, and of pessimism to falling prices. For the first part of the Edwardian period, the effects of industrial boom were a slight overall improvement in conditions for wage-earners. The rich throughout got richer, and thus, towards the end of the period, when wages remained static while prices continued to rise, the contrast between rich and poor stood out more sharply than ever. The years after 1910 were marked by much industrial conflict.

More crucial than the trade cycle, however, are the performance of the economy relative to other countries, and the principles upon which economic affairs are conducted. Britain was the world's greatest trading nation (35 per cent of all world trade in 1900), but her share was insistently being eaten into by other powers, particularly Germany and America. She was still holding her long lead in the older heavy industries, though this too was being overhauled. It was disquieting that her single most important export industry was actually based on a raw material – coal – not on manufactured goods. In the new and portentous chemical, electrical and motor industries, Britain was behind her foreign competitors. The situation in the Edwardian period must not be exaggerated: for all the poverty of that society, Edwardians at all levels were much better off than their German counterparts. But without doubt, the origins of future British economic problems are apparent at this time; so too was a determination not to do anything about them. Direct investment in technological education sat uneasily with, if not directly contrary to, the prevailing economic orthodoxy, that of laissez faire, of leaving everything to the free operation of market forces. The state, of course, had long taken on many of the functions assumed in the definition of modernization quoted at the beginning of this chapter; but, as Professor R. H. Tawney once put it, 'the Government, apart from the Post Office and a few naval and military establishments, did not own or administer business undertakings, did not concern itself with the organisation of industry or the marketing of its products, did not attempt directly to influence the course of trade, and rarely intervened, except as a borrower, in the money or capital markets.'[8]

## Social Structure

Whatever arguments may rage today over whether or not contemporary Britain is a class society, any such arguments would have sounded strange to Edwardian ears. Indeed, it can cogently be argued that this period marked the culmination of the evolution of a carefully delineated class structure embracing practically the whole nation, rather than just the most industrially advanced parts of it. Such a statement would need the qualification that some aspects of consolidation within classes continued into later periods; but, in general, future developments were more usually to be towards compression of the social pyramid, disruption of class categories, and blurring of class lines.

It should be noted that there is no complete consistency of usage in the Edwardian language of 'class' (the simple and familiar word which I prefer: pedants say 'social stratification'; polemicists insist that the word be confined to the narrow technical usage of Marxist-Leninism). Distinguishing three major classes and one 'under-class', the Edwardian social commentator C. F. G. Masterman labelled them, respectively, the 'conquerors', the 'suburbans', the 'multitude', and the 'prisoners'. Equally readily one could speak of the upper class, the middle class (or, more usually, 'the middle classes' – contemporaries recognized the range of occupations and incomes comprised within this one class), the working class (or, again, 'the working classes'), and the 'residuum' or 'sunken people' (to use Victorian and Edwardian labels) or 'under-class' (to use the phrase favoured by present-day sociology).

The middle class did *not* overthrow the aristocracy at the time of the Great Reform Act of 1832 or of the Repeal of the Corn Laws in 1846 (or at any other time); nor does it make much sense to speak pejoratively of the bourgeoisie 'selling out' to the aristocracy, though what such quaint phraseology does reflect is the important fact that in the nineteenth century the older landed class amalgamated with top business and professional people to form the upper class as it was in the Edwardian period. This class had a near monopoly of political power, dominated business and finance, and held about two-thirds of the country's total wealth. It had its own particular institutions, the handful of oldest established and most prestigious public schools, certain colleges – or certain societies within these colleges – at Oxford and Cambridge, certain clubs and certain regiments, its rituals and *rites de passage* (country house parties, débutante balls) and its special role in such events as Royal Ascot and the Henley Regatta. At the Royal Academy's annual private view (subject of a famous late Victorian painting by William Powell Frith) members of the upper class viewed not the paintings, but each other, and the handful of aspirants to upper-class status. In *Plate 4* the Hon. George Crichton, second son of the fourth Earl of Erne, married to Lady Mary Dawson, the youngest daughter of the second Earl of Dartrey, a captain in the Coldstream Guards, is seen emerging (wearing top hat) into Piccadilly. There his presence is registered by several middle-class bystanders (in bowlers), and one conspicuously working-class one (in cloth cap). The photographer, wittingly, was interested in the two celebrities and their companion; unwittingly he clearly presents the three Edwardian classes.

The Crichtons, with their blue, if not terribly ancient, blood, can be compared with another eminent figure who had just about made it into the border territories between the upper class, and what we can reasonably term the upper-middle class. The *Birmingham Magazine* in 1899 had described the Grange, Erdington (*Plate 5*), as 'a perfect example of all that the home of a cultured English gentleman should be'. The same magazine, however, also referred to the residence as 'a typical English dwelling', adding, most revealingly:

> It is manifestly the home of a man of taste and culture; the exterior and the interior unite to proclaim that the occupant is one to whom the mart and the counting house are not the be-all and end-all of existence.[9]

Benjamin Stone was born in Birmingham in 1838, the son of the manager of the glass manufacturing business of George Bacchus and Sons. In 1860 father and son became proprietors of this company, changing its name to Stone, Fawdry and Stone, diversifying almost immediately into paper manufacture, founding the company of Smith, Stone and Knight in 1862. While the original company making high-quality engraved glassware soon started losing money, the second more utilitarian business, making wrapping and corrugated paper, and paper bags, prospered. By the end of the century Benjamin Stone owned three factories in Birmingham and one in Bristol. He had also established the Cliffe Hill Granite Company which found its own profitable niche in the urban growth of the time

4 The Hon. George Crichton leaving the private view of the Royal Academy, 1 May 1914, with his wife Lady Mary Crichton. 'Society' news photo.

5 Afternoon tea at the Grange, home of Sir Benjamin Stone, July 1899. The *Birmingham Magazine* described the house as 'a typical English dwelling. It is reached from Birmingham by pleasant country roads, and lies embosomed in trees in the midst of a stretch of farmland. The drive to the entrance is bounded by stately lime trees, and the grounds are covered with clinging ivy.'

by using granite from the company's Leicestershire quarries to build the streets of suburban Birmingham. Barron Road and Norman Road, in the Northfield housing estate, were named after two of Stone's own sons.

It was in 1877 that Stone, his wife and his six children moved to the Grange (today, having gone the way of many such dwellings, it is a nursing home). Active in local politics, he was a founder member of the Birmingham Conservative Association, and first Mayor of Sutton Coldfield in 1886. He received his knighthood in 1892 for his work on behalf of the Primrose League, and in 1895 he was returned unopposed as Conservative member for the East Birmingham constituency. Stone is a good example of the important provincial figure of the time whose own status signified that of the provinces; it is by this very token that he is not properly a member of the upper class, which is always characterized by its strong metropolitan links. To be a gentleman, it was not necessary to be upper class; it was, however, necessary to exhibit a certain scorn for 'the Mart and the

6 Looking across the beach at Scarborough, *c*.1913. Unwittingly, the photographer has pinned down for us in the foreground ordinary middle-class fashion.

Counting House'. For Stone, in fact, photography became a passion, and it was a member of his National Photographic Record Association who made the utterance which prefaces this book.

Below the upper-middle class of highly successful local businessmen, and the more prestigious professions, we come to the solid middle class of professionals, salary earners, farmers and other businessmen, the backbone of the many smaller provincial towns where there was no greatly developed industry. Their respectable, though hardly very splendid, garb appears on the foreground figures in the view over the quintessentially middle-class spa town of Scarborough (*Plate 6*). In the Edwardian period, if not earlier, it is particularly important to single out the lower-middle class, which sprang into being in response to the expansion in industry and commerce. Clerical work in a large office might in general contour appear similar to machinists' work in a medium-sized factory (*Plate 7*). But clerical work was clean; white collars and educated accents were *de rigueur*. In the picture of the Bournville General Office, no machines are in evidence; all work is done with pen and ink. The typewriter was only beginning its rise to prominence, a process which would bring with it a whole new type of women's employment, but which did not as yet seriously menace the male clerk.

Undoubtedly some clerical workers had working-class family backgrounds. Thus there is controversy among historians over exactly where the boldest class lines should be drawn. There is an argument that the 'respectable' working class was nearer to the lower-middle class than it was to the working-class 'roughs'. At the time, contemporaries spoke of the 'labour aristocracy'; some later commentators have used this group, with its alleged adhesion to middle-class values, to explain how a revolutionary sentiment in the working class was damped down. Yet, as has just been indicated, working conditions for manual workers, however highly skilled, *were* different from those of white-collar workers. While there is certainly a line to be drawn between those of the working class who had more or less regular employment, and those in the residuum with only casual, desperately badly paid, or no employment, most of the evidence, both subjective and quantitative, suggests a very real, if slightly porous, boundary between the lower-middle class and the working class. The rich, said Masterman, 'despise the Working People; the Middle Classes fear them.'[10] On the eve of the war the average wage for the adult male industrial worker was about £75 per annum; there was a colossal gap between that and the average annual income of the salaried class of £340.[11] Some upper-working-class families did, it is true, just manage to keep one servant; but the secure retention of the services of at least one servant was very much a badge of middle-class status. Class divisions were reproduced by the educational system: secondary schools were very much the preserve of the middle classes, few working-class children ever progressing beyond the rudimentary disciplines acquired in the free elementary schools. All in all, there were only 200,000 secondary-school pupils in 1914.

7 Bournville General Office, 1912. Record picture for the factory's own archive.

8 Family tea at
Christmastime, *c.*1900.
Almost certainly a
'respectable' working-
class family, though
could be a lower-middle-
class family.

The family shown at tea in *Plate 8* cannot be definitively ascribed to the
working class, rather than lower-middle class, though more of the indications are
of the former status – the Christmas decorations are somewhat meagre and
haphazard, the character in the corner appears still to be in his working clothes,
and the tea is very much a plain one. Class stereotypes were the meat and drink of
*Punch* cartoons. The *Punch* stereotype was of a rough working class, highly
distinct from the lower-middle class; the workers (*Plate 9*) are portrayed as
feckless, if sometimes humorous, rather than as respectable artisans.

The Edwardian upper class ate enormous meals. In common with the upper-
middle class its main meals were: breakfast, lunch and afternoon tea, then dinner,
eaten about eight o'clock in the evening. Any generalizations about the eating
times of the other social classes must be qualified by a re-emphasis of the
geographical variousness of British society. However, we do have specimen
menus (published during the First World War, but referring to prewar days) for
both a lower-middle-class household, and a labourer's household. The middle-
class menu was as follows:

FRIDAY

*Breakfast*: fishcakes, sardines, fried bacon, bread, butter, marmalade, tea,
coffee.
*Dinner*:    rabbits, potatoes, gooseberry tart, rice pudding, cream, sugar.

*Tea*:      bread, butter, jam, cakes, tea.
*Supper*:   cheese, biscuits, bread, butter, cakes, cocoa. . . .

## SUNDAY

*Breakfast*: bacon, poached eggs, bread, butter, marmalade, tea, coffee.
*Dinner*:   roast beef, Yorkshire pudding, roast potatoes, rice pudding, gooseberry tart, cream, sugar.
*Tea*:      bread, butter, jam, cakes, tea.
*Supper*:   cheese, biscuits, bread, butter, cake, cocoa, milk. . . .

## WEDNESDAY

*Breakfast*: fried bacon, sardines, bread, butter, marmalade, tea, coffee.
*Dinner*:   roast mutton, jelly, potatoes, cabbage, gooseberry tart, pancakes.
*Tea*:      bread, butter, cakes, jam, marmalade, tea.
*Supper*:   cheese, biscuits, bread, butter, cakes, cocoa, milk. . . .

## THURSDAY

*Breakfast*: chicken and tongue mould, bread, butter, marmalade, tea, coffee.
*Dinner*:   cold mutton, potatoes, salad, curry, rice pudding, stewed fruit.
*Tea*:      bread, butter, cakes, jam, marmalade, tea.
*Supper*:   cheese, biscuits, bread, butter, cakes, cocoa, milk. . . .

The labourer's prewar menu was:

## FRIDAY

*Breakfast*: bread, cheese, tea.
*Dinner*:   potatoes, bread, tea.
*Tea*:      bread, butter, tea. . . .

"LOR, BILL, WE 'VE GOT INTO A FUST-CLAWSS CARRIAGE."          "YER DON'T SAY SO! AND ME WIV ODD SOCKS ON!"          9 *Punch* cartoon, 1909.

SUNDAY

*Breakfast*: bacon, bread, toast, tea.
*Dinner*:　meat, potatoes, Yorkshire pudding.
*tea*:　　bread, pie, tea cakes, tea. . . .

WEDNESDAY

*Breakfast*: bacon, bread, tea.
*Dinner*:　meat, bread, tea.
*Tea*:　　eggs, 'dip', bread, tea.

THURSDAY

*Breakfast*: bread, butter, tea.
*Dinner*:　meat, bread, 'dip', tea.
*Tea*:　　meat, bread, butter, tea.[12]

Few in the working class, and none in the under-class, could aspire to this menu, which could really only hold good when times themselves were good. Most social surveys of the time concentrated on the very real problem of working-class poverty. The economist A. L. Bowley, using the bare definition of the 'poverty line' adopted by Seebohm Rowntree (a pioneer of social welfare policies) in 1901, found 16 per cent of the working class living in what he called 'primary' poverty, as distinct from 'secondary' poverty brought about by unwise disposition of available income. His unequivocal conclusion was that 'to raise the wages of the worst-paid workers is the most pressing social task with which the country is confronted today'. Poor diet gave the working class another characteristic which distinguished them from the rest of society, their small stature.

Though the leasing of town, or even country, residences by the upper class was not unknown (almost invariably in the case of a second property), the standard practice for most of the middle class was the actual purchase of a house; the inheritance of a home thus became a reasonable prospect, at least for eldest sons. The working class in general rented their homes, usually from private landlords. Middle-class houses had bathrooms, working-class housing was not usually so equipped. With an estimated shortage of houses in 1913 of between 100,000 and 120,000, much working-class housing was appalling. Of Carmarthen in Wales, the Medical Officer of Health reported that there were houses 'that may aptly be described as squalid hovels and hot-beds of diseases'.[13] Housing conditions in the Northumberland mining village of Stanley were described by Bowley as 'horrifying'. Many of the best known photographs from the Edwardian era are deliberate pieces of social reporting bringing out the dreadful character of the slums. *Plate 10* is in fact a record photo designed to give the authorities a measure of the social problems facing them: deliberate stress is placed on the one water-pump, still in 1906 supplying all the houses in this nineteenth-century court. Perhaps the photograph also symbolically stresses the central role of the working-class housewife.

We have noted state concern for social welfare as an assumed characteristic of the 'modern' state; we have also noted the laissez faire inclinations of Edwardian governments. One of the longest running controversies in twentieth-century historical studies is over the scope and status to be attributed to the social reforms of the Edwardian era: do they deserve to be regarded as forming the origins of the modern Welfare State, or were they merely the continuance of a late-Victorian tradition of minimal piecemeal reform? In power from 1906, the Liberals introduced free meals and free medical services in the elementary schools, non-contributory old-age pensions (five shillings a week – not nearly enough to live on – at age seventy, subject to means test and good character), labour exchanges, and an eight-hour day for the miners. *Plate 11* is an example of photography as an actual 'agent' in a social reform campaign, the campaign against 'sweated labour', usually, as here, carried out in a family's own home. The agitation against sweated labour led to the passing of the Trades Boards Act of 1910 which laid down minimum standards. The reality of sweated working conditions was appalling enough, though it is probable that the baby has been deliberately posed for maximum effect. Part 1 of the great National Insurance Act of 1911 provided basic health insurance and treatment for practically everyone earning under £250

10 A Liverpool court, 1906. Record photo by Liverpool Council.

25

11 Toymaking at home, *c*.1906. A 'campaign photograph'.

per annum (but excluding dependants); Unemployment Insurance (Part 2 of the Act) applied only to the $2\frac{1}{4}$ million members of the building, shipbuilding, and iron and steel trades, the ones most affected by fluctuations in employment. Without doubt there is room for legitimate debate among historians, but in my view these reforms fall within a limited, filling-the-gaps tradition, bearing no more than the faintest distant relationship to the idea of a comprehensive Welfare State.

The Edwardians had no detergents, no insecticides, let alone electrical mod. cons. Theirs was an age above all of spit and polish, of scouring, lighting fires and humping coal scuttles around. The divide between those who toiled and those who only toyed with work was almost absolute, as was the divide between those with servants and those without, the divide between those who were masters and mistresses and those who were servants. No wonder the divide was so jealously policed; no wonder there was such a meticulous hierarchy even among servants themselves. Domestic service was the single largest occupation in Edwardian Britain: of the 2,600,000 so employed, 2,100,000 were women. Very nearly as degrading an occupation – for both males and females – was that of living-in shop assistants. As a flood of evidence, tapped by the war experience, was to reveal, living – practically as a serf – under someone else's roof is what most irked the daughters, and some of the sons, of the Edwardian working class. Upon working-class women as a whole fell the task of fighting dirt and dust with the most rudimentary facilities. *Plate 12*, another record photo, this time for a section on

'London's street industries' in the book *Living London*, shows us London's step-girls. The photograph is accompanied by this descriptive statement:

> It is a curious calling, but those who follow it no doubt prefer it, with all its drawbacks, to employment which would impose restrictions on their liberty. As a class they are in a sense alien to the hard-driven sisterhood of more mature years who offer their services as charwomen.[14]

We shall consider the position of women in the next section; for the moment the obvious pride in appearance of these girls is well worthy of attention.

In recent years much vital scholarship has been directed at the particular cultural forms developed in, or for, the working class. Elaborate and sophisticated theories have been developed, representing popular culture as a mere tool through which the ruling class exercises hegemony. Others have seen Edwardian working-class culture as exhibiting a defensive mentality, a turning away from political activism to the soft joys of pub and music hall. Others again have detected a mix of authentic working-class cultural traditions with products and activities offered freely on the open market by entrepreneurs with nothing more sinister in mind than commercial gain. Mass professional football as a spectator sport had its origins in the desire of nineteenth-century upper-class and middle-class do-gooders to bring sport to the workers. But, as much as anything ever could be, the whole activity was taken over by the working class, though, of course, clubs were sponsored and run by local businessmen. *Plate 13* shows Liverpool supporters in London for the FA Cup Final of April 1914. First of all, it is noteworthy how far these working men had come in support of their team (both teams, indeed, in the 1914 final were from the North). In a new way the

12 Step-cleaning, *c.*1902. Obviously carefully composed, this is a record photo which gives a pretty authentic picture of the nature of the calling.

13 Liverpool supporters on their way to the Oval for the 1914 FA Cup Final, Liverpool v Burnley.

working-class masses were visible to gentlemanly commentators in the metropolis. The hired cart is primitive, though motor transport can be seen in the background: the main journey would have been by train. The starched collars are as striking as the elaborate insignia of club and local loyalty.

Heavy drinking, by both men and women, was a common feature of working-class life, though many 'respectable' working men, including many Labour leaders, were teetotal. In the early 1900s a Conservative government had been successful in closing down a number of licensed premises throughout the country. The drink trade was subject to regulation, but pubs throughout England were able to open at 5 or 6 am, closing at half-past midnight in London, 11 pm in other towns, and 10 pm in country districts; in Scotland the hours varied between 10 am to 9 pm, and 10 am to 11 pm. On Sundays pubs were closed in both Scotland and Wales, but in England they were open for a couple of hours in the middle of the day, then again in the evening. Recent work on music-hall songs has brought out the way in which they often reflected the deeper realities of working-class life. Film was the new working-class entertainment of the Edwardian era, a further point, perhaps, indicating that this age should be regarded as the genuine beginning of the twentieth century rather than the ending of the nineteenth century.

## Values

The fundamental unit of Edwardian society was the family – the point of the music-hall song 'My Old Dutch' was that the elderly husband was about to be split from his wife (the 'Old Dutch' – abbreviation of 'duchess') as they each went into a different section of the workhouse. Many women did hard, unpleasant work outside the home, but the ideal to which the Edwardian male – from the respectable working man upwards – aspired, was to have his wife at home to look after the house. Women in the upper and middle classes were essentially seen as ornaments and foils to their menfolk. Edwardian photographs (see, for example, *Plate 2*) so often show children with old faces, looking almost like little stunted adults. Life certainly was harsh for children; although there is evidence in all social classes of genuine affection for them, belief in their innate tendencies towards evil, in the need for violent punishment and in a harsh and austere regime generally, was still very strong. The school attendance laws looked better in the letter than in the practice; they were easily bent by employers who wanted cheap child labour, parents who wanted additional income from their children, and parents and children who saw little value in schooling. Officially, the school-leaving age was fourteen, but children who had secured a certificate of 'proficiency' or of regular attendance could leave at thirteen. In the respectable working class it was a sign of status to keep girls as well as boys at school until at least the leaving age had been reached. It was thought much less worthwhile to keep girls on at school thereafter than it might be for their brothers, so the girls would be seen off into one of the respectable but badly paid jobs, such as shop assistant or secretary.

Edwardian society still observed strictly most of the moral canons of Victorianism. In the highest social circles, centring on Edward VII himself, there was undoubtedly much permissiveness, but it was not a permissiveness that could ever be publicly boasted of, so that the risks for an Edwardian lady were always considerably higher, and the freedoms considerably lower, than for an Edwardian gentleman. Middle-class and respectable working-class society aspired, without much hypocrisy, to a genuine observance of Victorian standards; but behaviour which could be condoned, or not known about, in a man could spell ruin for a woman. Most feminists in the Edwardian period believed in what they called 'purity'; their aim was to get all men to observe the ideal standard which respectable women themselves had to observe. There were women in the Edwardian period arguing for 'liberation' for women, rather then 'purification' for men. But apart from the taboos and conventions from which it was hard for even the most resolute woman to escape, there was the problem of the chanciness of existing methods of contraception. Rubber male and female contraceptives had been developed in the previous century; and there was a whole range of other secret remedies on the market – spermicides, pessaries, and, of course, abortifacients, ranging from the dubious, to the irrelevant, to the downright dangerous. Upper- and middle-class families were practising contraception within the family unit: but the woman who sought to go outside the family was still in a world of menacing shadows.

After the long Victorian silence in which novels had come near to denying the existence of any sexual drives at all in women, some Edwardian novels and plays were beginning to hint again that women might have greater sexual appetites than men. Elinor Glyn's *Three Weeks*, first published in 1907, was a bestseller, though also violently attacked as being sordid and immoral. Glyn later said of her heroine that she was 'beyond the ordinary laws of immorality'. But usually even the most avant-garde Edwardian novels carried the implication that celibacy was no real hardship for a woman. One of the finest tributes to liberated but independent womanhood was made in the celebrated play of 1911 *Hindle Wakes*, by the Manchester figure already referred to, Stanley Houghton: after a series of speeches upon which the most ardent young feminist of today could scarcely improve, the factory-girl heroine refuses to marry the boss's son who has got her pregnant.

Where women worked outside the home it was in the worst and lowest-paid jobs. The average weekly wage of women in industrial work was 11s 7d (under 60p), a third of the average male industrial wage. Although they could vote in local elections, and serve on local councils, women did not have the parliamentary vote. Upper- and middle-class women, often in face of great difficulties, were making some progress in the professions, but the central cause of the 'Women's Movement', perhaps the single most important political phenomenon on the Edwardian scene, was the winning of the parliamentary vote.

Attention very properly focuses on the political, economic and social disabilities of women, yet it is also important to be aware of the crucial role played by women in Edwardian society. Managing the family budget, scrimping and saving, feeding and clothing the children, plotting and scheming in the search for accommodation, passing on the traditions of child care – in the typical working-class household these were onerous tasks indeed. Something of woman's central role is perhaps hinted at in *Plates 3, 8* and *10*. Of course fulfilling this role could be sapping and stultifying. There is a very real dilemma between wishing to give full recognition to the special roles and skills of women, too often treated contemptuously in relation to the special roles of men, and wishing to see women have at least the same freedom of choice as men. Many of the controversies over the Women's Movement are rooted in this dilemma.

However, before we take up the question of Votes for Women we must be clear that in regard to Votes for Men the other sex was not particularly well served in Edwardian Britain. In fact, one of the most notable features indicating that Edwardian society was not fully 'modern' (as understood by Stearns) was the franchise. A series of Reform Acts in the nineteenth century, as every schoolchild knows, had greatly extended the franchise; but the upshot was very far from being one-man-one-vote; on the contrary a complex set of qualifications, of which the most important was the householder franchise requiring proof of twelve months' unbroken occupation of the house in question, ensured that while a substantial number of wealthy individuals actually had several votes, two-fifths of all adult males had no votes at all. One has only to look at Edwardian election results to see how far the country was from being a democracy. In 1910, when George Lansbury (who, it was said, 'let his bleeding heart run away with his bloody head') won the Bow and Bromley seat (which two years later he resigned and lost on the issue of women's suffrage) he polled 4,315 votes to his opponent's 3,452, and this in a highly populated part of London's East End.

Many men, indeed, supported the cause of Women's Suffrage, as can be seen from photographs which have men in the platform party. *Plate 14* is more ambiguous: the preponderance of men in the audience is probably more reliable as an indicator of the difficulties women in a small Welsh town found in attending an open air meeting than of male support for the cause. Mrs Emmeline Pankhurst was a fine orator who, with her daughter Christabel, led the militant section, christened 'suffragettes' by the *Daily Mail*. The section advocating reform by

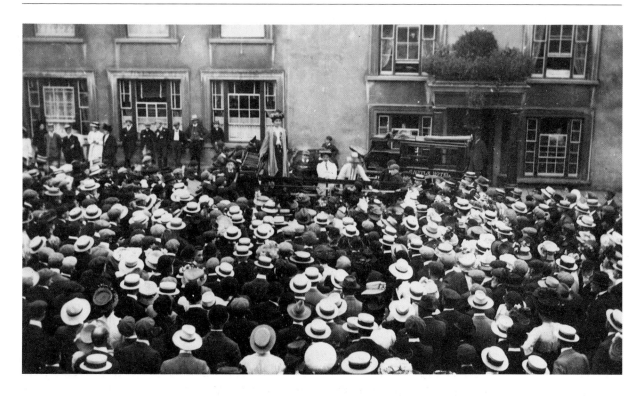

14 'The Suffragettes at Haverfordwest: Mrs Pankhurst Speaking'.

peaceful, constitutional means, the 'suffragists', was led by Mrs Millicent Fawcett.

The vile harassment of militant suffragettes, including forcible feeding, and then the 'cat-and-mouse' tactic of releasing hunger-striking women when they were on the point of death, then re-arresting them when restored to health, throws a revealing light on Edwardian concepts of law and order. No Marxist sophistry was needed to spot the class and sex prejudices, which from High Court Judge to local magistrate, to constable on the beat, informed law enforcement. Hanging, flogging, birching, penal servitude with hard labour were handmaidens to the system.

Nevertheless the political values of Edwardian society are not totally to be scoffed at. National pride, blatant enough, was no more so than in, say, France or Germany. Tories, believing in the utter sanctity of the United Kingdom, opposed any political concession to Irish national sentiment; Liberals expected to maintain the union through granting local self-government. Aided by maps in which the vast spread of British overseas possessions was indicated in red, children were brought up to believe in the special destiny of the British Empire. Even E. D. Morel, the age's great campaigner against Leopold of Belgium's imperial abuses in the Congo, liked to appeal to national pride: 'we who are of the race of Clarkson and of Wilberforce'.[15] The sentiments of tolerance and of liberty, meaning essentially the freedom of the individual vis-à-vis the state, were genuine: freedom of assembly and freedom of the press, however much abused, were realities. Violent hostility between Protestants and Catholics was endemic in the north of Ireland and in parts of such cities as Glasgow and Liverpool; but throughout most of mainland Britain a sort of 'secular anglicanism' prevailed, a

15 Proclamation of King
George V, Victoria
Square, Birmingham,
1910.

16 Coronation
Exhibition at the White
City: the opening
ceremony. Photograph
by Topical Press,
20 May 1911.

broad and deeply entrenched social consensus, which historians have traced back to the tolerant and undogmatic Anglican Church settlement of earlier, more religious centuries, though passionate arguments over the nature of religious instruction in schools still divided Anglicans and nonconformists. While much of the lower-working class was untouched by religion, Britain was still 'un-modern' in the extent to which religious belief and practice marked all of society from the respectable working class upwards.

The focal point for national, imperial and even religious feeling was the monarchy. The vast crowd assembled in the centre of Birmingham to hear the proclamation of King George V, with the statue of Queen Victoria prominent, suggests that public veneration of the monarchy was no exclusive metropolitan monopoly (*Plate 15*). The early twentieth century was very much an era of great exhibitions, glorifying international trade, the nascent consumer society and, of course, national and imperial achievement. The coronation of George V was accompanied by just such an exhibition. *Plate 16*, with its forest of millinery and top hats, well captures the folly and the grandeur of this Edwardian occasion.

In the 1930s a very young man achieved great success with a work of popular history entitled *The Strange Death of Liberal England*. Among other circumstances, the author, George Dangerfield, drew attention to the socially disruptive effects of the series of strikes, accompanied by some violence, which took place in the years 1910–13. With wages static and prices rising, harsh working and squalid living conditions, British workers had plenty of cause for militant action. But the fundamental cohesion of British society did not crack; liberalism was not yet dead. However circumscribed, the Edwardian liberals' instinct for reform pointed a finger of continuity.

Great violence there undoubtedly was in Edwardian society; and, not far below the surface, something of a 'will to war' can be detected – in invasion-scare

17 Gopsall Street School, 1906.

18 *Alcibiades*, one of the coloured designs from Wyndham Lewis' portfolio *Timon of Athens* (1913 or 1914), containing sixteen sheets, six with coloured, ten with black and white subjects.

novels, in speeches and prize-givings. Here is Lord Rosebery addressing the boys of Wellington in 1909:

> The stress that patriotism will have to bear in days not distant, and perhaps imminent, will be greater than has yet been known in the history of this country (*Hear, hear*). There never was a time when men were more needed to speak and act up to their faith (*Cheers*). I think that men will have to be more universally armed in the future than they are now (*Hear, hear*). . . . There are encroaching opinions which threaten patriotism, menace our love of country, and imply the relaxation, if not the destruction, of all the bonds which hold our empire together (*Hear, hear*). I would urge that so far as possible the study of patriotism should be promoted (*Cheers*).[16]

The most pregnant image of Edwardian society I have yet come across, however, relates to a much humbler seat of learning: Gopsall Street Elementary School in London (*Plate 17*). The military regimentation of the segregated boys in their closed-in playground is as touching as the thuggish presence of headmaster and teachers is threatening. These boys, though, are from the upper-working class: they do have reasonable clothing and, above all, footwear.

In the world of the intellect and the arts there was in the Edwardian era a development of the new modes and values established towards the end of the previous century: modernism was securely launched. Yet at least as striking was the persistence of older traditions and the resistance of the consumers of high culture to the disturbing disharmonies of Stravinsky and of the Post-Impressionist painters. Wyndham Lewis, disciple of the Italian Futurists and pioneer of Vorticism, was spurned as an avant-garde crank. Yet such paintings as *Alcibiades* (*Plate 18*) encompass very well that half-hidden 'will to war' which was assisting Edwardian society to the real source of its destruction: European war.

## Chapter Two

# The Great War
# and its Consequences

## War's Interrelationship with Society

There is a major controversy among historians over what effects, if any, the First World War had on British society. Actually, the controversy is not between those who argue that the war transformed totally all aspects of British society, and those who deny this. It is rather between those who say that within certain specific fields, always recognizing the importance of longer-term movements of change, the experience of war did have identifiable consequences, and those who insist that nowhere did the war bring about any significant changes. I stand firmly in the former camp and much of this chapter will be devoted to expounding my analysis of the relationship between the war and the social changes which, I would maintain, accompanied and followed it.

Those who lived through the war, it may be said, were – when they expressed an opinion at all – pretty clear that the war had had a cataclysmic effect. It is important, therefore, to consider why some historians have been so keen to reject contemporary testimony, and insist on the irrelevance of the war as an agent of social change. There would seem to be four reasons. First of all, historians have been struck (with much reason) by the conservatism of British society, and its general resistance to change. Postulating an overall framework of absence of change, they naturally find it difficult to detect any significant changes attributable to war. Secondly, and often rather closely related to the first point, historians of liberal or progressive sympathies find it hard to accept that war, that most horrible of all human activities, could possibly have anything but destructive effects upon human society. Thirdly, many historians are still very traditional in their approaches to historical sources and historical methodology: concentrating on politicians and political parties, they tend to concentrate on whether politicians, in the letters which they write to each other and which subsequently are stored in the political archives, actually reveal that through the influence of the war they have changed their opinion. Since they can usually show that politicians, being politicians, did not change much, they then conclude that no social change took place. But the arguments which I and others would wish to uphold are that *despite the politicians*, changes did in fact come about.

Finally, of course, there is no doubt that contemporaries did exaggerate the effects of the war, and ever since, there has been no lack of simpleminded generalists and popularizers, as well as glorifiers of war, to repeat untenable clichés about the 'impact' of the war. Historians naturally, and very properly, wish to debunk conventional and simplistic clichés. But, alas, this very proper instinct has led some of them into taking up an absurdly extreme position in which, in order to make their points, they have completely parodied those who have tried to formulate a careful appraisal of the exact nature of war's interrelationship with society.

Much of the argument depends upon what is counted as 'change', upon what sort of change one is looking for. In the more obvious ways, most physical aspects of both people and environment did not change much. This point is seized upon by Dr Paul Thompson, author of a brilliant book called *The Edwardians* (1975), who declares that the most remarkable thing about the war was 'how slight its permanent impact was upon British society as a whole'.[1] Dr Ross McKibbin, towards the end of a book which argued that the war itself had no influence on the evolution of the Labour Party, wrote:

> The towns were no larger than they had been; there were few new industries; there was no increase in the mobility of the population; despite fashionable forms of social dissent there was little of that political disorientation so noticeable on the Continent. Though the staple industries were soon to be in difficulties, they had also been in some before 1914, and the labour disturbances of 1917–1919 were no worse than those of 1911–13. The war had clearly extended the role of the state, but so had the most important social legislation of the Campbell-Bannerman and Asquith governments.[2]

More recently, Dr McKibbin has re-emphasized the somewhat bizarre argument that all political change must be attributed to the Reform of the Franchise in 1918, as if there could be no links between that reform and the war experience. Dr Martin Pugh has for long been insisting that rather than aiding the cause of votes for women, the circumstances of the war hindered it.[3]

On the other side of the argument, A. J. P. Taylor's *English History 1914–1945*, published in the same year (1965) as my own *The Deluge: British Society and the First World War*, put great emphasis on the social upheavals of the war and upon the drastically different role now assumed by the state. Working through much of the same ground as McKibbin and Pugh, Dr Close came up with the unequivocal statement:

> The war quickly made a vast expansion of the franchise inevitable, by establishing the claim to vote of new categories of people – especially servicemen and women – and by making intolerable the old difficulties of access to the electoral register, particularly the twelve-month qualifying period.[4]

If we are to make progress in what really is one of the most difficult areas of historical research we must unhook ourselves from the simple vocabulary which results in such statements as 'the war did this', 'the war did not do that'. Indeed we would be best (though it is difficult) to stop speaking at all of 'the war's impact', for we do not have two discrete factors, society on the one side, war on the other. We have to envisage a continuum, 'society at war': if we compare 'society at war' with 'society not at war' we can see clearly the characteristically different situations, problems and processes which affect 'society at war' and touch off all kinds of mechanisms of change, direct and indirect.

To illuminate the complex interaction between war and society it is useful to break war down analytically into four 'dimensions'. First is the immediately obvious *destructive* and *disruptive* dimension of war: building, shipping and other physical resources are destroyed, peacetime processes are interrupted, people are projected into new situations. Second is the *test* dimension. War brings new stresses, offers new challenges, and imposes new necessities. Institutions adapt; or they may even collapse. No value judgment is involved. The argument is not the militarist one that the best organized society is the one best equipped to win wars; it is simply that in meeting the test of war, societies will be forced to change, not necessarily in a desirable direction. Third is the *participation* dimension. When only minorities are involved in the waging of war only they are likely to derive any direct benefits from war, with deprivation and suffering probably being the lot of the mass of the population. But as wars more and more involve the participation of hitherto underprivileged groups in the community – and this is a characteristic of twentieth-century total war – those groups tend to benefit from such participation. Finally there is the *psychological* dimension. War, above all total war, is an enormous emotional and psychological experience comparable with the great revolutions in history.

However, in resorting to an analytical framework, we must not forget that the war lasted for four tragic years. Change was often slow, and in different areas it became significant at different times. In some phases we can see the circumstances of war actually highlighting the persistence of old traditions and prejudices. It is quite wrong to take the war as one homogeneous experience, as it is quite wrong, for example, to argue that because the role of certain women had not changed half way through the war, so, taking the war as a whole, it did not change at all. To give some sense of chronology, it is possible to make a fairly satisfactory division of the domestic history of the war into three parts: the first eight months, after a brief spell of panic and excitement, were dominated by the slogan 'Business as Usual'; thereafter, from the spring of 1915, right through 1915–16 we do begin to see the effects of the shortage of manpower, the imposition of conscription, and the need to organize society more efficiently for war; 1917 and 1918 were the years of very rigid state control, of shortages, and also of the clear emergence of the pattern of longer-term social change.

That there really had been a will to war seems to be demonstrated by the rush to the recruiting offices immediately upon the declaration of hostilities. By 15 September 1914, half-a-million men had enlisted. In November an increase in the army of another million was authorized, and by 21 December 1915 a third and then a fourth million had been approved. These volunteers, drawn from all social classes, were essentially enlisting for the simple Edwardian values of God, King and Country. Germany's violation of Belgian neutrality had provided the occasion for the British declaration of war, and the basis for the recruiting slogan 'Take up the Sword of Justice'. But equally prominent was the less complicated 'It's Our Flag' (*Plate 19*). This remarkably unposed photograph of the White City recruiting office, with men raising their arms to take the army oath, conveys well the naive enthusiasm, the simple sense of duty, even idealism, of the British after more than a year of the most horrific war in history; we see here, of course, an obvious continuity with Edwardian times. In essence simply a record photo, the picture was to have obvious propaganda value since much of the success of the early voluntary enlistment depended upon example: men were encouraged to enlist because that was what others were doing, and that was what they were expected to do.

19 Taking the oath: recruits at the White City, London, June 1915.

And yet these men, and millions like them, were to be projected into a new, unspeakable life, which could not but leave its mark on them. As soldiers' letters clearly show, it became impossible to maintain the old faiths in the face of the ruthless and irrational slaughter of war. 'Any faith in religion I ever had is most frightfully shaken by the things I've seen', wrote a soldier in March 1916.[5] Concentrating on global statistics, McKibbin detected no change in population mobility; but among the recruits were men from remote Welsh and Scottish villages whose acceptance of the old ways in many cases was totally disrupted. The decline of a particular type of God-fearing rural life may not be statistically significant, but it is very important in the evolution of British society all the same.

Extreme nationalism, amounting to xenophobia, was an evident feature of Edwardian society, yet even the mixed communities of the East End of London or of the Liverpool docklands enjoyed a relatively stable existence. Involvement in war brought a great intensification of xenophobic feelings – even Belgian refugees, on whom much vacuous sentimentality was initially lavished, became simply an irritant. The first rioting against those with German names was touched off by the German sinking of the Cunard liner *Lusitania* in April 1915. Right from the beginning of the war the *Daily Mail* had played its part, publishing, heavily leaded and prominently boxed, such delightful messages as:

> REFUSE TO BE SERVED BY AN AUSTRIAN
> OR GERMAN WAITER.
> IF YOUR WAITER SAYS HE IS SWISS
> ASK TO SEE HIS PASSPORT.

Because of his German origins, Prince Louis of Battenberg, First Sea Lord, had been forced out of office at the end of October 1914. Accepting the resignation, the First Lord of the Admiralty, Winston Churchill, got the disruptive tornado of war absolutely right:

> This is no ordinary war, but a struggle between nations for life and death. It raises passions between nations of the most terrible kind. It defaces the old landmarks and frontiers of our civilisation.

In the East End of London, there was serious rioting again in June 1915. In *Plate 20* the shop of the German-sounding E. R. Siebert has taken the punishment; a shop next-door, though boarded up, appears to be unscathed. The pub is open. The crowd appears to have organized itself for the photographer, rather than the photographer having organized them for his purposes. Children and men predominate; presumably most women had more important things to do.

20 Anti-German riots in the East End of London, June 1915. News photo.

Enthusiastic voluntary enlistment removed men from their homes, though the process did not become critical until the imposition of conscription – a sharp break from a much-vaunted tradition – in January 1916 (for unmarried men) and May 1916 (for all men). Domestic society knew of the horror of war through personal bereavement, through the long lists of casualties published in the newspapers, yet did not really comprehend it: a chasm opened betweeen the society of the trenches and society at home. It was part-and-parcel of the restraint of Edwardian respectability, a restraint similar to that observed in regard to sexual matters, that soldiers were inhibited from ever letting those at home know about the full obscene reality of life in the trenches: 'There are some things better undescribed', wrote one soldier. 'Perhaps in the afterwards when time has deadened matters, you will hear of them.'[6] That well brought up, yet rebellious upper-middle-class girl, Vera Brittain, got a sense of the truth when the clothes of her dead sweetheart, Roland, were returned:

> Everything was damp & worn & simply caked with mud. All the sepulchres and catacombs of Rome could not make me realise mortality & decay & corruption as vividly as did the smell of those clothes. I know now what he meant when he used to write 'this refuse-heap of a country' or 'a trench that is nothing but a charnel-house'...
> All that was left of his toilet luxuries came back – a regular chemist's shop – scented soap, solidified l'eau de cologne etc. We no longer wondered why he wanted them. One wants the most expensive things money can buy to combat that corruption.[7]

Subsequent work as a nurse with the Voluntary Aid Detachments in France brought her into direct contact with the sordid realities, yet neither in her diaries, nor in the more composed autobiography *Testament of Youth*, does the discreet conspiracy of restraint break down. The arrival of ambulance trains at major stations and the departure of ambulances was a depressing enough sight; but the true horrors of mutilation were not on view to the general public. As *Plate 21* suggests, the large crowds actually saw little of the wounded. The Bureau de Change notices, ironically, testify to a world of financial freedom, indeed frenzy, which disappeared with the war, but there is a fresh notice advertising the plight of Serbia.

The Vera Brittain diaries show no hint of a breaking of Edwardian moral canons: only a lament that on her last parting from Roland they had not even kissed. Yet, though the evidence, as always with such matters, is far from straightforward, there clearly were alterations in patterns of sexual behaviour. In the circumstances of war, both men and women were taken out of their sheltered family environments, opportunities for encounters between the sexes greatly increasing, particularly since the institution of the chaperone was also given a body blow: they were 'hard at work canteening and so on', one young lady explained, 'and people who gave parties did not want to feed and water them. And if they were elderly, they didn't feel like having to walk home after late nights.' Knowledge of mechanical methods of contraception spread, particularly when troops were given a free issue as a prophylactic against venereal diseases. When the slaughter of war was everywhere throwing civilized values in doubt, many of the older religious and social restraints were greatly weakened. 'War babies' were discovered by the press in April 1915. That year, in fact, proved to have an exceptionally low illegitimate birth rate combined with a phenomenally high marriage rate, many of the marriages, no doubt, taking place in some haste.

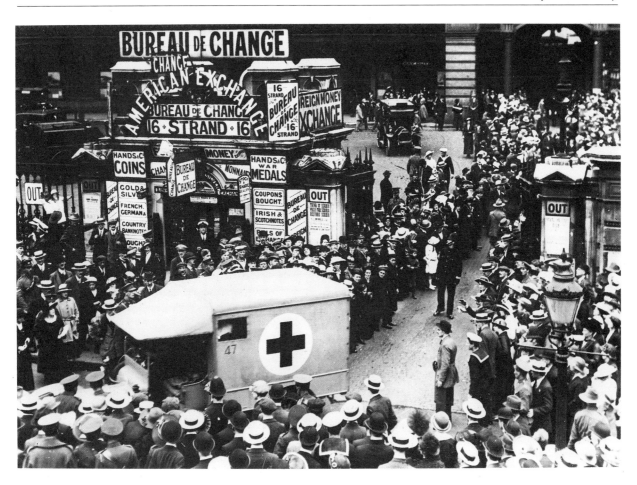

Marriage in haste was often to mean divorce at leisure: there was a nearly threefold increase in the number of divorces between 1910 (596) and 1920 (1,629). From 1916 onwards the illegitimacy figures did move steadily upwards, showing a total increase of 30 per cent by the end of the war. In general one can detect a softening of attitudes. The Secretary of the new War Babies and Mothers League explained: 'In the majority of cases, it is simply a matter of a young girl and a young man losing their heads when the man is going off to the Front.'[8]

The disruptions of war can be seen more directly in certain areas of social provision. On the eve of the war the Liberal government had announced plans for big increases in educational expenditure; these, as the Board of Education subsequently reported, were 'arrested by the outbreak of war'.[9] Soon local authorities were pressing hard for drastic relaxation in the school attendance by-laws. County magistrates argued that children should be released for 'national work', meaning, more often than not, work on the farms of the county magistrates. In fact, families whose one wage-earner was on active service overseas were often in dire straits and needed the potential earnings of their children. Addressing the House of Commons in August 1917, H. A. L. Fisher, President of the Board of Education, admitted that over 600,000 children had been put 'prematurely' to work. Children gave up schooling for 'excessive hours

21 Soldiers wounded during the Battle of the Somme leaving Charing Cross station, London, 8 July 1916.

of strenuous labour'.[10] Teachers left to fight in the trenches; many did not return. However, we now come to one of the great paradoxes attendant upon the disruptive influence of war. Educational provision was by this time so bad that something really positive had to be done about it. This truth quite clearly formed one of the motivations behind the Education Bill laid before the House of Commons in August 1917. As Fisher himself explained:

> It is framed to repair the intellectual wastage which has been caused by the war; and should it pass into a law before peace is struck it will put a prompt end to an evil which has grown to alarming proportions during the past three years – I allude to the industrial pressure upon the child life of this country – and it will greatly facilitate the solution of many problems of juvenile employment, which will certainly be affected by the transition of the country from a basis of war to a basis of peace.[11]

An exactly analogous process took place in the realm of housing. Concentration on the war effort meant that there was a complete cessation of normal private and local authority housebuilding. (In such great munition centres as Gretna, the necessities of war imposed pioneering state-sponsored housebuilding schemes which became something of a model for the interwar years.) Older industrial centres were crammed far beyond capacity with the influx of war workers. Housing at Barrow was described officially as 'a crying scandal.'[12] Reports proliferated of nightshift workers sleeping by day in beds occupied at night by dayshift workers – a feature, certainly, of Edwardian slum life, but less extensive and less commented on then. Short of 120,000 houses in 1913, the country needed 600,000 in 1918. So great, again, was the problem that it could be solved only by a massive state initiative: that, in any event, was the conclusion of the Salisbury Committee on Housing in England and Wales, and the Royal Commission on Housing in Scotland, both of which presented their findings during the last eighteen months of the war.[13] This paradoxical outcome of war's destructiveness need not surprise if attention is paid to the disaster studies carried out over the years by social scientists: war is in this respect analogous to natural disaster, to earthquakes and floods which, it appears, touch off reconstructive energies in human communities, generate a desire to build again, and build better than before.[14]

However, that war is essentially destructive should never be forgotten. Many of its disruptive effects were to have deleterious long-term consequences for British society. In particular we should note the overemphasis, caused by the immediate needs of war, on the older heavy industries, the upset to the delicate international trade mechanism from which Britain had benefited so greatly, and the loss of overseas markets. To these developments are related the slump which affected the British economy from the beginning of the 1920s, and they must be balanced against certain industrial innovations brought about by the test effect of war.

### The Test of War

The unreflective faith in private enterprise, and the casual neglect of science and technology, were both put to the test. In the first phase of excitement and emergency there was immediate state interference for certain limited purposes;

no one, however, saw these as directly challenging the basic economic orthodoxy. There followed a second phase, beginning in the spring of 1915, when it became clear that a total breakdown of the war effort would result if more positive state action were not taken to direct and control the economy. The attempts in this second phase were often blundering, half-hearted and ineffective. It was only in late 1916 that really whole-hearted efforts were made to come to grips with the economic problem.

The biggest step taken on the outbreak of war was government control of the railways, but there was nothing very surprising about this since such action had been allowed for in an act of 1871. Other immediate emergency actions concerned such matters as control of telegraphy, shipping, suspension of Stock Exchange dealing, printing of more paper money, and bulk purchase of foreign grain. Private traders continued to bid chaotically for scarce imports, including those needed for the munitions industries.

The first major point of change came in May 1915 when the crisis over munitions at the western front led to the formation of the first coalition government (with, however, the existing Prime Minister, Asquith, the Liberal leader, remaining in office). These were the surface signs of a much deeper crisis in which it was clear that the Liberal government had failed to respond adequately to the challenge of war. The most important development was the setting up of the Ministry of Munitions, involving direct government intervention in the munitions industry. Later in the year war agricultural committees were set up in an effort to exploit the full agricultural resources of the localities.

The next point of change, as nearly as it can be pinned down, is the autumn of 1916 when unrestricted German submarine attacks were resumed; informed opinion now coalesced into positive insistence upon more determined overall economic management. Disquiet with Asquith's policies finally brought his fall (and replacement by Lloyd George) in December 1916. Early in 1917 the government took control of the entire coal industry. This was followed by control of shipping and of the cotton industry; bulk purchase of all major imports was concentrated in the hands of the government.

Government emergency action in economic matters at the outbreak of war was paralleled by the setting up of a government Chemical Product Supply Committee under Lord Haldane, 'to consider and advise as to the best means of obtaining for the use of British industries sufficient supplies of chemical products, colours and dye stuffs of kinds hitherto largely imported from countries with which we are at present at war.' The result was the setting up of the not very successful National Dye Company. In May 1915 a deputation of professional scientists called for the establishment of a National Chemical Advisory Committee; a government White Paper of July went beyond that in outlining a form of 'permanent organisation for the promotion of industrial and scientific research'.[15] This Committee of the Privy Council for Scientific and Industrial Research was allocated £25,000 for its first year's work and £40,000 for its second. From 1 December 1916 it was re-organized as a separate government department with a ministerial head in the shape of the Lord President of the Council. A further step in the consolidation of centralized control of scientific research was taken a few months later when the National Physical Laboratory was transferred from the Royal Society to this newly christened Department of Scientific and Industrial Research. Only in war did the Medical Research Committee get off the ground; its annual reports refer to the war as 'a great stimulus' providing 'unequalled opportunities for study and research, of which the outcome may bring lasting benefits to the whole future population': work of the utmost value was indeed sponsored on dysentery, typhoid, cerebro-spinal fever, and new antiseptics. Seventeen months after the end of the war the new status and new permanency was recognized in the new title, Medical Research Council.

In the production and exploitation of motor vehicles Britain was a laggard nation in Edwardian times. Such as it was, the domestic motor car industry came to a standstill with the outbreak of war. But the War Office intervened directly, first of all subsidizing the production of vehicles, then requisitioning the whole output of all factories able to produce suitable machines, of which a great variety was developed, ranging from lorries and ambulances to – eventually – tanks. *Plate 22*, set in the context of the desolate wastes of battle-torn France, brings out the vital importance in this war of motor transport.

Before the war Britain was so heavily dependent on other countries for aero-engines that in the Aerial Derby of 1911 only one of the eleven machines had a British engine. Altogether at the outbreak of war the British air services had a total of 272 planes, which in the early stages of the war were mainly used for reconnaissance over enemy lines. According to the British Association for the Advancement of Science, 'By the end of the war . . . British aero-engines had gained the foremost place in design and manufacture, and were well up to requirements as regards supply.' The aeroplanes sent out with the British expeditionary force in 1914 had a maximum speed of 80 mph, a rate of climb from ground level of 300 or 400 feet per minute, and were equipped with engines of 60 to 100 horse-power. In 1918 the fastest machines could reach 140 mph and had a rate of climb from ground level of 2,000 feet per minute. The Handley-Page V/1500, which had its first test flight in May 1918, was capable of developing over 1,300 horsepower. The maximum flying height had been raised from 5,000 to 25,000 feet. Three days before the armistice two Handley-Page bombers stood fully equipped awaiting the order to start for Berlin. By this time there was considerable interest in the possible civilian uses of aircraft. In April 1918 the government formed a Civil Aerial Transport Committee under Lord Northcliffe, and Handley-Page, together with another leading manufacturer, Holt Thomas, anxious to exploit their new productive capacity, announced their plans for the development of civil aviation.[16]

Wireless likewise proclaimed its potential during the war, British valve transmitters being developed for the first time mainly for contact between the ground and planes on reconnaissance. As supplies from the main pioneer companies in this field, Marconi, Edison, Swann and A. C. Cosser, were insufficient, contracts for radio valves were given to the main manufacturers of electric light bulbs, the General Electric Company Limited, the British Thompson Houston Company Limited, and the British Westinghouse Electrical and Manufacturing Company Limited. The commitment of these three companies to the nascent radio industry was, by the end of the war, so great that it was they who exerted some of the strongest pressure on the government to permit

broadcasting in the postwar years. The first actual broadcasters were in many cases men who had gained experience of wireless during the war.

Existing resources were inadequate to the new power demands of the war effort. Thus, between 1914 and 1919, the capacity of electrical generating stations, both municipal and private, had to be doubled. Here, as with chemicals, we are talking about industries crucial to the shaping of twentieth-century society, to – as some would have it – modernization: yet because in size, though not in significance, they are tiny in the macro-economic picture of the British economy chosen by McKibbin, he ignores them.

There had been many other constraints upon industrial efficiency apart from neglect of economic organization and of technology. Early in 1915 Lloyd George made a dramatic denunciation of what he perceived as one of the most serious of these: 'We are fighting Germany, Austria and Drink and, as far as I can see, the greatest of these deadly foes is Drink.'[17] Lloyd George's concern was with alcohol as a cause of incapacity for work; there was also the problem that its manufacture consumed scarce cereal needed for animal and human consumption. Preparing the ground carefully for action, the government carried out an investigation into bad timekeeping in the shipbuilding, munitions and transport industries. Although there were no doubt many reasons for loss of time, the report, presented on 29 April 1915, concluded that the most important was the ease with

22 Men of the 16th (Irish) Division going back for rest after the Battle of Guillemont, 3 September 1916.

45

23 Glasgow Cross, early 1916.

which men now enjoying full employment and high wages could obtain beer and spirits. Thus came the establishment of the Central Control Board (Liquor Traffic), not intended to impose its rule uniformly across the country, but rather to take over control of liquor licensing in those areas where excessive drinking could be held to be an impediment to the war effort. By 1 October control had been taken of fourteen such areas, and, among other limitations, an important general order was put into force, restricting sale, whether for consumption on or off the premises, to two-and-a-half hours in the middle of the day and to three or, in some cases, two hours in the evening.

The sale of alcohol, that is, was prohibited before midday and throughout the afternoon after 2.30 pm. The photograph reproduced in *Plate 23* was deliberately taken to show a Glasgow scene at the time when Lloyd George was preoccupied with the troubles in the Glasgow Engineering works. Life, one can see, goes on in wartime. Unwittingly, the photograph shows the effects of liquor control through the advertisements for the expensive, but weak, 'Munitions Ale'. Reductions in the output and strength of beer were enforced during 1916, while prices went up. Whatever the dark mutterings over 'government ale', there could be no doubt that by the end of the war a salutary change had come about in one of the nation's most melancholy social habits: in 1914 average weekly convictions for drunkenness were 3,388 in England and Wales; by the end of 1918 they had fallen to 449. In Scotland the weekly average fell from 1,485 immediately before October 1915 to 355 in 1918. The Control Board now had a total of 38 million people within its aegis. In a tidying-up operation, designed to perpetuate the changes accomplished during the war, the Licensing Act of 1921 was passed extending state control, and particularly the restricted opening hours, to the entire country.

## Participation in Wartime

Men were needed in the trenches, men were needed in the factories: the market position of labour was transformed, it could successfully demand higher wages and better living standards. If the war were to be won, the co-operation of labour must be secured, and its morale maintained; thus working-class organizations gained a new status. There was a feeling, too, that through social reforms the working class should be rewarded for its vital participation in the national effort. The advance was by no means a steady one: many working-class families endured intense privation due to high wartime prices, or the loss or departure of a principal wage-earner; men, women and children were often worked to the utmost levels of endurance in overcrowded, ill-equipped factories; it was from the working class that the bulk of the British armies, crucified and decimated at the Front, were drawn. In the struggle to secure increased production many cherished trade union rights were set aside. But if the short-term picture is of many real and deep-felt grievances, the long-term reality was one of genuine gains, despite even the postwar slump, when the workers again were the major victims.

As early as February 1915 an upward movement in wages due to constant employment, longer hours, and war bonuses was apparent. The gains were most marked among the under-class of prewar days, who now began to be absorbed into the working class proper. On the other hand, better-off sections of the working class were being hit by rising prices. However, where the workers were prepared to strike, their demands were almost invariably met: the government simply could not afford a cessation in necessary war production, and employers, with quick profits to be made, were often ready, in conditions of labour shortage, to offer special war bonuses. Nonetheless working-class discontent with high prices and other irritations brought about by the war reached a peak in 1917 when the government appointed a special commission of enquiry into industrial unrest. This reported that:

> The high prices of stable commodities have undoubtedly laid a severe strain upon the majority of the working classes, and in some instances have resulted in hardship and actual privation. It is no doubt true that in some industries wages have risen to such an extent largely to compensate for the increased cost of living, but there are workers whose wages have been raised very slightly, if at all, and some whose earnings have actually diminished.[18]

But in the last months of war and in the first months of peace labour's strong bargaining power, product of a continued labour shortage, ensured further advances in wage rates. By July 1919 a bricklayer in full employment, who in July 1914 would have had an average weekly wage of 42s 10d, was earning 79s 2d; in

1920 this had risen to 100s 7d. His labourer's earnings at the same three points in time were 29s 1d, 65s 2d and 87s 4d. In the engineering and shipbuilding trades a pattern-maker's average wage rose from 42s 1d in August 1914 to 86s 8d in February 1920; the corresponding figures for a riveter were 37s 9d and 80s 5d, and for a labourer 22s 10d and 63s 11d. Engine drivers earning about 42s a week in 1914 were earning up to 90s in 1919; firemen had risen from 26s to 66s. The significant way in which greater increases took place in the poorer paid employments can be clearly seen in the worst paid of all manual occupations: the agricultural worker, who averaged 13s 4d in 1914, was by 1920–21 earning 46s a week. The average income of all working-class families between 1914 and 1920 rose by 100 per cent, which slightly more than cancelled out the rise in the cost of living. After 1920 price levels fell, while, with some exceptions, the new wage levels were successfully defended, so that by the early twenties the working classes, provided they were not unemployed, were in real terms about 25 per cent better off than before the war. In addition, between 1914 and the early twenties the average working week fell from fifty-five hours to forty-eight.

Recognition of the new status of labour came through the inclusion of Arthur Henderson, Labour Party leader, in the first coalition government of 1915, and still more in his inclusion in the small War Cabinet formed by Lloyd George in December 1916, when six other Labour men got government posts of varying importance. The Munitions of War Act of 1915 aimed heavy blows at many trade union privileges, including the enforcement of 'dilution' arrangements – that is to say the upgrading of unskilled labour – in government factories, and the 'leaving certificate' scheme which obstructed the free mobility of labour. On-the-ground struggles by shop stewards did succeed in preventing the extension of dilution to private work and, eventually, the dropping of the leaving certificate scheme, whereby the employee was obliged to obtain a certificate from his employer before taking up a job elsewhere. The Labour Party before the war had really been little more than a sidekick to the Liberal Party. Labour's new belief in itself and its determination to voice its grievances and aspirations were well demonstrated at the 1917 Conference of the TUC, which, as *The Observer* commented at the time, signified a change of mood throughout the entire Labour movement.[19] Through its wartime experience the Labour movement was greatly changed.

For women, the first effects of the war were very largely disastrous. The slight expansion of opportunities for clerical work in banking and commerce, the new openings in ordnance factories, and the growth in the numbers of women running small businesses in place of their absent husbands, no more than cancelled out the unemployment caused by the slump in the women's luxury trades. The most notable characteristic of the early months of 1915, in fact, is the gap between the obvious desire of women, particularly in the upper and middle classes, to undertake war service, and the opportunity offered to them to satisfy this desire. In Glasgow, where dilution was already being successfully applied in the engineering shops, the municipal tramways led the way by taking on two women conductresses on a week's trial; the experiment was soon extended, the women being fitted out with neat uniforms in Black Watch tartan (*Plate 24*). The government, despite the fact that in March it had compiled a register of women willing to do industrial, agricultural or clerical work, was not really enthusiastic about encouraging the employment of women, and many trade unions were actively hostile. On Saturday 17 July, Mrs Emmeline Pankhurst, encouraged by Lloyd George, organized a demonstration of 30,000 women on behalf of women's 'right to serve'. To the demonstration Lloyd George contributed £2,000 of Ministry of Munitions money *and* one of his finest phrases, encapsulating one vision of women's participation: 'Without women victory will tarry, and a victory which tarries means a victory whose footprints are footprints of blood.'

The two crucial turning points in the expansion of women's employment, however, were the establishment of the Ministry of Munitions in June 1915, and, still more important, the institution of universal conscription for men in May 1916. The Ministry of Munitions deliberately set out to recruit women, and what was more, it also deliberately set out to ensure that some sort of fair wage was paid to them, but there was always enough small print in its circulars to ensure that women never quite got what a man doing the equivalent job would have.

Only munitions factories were formally under government control, but the government and local authorities participated in appeals which other private employers might make for women's labour. In the cases of the more adventurous and active young women we find that during the war they moved in and out of different types of employment, sometimes for one of the voluntary semi-military corps, sometimes for private employers, sometimes in government-sponsored munitions schemes. Entirely in keeping with the attitudes of the time, there was still much overlap between private initiative and official initiative. On 19 July 1915, Lady Moya and Lady Cowan established at Lesney House, Erith, Kent, a scheme for training leisured ladies to do weekend work at Vickers Armaments factory at Erith. Eventually many of the leisured ladies moved on to doing a full week's work. The first skilled women workers in a privately owned munitions factory were those who began at Sir William Beardmore's engineering works in Glasgow in June 1915. The idea of training upper-class ladies for part-time work was extended to this factory in November 1915. In July 1914 there had been 212,000 women employed in the various metal and engineering industries that were to become the ones most directly connected with war production. The figure for July 1915, 256,000, shows only a relatively small increase; but the greater expansion of later 1915 is seen in the next July figure, 520,000, an increase of over 100 per cent. Most of the new munitionettes were working-class in background, and the biggest single identifiable group among them were former domestic servants. In the autumn of 1915 a change in male trade union thinking begins to become apparent: the attempt to exclude women is changing to an insistence that women be paid the same rates as men.

The imposition of universal conscription for men was an event of central importance in the social history of the war: it began the second and definitive growth in women's employment and determined that the changes involved should go far beyond a limited expansion and upgrading of industrial labour, given additional piquancy by the entry for the first time into hard physical work of a few adventurous members of the upper classes. Just two weeks after the passing of the Act, the government launched its first national drive to fill the places vacated or about to be vacated by men. Only now did the wartime pattern of women's employment begin to assume its final shape. When, in early 1917, an official National Service Scheme was introduced to cover all aspects of civilian

24 Glasgow Corporation Tramways Department conductress. A very posed record photograph to bring out Glasgow Corporation's pioneering spirit in the employment of women.

25 Woman worker scraping aeroplane propeller in preparation for glasspapering at Frederick Tibbenham Ltd, Ipswich.

and non-combatant employment, it was concerned as much with women as with men. By July 1917 the total number of women employed in the munitions industries was 819,000; in the last year of the war there was a further increase of over 100,000. In industry as a whole the total employment of women and girls over ten had increased between 1914 and 1918 by about 800,000, from 2,179,000 to 2,971,000. The newer industries (*Plate 25*) tended to welcome women more enthusiastically than the older ones; but aeroplanes were still largely made of wood. The Voluntary Aid Detachments (*Plate 26*) were established shortly before the war and then recruited both men and women. Women predominated during the war, and, working mainly as nurses, came into contact with most of the most sordid, and some of the most dangerous aspects of warfare.

Although later in the war men at the Front were often upset by rumours that conscription for women was about to be imposed, there never was any conscription for women during the First World War. Yet some women, looking back through the hazy mists of memory, do write of having been 'called up'. The position was that both in the various voluntary schemes, and then in government schemes such as the National Factories, Women's Forage Corps, and, later, the Land Army, women were required to go through a form of enlistment, signing a definite contract committing themselves for six months, or a year's service. In factories they were constrained by the system of 'leaving certificates', which was also a great grievance to male trade unionists.

26 VADs running to their ambulances when an ambulance train was signalled, Étaples, 27 June 1917.

Even in factories where most of the workers were women, almost inevitably given the attitudes of the time, the supervisory roles were filled by men. *Plate 27* shows one of the factories directly run by the Ministry of Munitions but, as can be seen, the positions of authority are still occupied by men. We see the characteristic munitionette's outfit, including mob caps and – stunning innovation – dungarees. Equipment in these national factories was relatively up-to-date, with, for example, electric trollies assisting women in the undertaking of heavy manual labour. Many of the jobs done by women were extremely dangerous: there were several fatal explosions, and women working with TNT often became quite seriously ill, though they were sometimes jocularly referred to as 'canaries' because of the discoloration of the skin brought about by TNT poisoning. At the same time, a great impetus was given to the provision of proper factory welfare and canteen facilities (*Plate 28*), something from which men were also to benefit.

Much recent research, particularly by feminist historians, has stressed the continuing hostility to women's employment during the war, the strong male backlash against it in the immediate postwar years, and the large numbers of women who left the jobs they had taken up in wartime.[20] The global statistics certainly do not support the case of there being an impressive change in women's employment opportunities. In 1914, there were rather less than six million women in paid employment in Great Britain and Ireland. At the end of the war

27 National Shell-filling Factory, Chilwell, Nottinghamshire.

this had risen by well over one-and-a-quarter million to between seven-and-a-quarter and seven-and-a-half million. By 1920 almost two-thirds of those who had entered employment during the war had left it again. A year later, with the onset of the long period of trade depression and unemployment, the figure for women's employment was not much higher than it had been in 1914. Where employment opportunities were held on to, this was almost exclusively in professional and commercial occupations: the figures are small, but again, I would argue, of great significance. But, undoubtedly, any changes in women's position must be seen within a general framework of the persistence of the traditional idea of women's basic role being that of home-builder. We should not project too many contemporary preoccupations upon the past: it has to be remembered that the understanding upon which most women took employment during the war was that of a temporary contribution to the national effort. Great numbers of women were forced back into domestic service, but after their wartime experiences they were more ready to resist, and successfully resist, the degrading conditions of prewar times; many did not, in fact, live in. Likewise in the world of the shop assistant, 'living in' had disappeared totally amid the food shortages of war: though many women, no doubt, would have preferred not to be forced into that occupation, it was at least a more dignified one than it had usually been in Edwardian times.

The real change, then, is to be found in women themselves, rather than in the outward trappings of the roles they seemed to be playing. During the war, the Chief Factory Inspector in his Report for 1916 referred to 'the new self-confidence

28 Another aspect of the National Factory at Chilwell: the women's canteen.

engendered in women' by the changed conditions of work.[21] The *New Statesman*, too, reported:

> They appear more alert, more critical of the conditions under which they work, more ready to make a stand against injustice than their pre-war selves or their proto-types. They have a keener appetite for experience and pleasure and a tendency quite new to their class to protest against wrongs even before they become 'intolerable'.[22]

In his classic autobiography, *The Classic Slum*, Robert Roberts speaks of the new assertiveness of women, even if activated only within the family circle:

> By the end of the war working-class women, as we have seen, had gained far more than a limited right to vote. For years now, in their menfolk's absence, many had reared a family, and found in the responsibility a new freedom. Women were more alert, more worldly-wise. Yet the liberty won, some felt they would have to fight hard to retain it once the warriors returned. But with surprise they discovered that husbands, home again, were far less the lords and masters of old, but more comrades to be lived with on something like level terms. Women customers in the shop commented on this change time and again.[23]

Finally, a recent important thesis on women engineering workers during the war also stresses the new levels of consciousness attained through their efforts in the war.[24]

### The Psychological Dimension of War

In war, feelings of solidarity with 'in-groups' are strengthened; feelings of hostility towards 'out-groups' are intensified. Early in the war there were attacks on those with German-sounding names or German associations (*Plate 20*). Those who argued that the war was wrong, or a mistake, who opposed conscription, or who argued for a negotiated peace, generally aroused hostile reactions (*Plate 29*). Organized propaganda was scarcely necessary in the first two-and-a-half years of the war. Artists and cartoonists readily contributed their absurd stereotypes of German militarism and its attitudes, and these featured in cartoons, film and posters. *Plate 30* combines stereotypes of the 'wicked Hun' with the familiar appeal to women who were being relied upon to make sure that their menfolk enlisted.

The sense of in-group solidarity which the upper and upper-middle class felt towards the rest of the community helped to strengthen the movements towards general social reform which we have already noted. In the working class, however, strengthened in-group feelings tended to show themselves as much in increased working-class awareness and solidarity with working-class institutions as in any uncritical patriotism. Here we have the clue to the paradox that while, quite definitely, feelings of national solidarity did increase, at the same time workers showed no reluctance to resort to the strike weapon: the combination, in fact, was a potent one – what the working class was now more determined to demand, the upper classes were more ready to concede.

Another important psychological aspect of the war experience was the way in which it ratified aspiration after change. In April 1916 R. D. Blumenfeld, editor of the *Daily Express*, noted in his diary, 'The war has simply turned the whole world topsy-turvy'; in October 1917 he was writing, 'That horrible ogre, Tradition, lies in the dust.' Writing in August 1916, the distinguished civil servant Sir Michael

29 Crowds gathered
outside a 'peace' meeting
in London, 1917.

30 War poster.

Sadler saw the war as a time of 'gestation of a new social ideal'.[25] The historian W. H. Dawson, writing in late 1916, expressed very well the whole mood, the whole feeling that so great and horrific a war, must be for something, must bring change:

> We are living at a time when days and weeks have the fullness and significance of years and decades. Who does not feel that since August 1914 England has in many ways broken with her past and entered an entirely new epoch in her history, marked by transformations of every kind, so that when the day of peace arrives, be it soon or late, we shall be confronted at home by an altogether altered situation?[26]

These are thoughts, perhaps aspirations, not concrete evidence that change actually was taking place; but they are not empty phrases, for the feeling that the war ought to bring change helped to boost the other forces which were making for change.

But we must not neglect the desperately negative effects of the war, not so apparent while the war was still being waged, but very evident in the aftermath. It was difficult for liberal-minded men to go on believing in the old liberal absolutes in face of the horrific slaughter of war. A divide developed between the unspeakable society of the trenches, and the still comfortable society at home. It is from poets and painters, more than from soldiers' letters, that we understand the bitter trauma of the war for those who actually fought it. A letter from Paul Nash to his wife in November 1917 is eloquent of the effect of the war upon him both as soldier and painter.

> We all have a vague notion of the terrors of a battle, and can conjure up with the aid of some of the more inspired war correspondents and the pictures in the *Daily Mirror* some vision of a battlefield; but no pen or drawing can convey this country – the normal setting of the battles taking place day and night, month after month. Evil and the incarnate fiend alone can be master of this war, and no glimmer of God's hand is seen anywhere. Sunset and sunrise are blasphemous, they are mockeries to man, only the black rain out of the bruised and swollen clouds all through the bitter black of night is fit atmosphere in such a land. The rain drives on, the stinking mud becomes more evilly yellow, the shell holes fill up with green-white water, the roads and tracks are covered in inches of slime, the black dying trees ooze and sweat and the shells never cease. They alone plunge overhead, tearing away the rotting tree stumps, breaking the plank roads, striking down horses and mules, annihilating, maiming, maddening, they plunge into the grave which is this land; one huge grave, and cast up on it the poor dead. It is unspeakable, godless, hopeless. I am no longer an artist interested and curious, I am a messenger who will bring back word from the men who are fighting to those who want the war to go on forever. Feeble, inarticulate, will be my message, but it will have a bitter truth, and may it burn their lousy souls.[27]

Among the many 'messages' transmitted by Paul Nash was Mont St. Eloi, one of the most fought-over landmarks on the western front (*Plate 31*). Of Nash's exhibition 'Void of War', held at the Leicester Galleries in May 1918, the novelist Arnold Bennett wrote:

> Lieutenant Nash has seen the Front simply and largely. He has found the essentials of it – that is to say, disfigurement, danger, desolation, ruin, chaos – and little figures of men creeping devotedly and tragically over the waste. The convention he uses is ruthlessly selective. The wave-like formations of shell-holes, the curves of shell-bursts, the straight lines and sharply defined angles of wooden causeways, decapitated trees, the fangs of obdurate masonry, the weight of heavy skies, the human pawns of battle – these things are repeated again and again, monotonously, endlessly. The artist cannot get away from them. They obsess him; and they obsess him because they are the obsession of trench-life.[28]

31 Painting by Paul Nash: *Mont St. Eloi*, 1917–18.

The war did not create a new movement in the arts, but it gave an accelerating currency and relevance to the modes of modernism. P. G. Konody, Art Critic of *The Observer*, put it well:

> It is fairly obvious that the ordinary representational manner of painting is wholly inadequate for the interpretation of this tremendous conflict in which all the forces of nature have to be conquered and pressed into service against the opposing enemy. A more synthetic method is needed to express the essential character of this cataclysmic war, in which the very earth is disembowelled and rocky mountain summits are blown sky-high to bury all life under the following debris. How could even a faint echo of such things find its way into that species of enlarged and coloured newspaper illustration that continues to represent the art of the battle painter on the walls of the Royal Academy.[29]

## Consequences of the War

In attempting to assess the consequences of the war, some historians, conscious that in certain respects society in the 1920s was different from society in the Edwardian era, but also very aware of the significance of long-term developments, have tended to resort to metaphor: the war is said to have 'accelerated' social change, or to have acted as a 'catalyst'. Neither of these rather simple metaphors is adequate to describe the complex interactions touched off when a society is at war; and to talk of total war 'accelerating modernization' is simply to substitute rather trivial phraseology for real explanation.[30]

The major pieces of social legislation enacted at the end of the war can be quickly listed. The Fisher Education Act of 1918 called upon local education authorities to draw up schemes covering all forms of education for their districts,

enforced the universal minimum leaving age of fourteen, and abolished all fees in public elementary schools; nothing, however, was done to remedy Britain's weaknesses in industrial training. The Ministry of Health Act of 1919 involved the government for the first time in a formal commitment to health throughout the country; it placed new basic health responsibilities on the local authorities. The Housing Act of 1919 marked the direct entry of the state, for the first time, into the business of building subsidized housing for rent. The Unemployment Insurance Acts of 1920 and 1921 totally transformed the extremely limited unemployment insurance provision of the prewar era; all members of the working class, whatever their job, now had unemployment insurance cover. Finally, the Maternity and Child Welfare Act of 1918 recognized the new concern which had developed during the war for mother and child. The building of community welfare and maternity centres (*Plate 32*) in the 1920s, ignored by male historians, and dismissed by many feminists, marked in fact an important stage in creating a better life for mother and child, while, of course, stressing the family and childbearing aspect of women's lives.

"Votes for Women," November 26, 1915.        Registered at the G.P.O. as a Newspaper.

## The War Paper for Women

# VOTES FOR WOMEN

### OFFICIAL ORGAN OF THE UNITED SUFFRAGISTS

VOL. IX. (Third Series), No. 403.     FRIDAY, NOVEMBER 26, 1915.     Price 1d. Weekly (Post Free)

## VOTES FOR HEROINES AS WELL AS HEROES

**CHIVALRY :** "Men and women protect one another in the hour of death. With the addition of the woman's vote, they would be able to protect one another in life as well."

*(The Anti-Suffragists used to allege, as one reason for refusing women the protection of the vote, that women were already protected by men's chivalry—as in a shipwreck, when the women are always saved first. When the hospital ship Anglia went down, last week, the women nurses refused life belts, saying, "Wounded men first.")*

32 Glasgow Child Welfare Centre, 1922 record photo.

33 'Votes for Heroines as well as Heroes': cover from the war-time suffragist paper (on which men were as active as women), *Votes for Women.*

The other reforms were all severely affected by the drastic economic cuts of the early twenties. It is, however, misleading to speak of 'the failure of social reform', just as, from the opposite point of view, it is misleading to think that because an Act of Parliament is passed actual reform will inevitably follow. By the early twenties new standards of social welfare, rather different from those prevailing in Edwardian times, had been laid down, and there were energetic local authorities, particularly Labour-controlled ones, ready to insist on the maintenance of these standards.

The Labour Party, in fact, did not do well in the 1918 General Election, but with its new party constitution it was now for the first time a genuine national party, clearly dissociated from the Liberals; it did well in local elections, and by 1923 was clearly recognized as the main opposition party, totally supplanting the Liberals. Labour leaders had been tested and proven competent in the war and were now before the public eye. Working men had become more class-aware, more ready to give a definite allegiance to the Labour Party. Of course, the new mass electorate enfranchised by the 1918 Representation of the People Act was extremely important, but it takes a particular type of academic mind to deny any relationship between this act and the experience of the war.

In fact, as an abundance of evidence shows, politicians felt bound to bring in the new Act, first, because many of those who went out to fight for their country or move to other areas at home in order to work in munitions factories lost their right to vote, based as it was on residence; secondly, many of the patient and heroic soldiers in the trenches had never in fact had the vote in the first place. It was entirely within the logic of military participation that the franchise should be extended to all men, just as all men had been eligible to fight (it is noteworthy that at the same time conscientious objectors were disfranchised).

As long as all issues related to the franchise were shelved for the duration of the war, the suffragists and suffragettes were prepared, also, to give up their agitation. But as soon as it was proposed to extend the franchise for men, the Women's Suffrage Movement came back into action. The cartoon reproduced as *Plate 33* brings out very graphically the way in which women's participation in the war effort was deployed to support the case for women's suffrage.

Again the evidence on this point is abundant, and it seems tortuous in the extreme to deny it. Mrs Fawcett may be regarded as a more reliable authority than some latter-day historian: she was quite clear about the direct connection between women's war work and the winning of the vote.[31] It is true that a small property qualification was retained for women, and that the vote was not granted to any woman under the age of thirty. But Mrs Fawcett and her colleagues recognized this as a tactical concession made, in particular, to appease those, of whom there were many in the Labour movement, who simply feared having women in an overall majority in the electorate. Mrs Fawcett knew that the vital principle having been conceded (and the point is that for all the talk and all the resolutions in prewar years, it never had been conceded) the vote would soon be given to women on the same terms as it was given to men; and this did indeed come to pass in 1928.

The winning of the vote was both a practical and a symbolic gain; it was immediately associated with the abolition of other legal inequalities. But vitally important as it was, a too narrow concentration by political historians on the question of whether or not the war was a critical factor in the enfranchisement of women has directed attention away from the crucial point that winning the vote was only one aspect of a great complex of changes which affected both men and women.

## Chapter Three

# The Twenties

### Working-Class Militancy and Economic Depression

Twenty, or even ten years ago much of the historical discussion over the first postwar decade centred on the question 'why was there no revolution in Britain?' Even today much energy and subtlety is still being expended on this question. Marxist writers, who are foremost in believing that a revolution *ought* to have taken place, have stressed both the long-term quiescence of the British working class and such short-term factors as the national solidarity fostered by war, as well as the skilful policies of Britain's governments.[1] Recently an American scholar, James Cronin, one of the leading proponents of that form of social history which, in the tradition of the continental sociologists, concentrates on the shifting relationships and conflicts between different economic interest groups, has restated the argument that there was a special 'crisis' in Britain in 1919–20 which, but for the skilful containment policies of the government, might have issued in revolution.[2]

Cronin's arguments, however, take us into another controversy which, in recent years, has tended to eclipse the old one about the possibilities of revolution. This controversy centres on the thesis that the readjustments between government, unions and employers which took place in response to the problems of war, and continued to take place in response to the disruptions and crises of the postwar years, marked a significant stage in the evolution of the corporatist state. A corporatist state is to be distinguished from a genuine parliamentary democracy in which decisions are taken by representatives of all of the people; in a corporatist state decisions are taken by the direct interaction between government and such powerful groups as unions and large employers and their organizations.[3]

A further trend in recent historical writing has been a re-examination of postwar economic policy with eyes made sympathetic by a consideration of the dire straits in which the British economy finds itself today. While once the governments of the early twenties were excoriated for their savage economy measures, now attention is given to the potentially inflationary effect that the concession of wage increases and the maintenance of government expenditure would have had – and to the general question of what the country actually could afford in the way of social benefits and working-class earnings. Finally, there has been debate over whether the record of British industry in the interwar period was as bad as tradition would have it; more attention, it has been argued, ought to be given to the new industries which were expanding. This first section concentrates mainly on the economy, and on the question of the revolutionary potential of working-class militancy; the question of corporatism will be returned to in the final section.[4]

Whatever glimpses of silver lining there may have been in the new technologies and the new amenities of life, any study of the interwar years must begin with the long cycle of depression which began in late 1920 and came to an end only in the first year of the Second World War. The cycle began in the classic style of the nineteenth-century capitalist economy. War-boom conditions continued and accelerated through 1919 and into 1920: the index number of prices, standing at 192 in 1918, 206 in 1919, and 265 at the April peak of 1920 collapsed to 155 in 1921 and 131 in 1922. The slump had set in, and despite a temporary recovery during the French occupation of the Ruhr coalfield in Germany in 1923–4, and the appearance of modest progress between 1924 and 1929, it persisted till it was engulfed in the still greater economic crash of 1929–31. Unemployment quickly reached $1\frac{1}{2}$ million, and remained there till it started climbing steadily in late 1929. It should not be thought that governments were unconcerned about unemployment, or did not, in their way, prepare for it. From the moment the end of the war had appeared in sight, the politicians got ready for the worst, though of course in so doing they helped to bring about the worst. Carefully planned demobilization schemes caused soldiers' demonstrations and riots because they were completely inequitable, although the principle on which they were based was not a silly one: it was that by first releasing those in certain 'key' occupations a smooth transition to peace, without the unemployment to be expected when soldiers flooded back in the labour market, would be achieved.

In August 1920 a special Cabinet Committee was appointed, charged with the responsibility of finding remedies for unemployment. Governments, however, were constrained by the financial orthodoxies of the time; although some of the experiments of the war were to be continued, or returned to later, the prevailing view was that conditions of a free market must be restored, expenditure curtailed, and budgets balanced. This orthodoxy was rendered specially impregnable because of the preponderance within the upper class of those whose interests were in finance rather than in industry. The rewards and prestige of finance were great; though there were industrialists of great social and political power (such as Stanley Baldwin, Andrew Bonar Law and Alfred Mond) much of industry was still organized on a relatively small scale, and run by men whose status was middle class rather than upper class. Most industrialists, whether upper class or middle class, were unadventurous and conservative in outlook (not all: William Morris, the future Lord Nuffield, could have walked straight from the pages of an early Victorian account of the buccaneering capitalists who made Britain great). John Maynard Keynes passed sweeping, but not wholly undeserved, sentence:

> The mishandling of currency and credit by the Bank of England since the war, the stiff-neckedness of the coal-owners, the apparently suicidal behaviour of the leaders of Lancashire, raised the question of the suitability and adaptability of our Businessmen to the modern age of mingled progress and retrogression. What has happened to them – the class in which a generation or two generations ago we could take a just and worthy pride? Are they too old or too obstinate? Or what? Is it that too many of them have risen not on their own legs, but on the shoulders of their fathers and grandfathers?[5]

It is actually rather difficult to argue that Britain's entrepreneurs showed any great awareness of the potential of the 'new industries' – electricity, rayon, motor vehicles, patent foods, luxuries – or that the expansion of these industries was in any way impressive: amounting to 6.5 per cent of Britain's total industrial output in 1907, they contributed (to a large extent because of the enforced transformations of the war) 12.5 per cent in 1921, but as late as 1928 still only 16.3 per cent. However, despite the well-known, and undoubtedly sustainable arguments about the preference of Britain's upper class for 'gentlemanly' pursuits rather than business enterprise it would be inapposite to focus attention on industrialists and entrepreneurs as an occupational group, rather than upon the upper class as a whole, and its politically active members in particular. Businessmen were inhibited by macro-economic policies which restricted credit and made investment difficult.

Without doubt top civil servants in the Treasury shared the outlook of other top people in the financial institutions of the City of London; their concern was Britain's role in the world of international finance, rather than with industrial productivity. Still, economists, civil servants and politicians do not control the state of the economy. The war had seriously disrupted the international trading system. The confidence which had enabled Britain to maintain its international financial role on remarkably low reserves was all but totally destroyed. Britain's older heavy industries, in reality less in demand in a world at peace, had been artificially stimulated during the war. All round the world markets had been lost, or were now open to vigorous competition from newcomers. During the war lavish levels of government expenditure had kept all productive resources at full pitch: many of the products had simply been destroyed in the war; there was a raging inflation, though – and this has to be stressed – thanks to relatively prudent management and the use, in particular, of a progressive tax system, this inflation was much less than that suffered by other European countries.

It was not apparent to anyone – not even, at this stage, to Keynes – that as expenditure was curtailed in the postwar years so it would be impossible to keep all productive resources fully employed. Nineteenth-century theory, to be sure, as embodied in Say's law envisaged brief cycles of depression and underemployment, but expected a natural adjustment of interest rates to bring the economy into equilibrium and again ensure the full employment of all resources. In the disturbed conditions of the postwar world this failed to happen, for, as Keynes later described it, there was a high 'propensity to save'. In other words the old nostrum of thrift, which equated saving with investment, was no longer valid: the thrifty classes were saving, but they were not investing, hence there was a shortfall in the total amount of money circulating in the community, a shortfall which brought about stagnation and unemployment.

Although, as just noted, the full analysis of this problem was worked out by Keynes only in the 1930s, there were a number of critics pointing in the right direction: the problem was that that direction was abhorrent to those in control of economic policy. The Independent Labour Party, on the left of the Labour Party, developed the idea of 'the living wage' which, it was argued, would encourage expansion and fuller employment by stimulating consumption. (The contrary argument, more fashionable now than it was ten years ago, is that without a guarantee of real increase in production, the result would simply have been inflation.) Keynes and others also protested vigorously over existing economic policy.

But in the government's own analysis of the problem, carried through in early 1920 by the Cunliffe Committee, treasury and financial interests predominated: on the recommendations of this committee the money supply was severely cut by raising the bank rate (in April 1920) to 7 per cent and drastically reducing the fiduciary issue (the amount of paper money in excess of actual holdings of gold). In August 1921 the government set up an Economy Committee under Sir Eric Geddes. Early in 1922 the 'Geddes Axe' chopped away a substantial section of public expenditure, thus further reducing the spending power of the community. Factors far beyond government control had begun the vicious process: government policy turned it into a circle.

The desire to bring the 'natural' discipline of 'economic laws' into the labour market, combined with the wish to restore in full Britain's respectability and status in the international financial market, was responsible for one other serious error. In 1925 Winston Churchill, now Chancellor of the Exchequer, was prevailed upon to return the country to the gold standard at the prewar parity of pound to dollar, regardless of the fact that the pound had meantime dropped in relative value by at least 10 per cent. Sir Roy Harrod has described the background to the move in the following terms:

> In the second half of 1924 sterling began to rise in a sinister manner in the foreign exchange market. The originating impulse was obscure; it may have been connected with Federal Reserve Policy; America had a minor trade recession in that year, and the Federal Reserve System, in accordance with its now well-established practice, proceeded to pump in credit in order to stimulate trade; this may have been the initial cause of the weakening of the dollar against sterling. Be that as it may, there is no doubt about what was responsible for the continuing major upward movement, a return to the old Gold Standard was definitely in the air now, and bulls were buying sterling at a discount in order to make a profit when the old parity should be re-established. The important thing to notice was that the rise in sterling did not reflect a reduction in British costs or a rise in American prices.[6]

In the interests of the prestige (and profit) of the City, British industry was presented with the gratuitous handicap that foreigners were now expected to pay 10 per cent more for British exports (4.25 dollars for every pound's worth, instead of 3.85 dollars). Many industrialists felt that the only way out (and this was part of the intended 'discipline' anyway) was to reduce costs through wage cuts equivalent to the 10 per cent.

These are the broad and dismal outlines; but some further detail must be shaded in, some of it good from the point of view of the country and its workpeople, some arguably good for the country in the long term, though less so for its workpeople, some perhaps bad for both.

Many of the more doleful tunes of the decade were rehearsed by Lloyd George at a Cabinet meeting of 5 August 1919, when he initiated a review of the 'whole position of the country' now that the peace treaty was concluded. Apparently in one of the moods of mystical depression which seized him from time to time, the Prime Minister declared that Britain was now a debtor country. In this he was immediately controverted by Bonar Law: strictly speaking Bonar Law was correct (Britain's wartime allies owed her more than she owed the Americans – and anyway she defaulted on part of her American payments), but it was the gloomy view of Lloyd George which governed subsequent economic policies. There were, Lloyd George continued, two problems facing the country: strikes and, more serious, declining productivity. The Bolsheviks, he said – launching upon one of the flights of fancy which, unhappily for the country, had a firm hold over his mind – had captured the trade union organizations. At the same time the working class had legitimate grievances, among which he stressed profiteering and bad housing. As a remedy for the former, he touched on the possibility of a programme of nationalization, and immediately met strong hostility from the other members of the Cabinet, who clearly preferred his vague references to stimulating agriculture and watching expenditure. Then Lloyd George came to the very heart of the storms which were to rage over British domestic history between 1919 and 1922:

> ... they could not take risks with labour. If we did, we should at once create an enemy within our own borders, and one which would be better provided with dangerous weapons than Germany. We had in this country millions of men who had been trained to arms, and there were plenty of guns and ammunition available.

Risks, the Prime Minister continued, in a typical modulation of key, could be taken with external force, but not with the 'health and labour of the people'. This was a critical discussion, and recognized as such, for it was decided that not a hint of it should be allowed to appear in the Press.[7]

The storm centres of working-class militancy can be precisely identified: the readjustment to peacetime conditions, leading, after 1920, into the wider problem of mass unemployment; the coal industry, where the miners were puzzled and embittered to find that, having been the highest-paid sector of the working class in prewar days, and having been the industrial workers upon whom the British war effort had seemed to depend, they were now entrapped in a declining industry; and, of transient importance only, the fear that a government which in 1918 had adopted the war aims of the Labour movement might now involve the country in a war against Soviet Russia.

Was there a revolutionary situation in 1919, or at least 'a profound crisis of legitimacy, pervading and threatening the political and social order as it had evolved to 1918'?[8] The photographic images of working-class militancy and the response of authority (*Plates 34 and 35*) are impressive enough. 'The question uppermost in the minds of all Britain today', declared a large industrialist, 'is whether, now that the Germans are beaten, there shall be peace or war in industry.' 'Trade union organisation was the only thing between us and anarchy', said Bonar Law; 'but there was not enough of it', Churchill lamented. 'Clearly, it was not the leaders but the mass of the men who had gone "red"', observed Beatrice Webb. Reviewing 1919, Basil Thompson, Director of Intelligence for the Home Office, warned:

> The year opened ominously, for the defeat of the pacifist and revolutionary candidates in the General Election brought into being an underground movement for Direct Action on the plea that the House of Commons had ceased to represent the country as a whole.[9]

Without any doubt the war experience had created a more coherent and unified, a more assertive, a more self-confident, a more class-aware, perhaps even more class-conscious, working class. With official trade union leadership stifled in the embrace of government during the war, all kinds of rank and file organizations had sprung into being. These points, together with the citations of upper-class opinion, are made by James Cronin in support of the 'crisis of legitimacy' idea. He also quotes a young Welsh miner as explaining, 'now we're ready to take over the job of runnin' the country'. The events of 1919–20 certainly provide impressive testimony to the willingness of large sections of the British working class to take direct action against the indignities of their condition and in favour of their legitimate aspirations, and they certainly should not be glossed over.

But the notion that there was something extra-special about this moment in time, never before achieved, and never again to be repeated, seems to me to be misconceived. Despite the appalling setbacks of the Depression, the working class was to proceed to further triumphs even if still, in society today, denied the life chances annexed by the more prosperous classes. Cronin brings into the argument the new Labour Party constitution and programme of 1918, and the new constituency parties spread across the country. These indeed regularized the accession of power to Labour gained through participation in the war effort; they were, however, important agencies through which reforms on behalf of the working class were secured *within* the existing parliamentary system; they were not agencies used *against* the system. In fact, Cronin seems to recognize the weakness of his own case when he states, very accurately:

> Of course, the bulk of the working class were far from being committed socialists in these turbulent years, and the general situation was far from revolutionary. Most important, the governing élite never lost the capacity or will to rule, nor were they rent with divisions sharp enough to paralyse administration.

The proud claim of the young Welsh miner, it seems to me, can easily be set within a context in which Labour men had been in government and in which Labour leaders had to be consulted by government; a context in which some social reforms had been passed, and in which Labour was coming to power on a number of local councils. It is important, too, not to overplay the argument about the skill and cohesion of the upper class. Marxists, believing that there *ought* to have been a revolution, are forced to do this. Thus Walter Kendall: 'Put to the test, the maturity of the ruling élite proved far greater than that of the revolutionaries who sought its overthrow.'[10] Such statements put too little emphasis on the belief within the working class in the existence of their own freedoms, the belief that, though extremely militant action might be needed from time to time, institutions were themselves adaptable and indeed would be adapted to realize working-class aspirations. The war experience had brought a more consolidated and homogeneous working class; it had also created grave sources of tension and discontent: but beyond that it had revealed that through the carefully articulated class structure there was a great residuum of national unity and faith in British institutions. There is more than one resonance to the phrase: 'Britons never never never shall be slaves'.

So, in no way undervaluing the significance of working-class militancy, let us turn to the stirring events themselves. The year 1919 opened with soldiers' demobilization riots, followed immediately by the forty-hour strike in Glasgow. The wartime Clyde strikes had been spontaneous and broad-based; now when the Clydeside workers' leaders called for a general strike on Monday 27 January,

34 'William Gallacher being brought round after an encounter with a police truncheon, City Chambers, George Square, 1st February 1919, Glasgow'. An excellent piece of newspaper photography, even if the caption fails to maintain the same standard.

to press their very practical demand for a forty-hour week as a means of absorbing returning servicemen, they were fully supported in all the principal factories: three mass demonstrations took place on the 27th, the 29th and the 31st. The third the government anticipated by concentrating troops, tanks and machine guns on the city, though the actual 'Battle of George Square' on 1 February was fought with policemen's truncheons (*Plate 34*) and lemonade bottles. It appears that not only the prostrate Willie Gallacher, one of the leaders of the demonstration, but also the civilian in the background had been struck; the strong police presence is very evident. A little later the tanks moved in upon the deserted battlefield: the strike continued for a further ten days. The press was filled with all kinds of alarmist tales, special attention being devoted to the running up of the Red Flag by the strikers: it is too often forgotten that the Red Flag in Britain was as much a symbol of working-class solidarity as of revolution – even if many members showed that they knew neither the words nor the tune, the Red Flag was the song of the distinctively non-revolutionary Labour Party. The readiness of many members of the government to wage their own form of class war was made clear in cabinet by Winston Churchill:

> The disaffected were in a minority, and, in his opinion, there would have to be a conflict in order to clear the air. We should be careful to have plenty of provocation before taking strong measures. By going gently at first we should get the support we wanted from the nation and then troops could be used more effectively.[11]

A dozen of the leaders were arrested, but against only two could a successful charge be made out, and that scarcely implied any deep subversion of the established order: Willie Gallacher, himself, and Emanuel Shinwell were imprisoned for 'inciting to riot'. Looking back ruefully many years later, Gallacher unwittingly went straight to the heart of the situation: 'We were carrying on a strike when we ought to have been making a revolution.'[12] In fact nothing which has been published on the early history of the British Communist Party suggests that native British communists had the faintest idea of how to set about having a revolution. The government, nonetheless, sent a secret military circular to all commanding officers in Britain asking whether their troops would respond to orders necessary for preserving public peace, and whether they would participate in strikebreaking. A few days later a permanent anti-strike organization, in the form of a Committee of the Cabinet, was established under the headship of Sir Hamar Greenwood, later notorious as the sponsor of the Black and Tan terror tactics in Ireland.

The first mining crisis also came to a head in January 1919. Mainly because of the coal owners' resistance to paying war bonuses, the coal industry had been taken over by the government during the war. Miners now wished their gains of the wartime period to be safeguarded and nationalization to be made permanent, and in January they threatened a national mining strike in support of these demands. However, Lloyd George was able to avert trouble for the time being by setting up a special Statutory Commission to investigate the condition of the coal industry. Much of the evidence heard by the Commission clearly supported nationalization, but the Commission itself was divided in its verdict, and eventually on 18 August Lloyd George, under pressure from Conservative Cabinet colleagues, announced his rejection of the idea of nationalization. For the time being, however, government wartime control of the industry continued.

There had been short police strikes towards the end of the war, and early in August 1919 further police strikes broke out in London and Liverpool. Between Friday 1 August and Sunday 3 August there was extensive rioting in Liverpool as the lawless elements in that great sea port exploited the absence of the usual law enforcement officers. The riots may well be significant as showing how large a proportion of society remained indifferent to the principles of law and order, but they do not provide any evidence of revolutionary intentions on the part of organized labour. The *Morning Post* reported

> After the first outbreak in the neighbourhood of the Rotunda Theatre, where a shop was attacked and looted, had been answered by the reading of the Riot Act, a body of soldiers fired a warning volley, pointing their rifles over the heads of the crowds. Thereafter they paraded the districts where the mob were threatening activity, without, however, actually interfering. Their passivity being cunningly sensed, no sooner were they out of reach than shop windows were smashed, and the law-breakers, many of them young women, pressed forward to help themselves to the contents. Four tanks, which moved in yesterday to support the men of the Notts and Derby and the South Staffordshire Regiments who composed the occupying military force, stood silent sentinels on St. George's Hall platform, while within a stone's throw away scenes of lawless effrontery were witnessed.[13]

Altogether 2,600 troops were brought in, as well as four tanks (*Plate 35*), *HMS Valiant* and two destroyers which stood off Liverpool port. After a round of shots one civilian died of wounds, and there were bayonet charges on the Saturday

35 Liverpool police strike, 1919: tanks posted outside St George's Hall. Another valuable piece of photojournalism, from the *Illustrated London News*, 2 August 1919.

night. Despite its own careful eye-witness reports (corroborated in other newspapers) the *Morning Post* in its leading articles continued to assert that the Liverpool violence and the various minor strikes throughout the country could be explained only by the two words 'attempted revolution'. Historians, however, have no need to ape the lunacies of the *Morning Post*.

The government still controlled the railways and proposed to cut back some of the wage gains made during the war. To resist this cut, the railwaymen called for a national railway strike on 30 September. The government now renamed the Committee on Industrial Unrest the Strike Committee and extended its powers: the country was divided into twelve divisional areas, each with a commissioner and staff. Under the unrepealed wartime Defence of the Realm Act, a state of emergency was declared as soon as the strike broke out. On Friday 3 October the Home Secretary appealed to all citizens to join the formation of 'citizen guards in face of the menace by which we are confronted today'. But the railwaymen's case was supported by Arthur Henderson and J. R. Clynes, both of whom had served as Labour members of the wartime Coalition governments, and the strike ended on 5 October when the government decided to abandon the proposed wage cut.

There were several other strikes of a similar nature; then, half-way through 1920, there came a series of events which seemed to indicate that Labour was prepared to use its industrial power to influence the foreign policy of His Majesty's duly elected government. Three questions are involved: was this action 'potentially revolutionary', did it have any effect, and what does this episode tell us about the nature of working-class activism at this fabled historical moment? The object once again was a concrete one: to stop Britain being involved in a war on behalf of Poland against Soviet Russia. Unconstitutional perhaps, but a very different thing from aiming at the overthrow of established government. Indeed, although windbags like the railwaymen's leader J. H. Thomas might like to stress the seriousness of Labour's intentions by talking of a 'challenge to the whole Constitution of the country', the term 'unconstitutional' is scarcely really relevant: one does not have to swallow the whole corporatist thesis to recognize that decisions in modern British society have always been affected by the pressure of relevant interest groups, such as the medical profession or the big insurance companies (both important in Lloyd George's planning of health insurance in 1911).

Did it have any effect? The first event was the refusal on 10 May 1920 of a gang of London dockers to coal the *Jolly George*, believing it to be carrying munitions bound for Poland. The incident does not seem to have disturbed the Cabinet, which was absorbed on 10 May in Coal Prices, the Amritsar Massacre and the Mural Decoration of the Foreign Office, and, on 12 May, in Ireland, India, Turkey and Asphyxiating Gas.[14] On Sunday 8 August a series of Labour demonstrations against the possibility of British intervention on behalf of Poland were organized, followed on 9 August by the setting up of a Council of Action to implement a joint Labour Party–TUC decision to use 'the whole industrial power of the organised workers' against war. There was in fact no British intervention against Russia. But the Cabinet papers for the period between the *Jolly George* incident and the final Labour outburst make it clear that whatever Labour thought or did the government was by no means hell-bent on supporting Poland. All the Labour agitation achieved, in conjunction with that of the Liberals who followed the leadership of Asquith, and sections of the press, was the strengthening of the hand of the government in its dealings with the French, who were much more belligerent on this issue.

In a conference with the French which took place during the same weekend as the first labour demonstrations, Lloyd George stressed that 'the working classes were frankly hostile to intervention and this view was shared by Conservative opinion, as was clearly indicated in the Press'. By 10 August any danger of intervention was really over, for the Cabinet decided that the Russian terms for an armistice with the Poles were reasonable, and since 'Labour was in a very irritable frame of mind at present', a disavowal of any interventionist intentions might be issued.[15] Local Councils of Action, of which there were at least 250, remained in being for some time, so that the whole episode is of importance in demonstrating once again the maturity and coherence which the working class had now attained. That the trade union movement has not since contemplated action of quite the same type is not so much because it has meantime become less revolutionary, but because it now has other means of asserting its influence.

In October 1920 there took place the 'Battle of Downing Street'. The wartime boom was coming to an end, and the mass unemployment which everyone feared was becoming a reality. A deputation of London mayors led by George Lansbury, with the unemployed marching behind in their thousands, had demanded an interview with Lloyd George to discuss the unemployment problem in their boroughs. A peaceable demonstration erupted into violence when the police suddenly decided to clear Whitehall by means of mounted baton charges.

Government control of the coal industry was due to end on 31 March 1921. The coal owners, insisting that the only way to deal with the depression in the industry was to lower labour costs, posted their new terms, which in most cases involved substantial wage cuts for the miners. The miners' leaders, cheated, as they believed, of nationalization, argued strongly for a national wages agreement, so that the relatively prosperous mines could subsidize the uneconomic ones, and maintain existing wage standards. The miners also declared that the attack on their standards was merely a prelude to a general attack on working-class living standards. British trade unions now had the rudiments of a central organization in the form of the General Council of the TUC established in 1920. But at this stage the miners looked to a grouping which had been established before the war, the Triple Alliance of Miners, Railwaymen and General Workers.

The Triple Alliance did not in fact agree to take sympathetic action on behalf of the miners till 8 April. The government declared a state of emergency under the Emergency Powers Act which had been passed in October 1920, prepared for the call up of the army reserve, and approved the setting up of a special defence force of 'loyal ex-servicemen and loyal citizens'. According to Lloyd George, 'the country is facing a situation analogous to civil war'. Over Saturday and Sunday 9 and 10 April, military encampments were set up in parks, on the outskirts of the main cities, and in disused military bases. The following week there were movements of troops, transports and tanks, while troops equipped with machine guns moved in on the Fife coalfield. Bitter rioting broke out in Lanarkshire, Fife and South Wales when managerial staff tried to man the pumps.

The sympathetic strike by the whole Triple Alliance was due to begin at midnight on Tuesday 12 April, unless, as J. H. Thomas and a deputation of railwaymen and transport workers put it to the Prime Minister, negotiations with the miners were resumed. The Triple Alliance case was this:

> We are not proclaiming a revolution, we are standing shoulder to shoulder for fundamental trade union rights. If these are denied to us now they will be denied to the whole trade union movement later. The fight must be won; it will be won; British trade unionism will triumph against the united effort of British organized capital in its attempt to destroy the trade union achievements, legitimately gained by years of hard work and sacrifice.[16]

In these circumstances, the government did in fact institute negotiations with the mine owners and the miners, and the Triple Alliance strike was called off. But there remained the basic stumbling block of the question of a national agreement on miners' wages, something to which the government was strongly opposed. With the breakdown of negotiations on this issue, the Triple Alliance strike was rescheduled for midnight on Friday 15 April.

But that strike never took place. On 14 April a meeting of Coalition MPs, attended also by the miners' secretary Frank Hodges, suggested a possible compromise which Lloyd George immediately seized upon: on the fateful Friday he offered the miners a temporary arrangement on wages, provided the national agreement question was shelved. The Triple Alliance leaders, alarmed in a time of mounting depression and unemployment at the prospect of granting the miners *carte blanche*, urged the miners to discuss this proposal. The miners, who felt that they had been duped once too often by Lloyd George, refused. But the Triple Alliance leaders cancelled the strike. April 15 became 'Black Friday' in British labour history. The miners fought on alone, finally on 1 July being forced back to work, to local agreements and, in most areas, to substantial cuts in wages.

Given the extent of the Depression and the accompanying unemployment, it is not surprising that strikes in various other industries during 1922 were unsuccessful in resisting wage cuts; it should be remembered, too, that along with wages the cost of living was dropping from the postwar peak. At the end of 1922 the Labour Party began to show signs of shaking itself out of the lethargy which had afflicted it since 1918. There was a steady drop in the incidence of strikes. The centre of militant working-class activity tended, therefore, to move back to the unemployed. On Armistice Day 1922, 25,000 London unemployed tacked themselves on to the official ceremony, carrying at their head a large wreath inscribed: 'From the living victims – the unemployed – to our dead comrades, who died in vain.' It was at the end of 1922 that the first Hunger Marches began, organized by Wal Hannington in the south and by Harry McShane in Scotland. Again there was a ready propensity among the prosperous classes of people to see in marches, demonstrations and 'Unemployed Sundays' the sinister hand of revolutionary intent: references to unemployed marches in *The Times* are indexed during the twenties under the heading 'Russia: Government Propaganda'.

Members of the National Unemployed Workers Committee Movement took an oath 'to never cease from active strife against this system until capitalism is abolished, and our country and all its resources belong to the people'. But the active Communist element remained a minority among the unemployed, and the unemployed themselves were to some extent cut off from their fellow-workers lucky enough to be employed. In any event Hannington, McShane and their associates concentrated their energies on specific abuses within the administration of the unemployed insurance scheme and within the Poor Law (which concerned those who did not qualify for insurance or who had exhausted their benefits).

Rates of poor relief were at the discretion of the local Boards of Guardians: the NUWCM directed its fire at the niggardly ones, while the more generous ones, such as the Poplar Board, fell foul of middle-class opinion. In protest against the heavy burden being imposed on borough rates and against the attempt of the government to control expenditure on poor relief, George Lansbury and the Poplar Council refused to pay their precept to the London County Council. The thirty councillors were imprisoned for over a month, but, as did some of the protests of the unemployed, their gesture brought its reward: an act was passed spreading the costs of relief more equitably over London as a whole. That did not stop 'poplarism' being equated in the usual sections of the press with 'revolution'.

The first Labour government (a minority administration) came in 1923 under MacDonald and went nine months later. Unemployment remained above the $1\frac{1}{2}$ million mark. In 1925 came the return to the gold standard, and with it a resuscitation of all the bitter conflicts within the coal industry: the timetable of confrontation was in motion. On 30 June the coal-owners announced wage cuts to take effect on 1 August. Ten days later the General Council of the TUC promised the Miners Federation Executive support in 'the fight to preserve the standard of life of its members'. On 23 July the government reviewed the emergency plans (first drawn up in 1920); two days later the Railwaymen's, Transport Workers', and Seamen's unions agreed to put an embargo on coal movements from midnight on 31 July. On 29 July an official enquiry into the mining crisis by the Macmillan Committee came down on the side of the miners, and two days later, 'Red Friday', the government agreed to subsidize the coal industry until 1 May 1926 so that existing wages could be maintained.

Although Baldwin (now Prime Minister again) had called in March, before the return to the gold standard, for industrial conciliation, in his 'Peace in our Time' speech, and genuinely was himself a man of peace, the presumption is that the government's emergency plans were not yet in full readiness. At any rate, in August the government did two things: first, it set up the Samuel Commission to investigate the coal industry; but second, under the Emergency Powers Act it set aside £10,000 to establish emergency organization in the event of a General Strike, authorizing the recruitment of the Organisation for Maintenance of Supplies (OMS), which mustered about 100,000 voluntary recruits by 1 May 1926. On the other side, Walter Citrine, Secretary of the General Council, several times noted the absence of any kind of effective planning on the part of the TUC. A. J. Cook, Secretary of the Miners Federation, made a number of fiery speeches. On 18 April 1926 he declared: 'My last word to the Government is "count the cost". The cost of a strike of the miners would mean the end of capitalism. . . . This is a war to the death, and it is your death they are after.'[17]

The Samuel Commission reported on 6 March 1926, recommending (a) long-term reorganization of the industry; (b) immediate wage cuts. The coal-owners at once expressed hostility to the first of these recommendations, while the miners expressed total opposition to the second. On 29 April, the executives of 141 trade unions met at Memorial Hall, London, to authorize the General Council of the TUC to carry out negotiations on behalf of the miners and, if necessary, to call a national strike in support of the miners to begin on 3 May. The next day the coal-owners published their final terms, involving wage cuts of $13\frac{1}{2}$ per cent. Over that night and into May, the lock-out of miners who refused these terms began. Over the same period, and extending to 3 May, negotiations were taking place between a three-man Cabinet team and a three-man General Council team, consisting of J. H. Thomas, who never concealed his view that in any direct confrontation between unions and government constitutional propriety demanded that the government must win, Alonso Swailes, a left-wing militant, and Arthur Pugh who stood in the moderate centre, with the calmly efficient Walter Citrine as Secretary. At 1.15 am, Sunday 2 May, these negotiating teams issued a 'midnight memorandum' saying:

> The Prime Minister has satisfied himself, as a result of conversations he has had with the representatives of the Trade Union Congress that if negotiations are continued (it being understood that the [coal-owners' lockout] notices cease to be operative) the representatives of the Trade Union Congress are confident that a settlement can be reached on the lines of the report [on the future reorganization of the coal industry] within a fortnight.

But many members of the full Cabinet (including Churchill) saw this as representing capitulation to the unions; on the other side the Miners' Executive had already left London, and their Secretary A. J. Cook refused to accept this memorandum on their behalf.

11.30 pm, 2 May: news came through that printers on the *Daily Mail* had refused to print an editorial calling on the nation to support the government. Baldwin informed the General Council negotiators that because of this 'overt act' and the fact that telegrams had already been sent out in readiness for a national strike beginning at midnight on Thursday 6 May, negotiations were now at an end. Midnight, 3 May: 'first-line' workers (transport, railways, printing, iron and steel, metal and chemical industries, building and power-stations) were called out; 'second-line' workers (engineering, shipbuilding, textiles, woodworking, the Post Office and distributive trades) were instructed to remain at work for the time being. The strike was organized by local unions and councils of action throughout the country, and by Citrine and Ernest Bevin from TUC headquarters

36 The General Strike, fifth day: an armoured car passing through Oxford Street, London. Given the technical limitations of the single-shot photography of the time, this is a quite remarkable photograph.

in London. Communist Party members and even non-union Labour Party members were firmly excluded; funds from Russia were refused. The strike was overwhelmingly solid, as it was to remain save for, as the historian G. A. Phillips has put it, some 'fraying at the edges'.[18]

On 6 May the Liberal MP Sir John Simon declared to the House of Commons that since the strike was aimed at the government and not at employers it was 'an utterly illegal proceeding' and that therefore the union leaders were totally liable for damages. The next day informal discussions began between Sir Herbert Samuel (the Liberal lawyer who had chaired the Samuel Commission) and the General Council. The miners again made it clear that they would not accept any settlement involving immediate wage cuts. Nevertheless Samuel went ahead with the drafting of the Samuel Memorandum which advocated both reorganization of the coal industry and wage cuts.

11 May: the second-line workers were brought out. The strike was still very solid; there was some violence, but no loss of life. *Plates 36 and 37* illuminate aspects of the strike. In the bustle of Oxford Street the armoured car in *Plate 36* does not seem particularly ominous, especially since the citizens on top of the bus are looking on with interest and probably approbation. The motor-bike was the best form of transport that the upper-working class or lower-middle class could aspire to: three can be seen in this photograph, while there is only one car, an open tourer, the possession of a rather more affluent citizen. The way in which transport remained so largely open to the elements (particularly in the three buses seen) may suggest why the wearing of hats persisted during the twenties, though was to decline in the thirties. *Plate 37* is altogether more foreboding, but that is largely because of the earliness of the hour, the absence of civilians, and the presence of troops. The purpose, the convoying of food, interrupted of course by

37 'The General Strike,
seventh day: scene at
Hyde Park at 6 am,
10 May 1926, showing
armoured cars and
troops ready to escort
London's great food
convoy.'

the transport workers being part of the General Strike, was not in itself a directly menacing one.

8.30 pm, 11 May: at a joint meeting General Council members urged the Miners' Executive to accept the Samuel Memorandum as a basis for a return to work. This was rejected by the miners. 13 May: a General Council delegation to 10 Downing Street agreed to call off the strike without securing any conditions at all. May–November 1926: the miners remained on strike for a further seven months till driven back by starvation. However, some miners in Nottinghamshire and Derbyshire established the breakaway Spencer Union on the basis of collaboration with the coal-owners. 1927: the Conservative government introduced the Trades Disputes Act, declaring general strikes illegal, and changing the system of trade union financial support for the Labour Party from 'contracting out' to 'contracting in'. Labour Party finances suffered; and there was also, immediately, a decline in trade union membership. Bruised and shaken, the General Council, under the chairmanship of Ben Turner accepted the initiative of Sir Alfred Mond and entered into discussions over co-operation between employers and unions (*Plate 38*).

## Social Structure and Social Change

As well as irony, there is artistic licence in Wenam's *Punch* cartoon 'Capital-and-Labour Day, May 1st' (*Plate 38*). But it is not inaccurate in its portrayal of a very distinctive working class: flat caps and cravats, with one foreman figure in bowler hat and collar and tie, and an upper class of industrialists clearly assimilated into the aristocracy (top hats, wing collars, and note the monocle). The classic instance of industrial combination was the merger in 1927 between Brunner

Mond, United Alkali, British Dye Stuffs and Nobel Industries which created Imperial Chemical Industries (ICI). ICI in itself provides a marvellous case-study of the upper class, its attitudes, and its dominance of British society, economy and politics.

Sir Alfred Mond's father was born in Germany, but was so successful in business in Britain, that he was able to send both of his sons to public school and university. It was a token of the openness of the upper class that, having gone through the correct acculturation process, Mond was welcomed into it. In sponsoring the merger Mond declared:

> We are on trial before the eyes of the entire world, and especially the eyes of our fellow citizens and of the Empire. We are not merely a body of people carrying on industry in order to make dividends, we are much more: we are the object of universal envy, admiration and criticism, and the capacity of British industrialists, British commercialists and British technicians will be judged by the entire world from the success we make of this merger.

McGowan of United Alkali responded: 'Primarily of course the duties of a Board of Directors are to make dividends for their Shareholders, but in forming this combine we are doing something for the Empire.'[19] ICI boards thereafter perfectly exemplified the interchangeability of roles between business and government (in all its aspects) which characterized the upper class. Among those who served on the board during the later twenties and into the thirties were Rufus Isaacs, 1st Marquess of Reading, who had been Lord Chief Justice, and then, for five years, Viceroy of India (his son, incidentally, had married Alfred Mond's daughter Eva), Lord Birkenhead (the former F. E. Smith, successively in the 1920s Lord Chancellor and Secretary for India), Lord Weir, the Scottish shipping magnate and pillar of Toryism, and Sir John Anderson, permanent Under-Secretary at the Home Office, and director of the government's preparations against the General Strike; the first Treasurer was recruited from the Inland Revenue. Sir Alfred Mond himself shortly became Lord Melchett.

The new industrial giant had to have a head office. *Plate 39* shows the drawing produced by a run-of-the-mill but influential architect whom Mond had known at the Ministry of Works, Sir Frank Baines. The style is that best described as modern brutalism, enlivened with the pomposity felt to be appropriate to this special agent of the British Empire: note the columns and the statues. Just out of sight, round the corner on the left side of the drawing, was the site where the Transport and General Workers Union were building Transport House, which was also to be the headquarters of the Labour Party: a juxtaposition between capital and labour as close as that represented in the *Punch* cartoon. From this Millbank site, the Houses of Parliament, of course, were not far away either. The nine-storey block, housing 1,500 people, was erected in twenty-six months by the construction firm of John Mowlem.

Baines's stately (as he would have seen it) drawing can be most fruitfully compared with the Glasgow *Evening Times* cartoon 'Mond amalgamates everything within sight' (*Plate 40*). This rich product of a Glasgow provincial newspaper, whose vision of the new world is in the same category as Chaplin's *Modern Times*, René Clair's *A Nous la Liberté* and Huxley's *Brave New World*, repays close study. On the right is Mond himself, on the left the epitome of the mad scientist. Everywhere, the features which seemed most new and striking

38 Architect's drawing of Imperial Chemical House, Millbank, London. The architect was Sir Frank Baines (1877–1933).

39 *Punch* cartoon 1 May 1929. There is quite a heavy touch of irony about this, with a capitalist on the right carrying his cash box, and the slogans, 'give the men a chance' and 'give the masters a chance', but the stereotypes of capital and of labour are clear enough. The specific reference is to the conference usually described as the Mond–Turner talks.

40 Cartoon in the *Evening Times*, Glasgow, 19 September 1927.

CAPITAL-AND-LABOUR DAY, MAY 1ST
WITH MR. PUNCH'S BEST WISHES FOR THE SUCCESS OF THE CONFERENCE OF REPRESENTA-
TIVES OF TRADE UNIONS AND EMPLOYERS WHICH OPENED ON ST. GEORGE'S DAY.

PEEPS INTO THE WONDERFUL FUTURE

Mond Amalgamates Everything Within Sight

41 Ascot, second day:
June 1925.

about twenties society have been adapted to incorporate the name Mond. There
are the cosmetics, the soaps, the household cleaners, the large art deco cinema,
the Civil Aviation (British Imperial Airways, with a government subsidy, was
founded in 1924): the 'Alfrock Café' may even be a reference to T. S. Eliot's
*avant-garde* poetry and J. Alfred Prufrock.

This sense of the future is an important aspect of the 1920s. However, as
already indicated, the class structure betrayed much of the past. The basic
institutions and the great sporting occasions of the upper class remained
untouched. *Plate 41* is, of course, most carefully composed, though possibly the
photographer would have preferred to do without the intruding heads on the
lower right. The image is, in any case, redolent of Ascot as the quintessential
upper-class occasion.

We have to take a pinch of salt with the textbook stories of mass culture and
standardization of clothes and leisure activities bringing classes closer together.
From social surveys we do know of the significance to working-class life of the
new dance halls and cinema palaces, of the influence on fashions of Hollywood
films, and of the capability of the mass-produced clothing trade to meet some of
the demands put upon it. *Plate 42* shows one of the most famous of all of the
Palais de Danse. Almost all photographs and even cartoons of the time show
dances, even in working-class areas, as rather formal affairs. This photograph is
particularly valuable for its unpremeditated quality, and gives us a true insight
into the informality which had crept in since the war. Some of the women are

wearing hats, some not. There is one gentleman, but only one, in formal dinner attire. The chinoiserie is inescapable: within a few years the predominant influence would be the ancient Egyptian one released by the discovery of the tomb of Tutankhamun.

42 Palais de Danse, Hammersmith, March 1920.

 To be working class was still, essentially, to be performing physical labour in unpleasant conditions, and to be specially vulnerable to the vagaries of the trade cycle. Between working class and upper class were the different levels of the middle class. We can make a rough-and-ready distinction between an upper-middle class of lesser businessmen, managers and most professionals, and a lower-middle class of shopkeepers, elementary schoolteachers and the growing sector of white-collar workers. All of these lower-middle-class groups, however, aspired upwards: in their recruiting campaigns the Insurance Officers Union cited as their model doctors' and lawyers' professional organizations. The continuing decline in religious observance affected all classes, but probably the middle classes least. Religion, however, was still a matter of significance in governing circles. The reform of the official prayerbook of the Anglican Church aroused heated controversy in parliament. The educational system served to reinforce the existing class structure, while making possible, for individuals, perhaps slightly more mobility than had been apparent in prewar days. Essentially the very expensive public schools remained for the upper class or the upwardly mobile; the much less expensive grammar schools, with scholarships and free places, were for the middle class; and elementary schools for the working class.

43 'Parade of young
ladies wearing the
newest designs in
bathing costumes and
wraps at Southport
Lake', 18 May 1928.

44 *Punch* cartoon,
25 August 1926, by
Pat Keely.

*Mother.* "WHEN I WAS YOUNG, GIRLS NEVER THOUGHT OF DOING THE THINGS THEY DO TO-DAY."
*Daughter.* "PERHAPS THAT'S WHY THEY DIDN'T DO THEM."

*Plates 43, 44 and 45* draw our attention to issues which were not just a source of agitation in the press and cultivated newspaper-reading public, but which really did run right down through society. Since the war, young women had been openly behaving in ways which would have been considered utterly improper in Edwardian times. *Plate 43*, a very carefully set-up picture (in its pyramidal structure echoing *Plate 41*), gives the standard image of the 'gay twenties' and the decade's (allegedly) emancipated young women. Here, we clearly have actresses or showgirls playing parts which forty years later would be taken by professional photographic models: the footwear suggests that bathing is not a main purpose of these outfits. The cigarettes and the public application of make-up would generally have been considered bad taste in Edwardian society. The cartoon in *Plate 44* is cleverer than perhaps the artist appreciated. Word of mouth really is one of the most potent forces for change in the realm of manners and morals. The girl in the hammock is absolutely right: the frontiers of what could be thought, and what could be talked about, had been greatly pushed back during and since the war. Broadly, though, prudishness still ruled: Sir Roy Harrod narrates how a hearty Cambridge undergraduate in 1922 found 'unseemly and immoral' a reference to contraceptives made by Keynes when delivering a paper on Malthus. The Strube cartoon (*Plate 45*) may seem striking for its male chauvinism, though, as the *Punch* cartoon suggests, the point being made was as much a matter of generations as a matter of sexes. One is made aware of some of the more enduring features of the controversies over women's rights, since many reformulations of this cartoon (which, itself, is representative of a very large number at the time) are to be found again in the 1970s, when the Women's Liberation movement began to have an impact. There is shrewdness in the rendering of the benign Stanley Baldwin in the background, though, of course, nastiness in the portrayal of the old militant. Actually, for all that there was a surface controversy over the flapper

SHADE OF OLD MILITANT : " So this is what I fought for ! "    *April 29th*, 1927.

45 Strube cartoon, 29 April 1927.

46 £1,000,000 Motor
Show at Olympia, 13
October 1927: 'a first
peep at the Mystery
Morris'.

vote, this cartoon, and the others like it, get things wrong. The suffragists had
known that the total enfranchisement of women was only a matter of time, and
among serious politicians there was in reality little or no opposition to the act of
1928 which enfranchised all women, including those under thirty (the 'flappers'),
upon exactly the same terms as men.

Equality may seem fundamentally a moral issue; but gross inequality can in
fact result in economic inefficiency – the talents of certain individuals in
underprivileged groups may not be exploited to the common good, and certain
groups may not have sufficient purchasing power to enable the economy to
function at the highest possible level. Although the motor-car industry greatly
expanded in the twenties, there was no question of it having the same kind of
democratic aspirations as were being expressed at the same time in the United
States. In 1922 952,000 motor vehicle licences were issued; by 1930 the figure had
more than doubled to 2,218,000. This latter figure represents about one vehicle to
every five families, so we can see that the car is beginning to become a possibility
for many middle-class families, while it is still a total improbability for almost all
working-class families. Motor-cars, nevertheless, were a matter of great interest
far beyond those who could actually afford to buy one. *Plate 46* is illustrative
both of the great motor shows which were now being held at Olympia, and of the
continuing emphasis on luxury which rather characterized the British motor
industry. If the motor-car could scarcely be credited with bringing society

47 Prime Minister Stanley Baldwin at the BBC microphone.

together in any way, the motor-bus, along with trams and electric trolley-buses, played a very important part in improving communications: by 1929 100 municipalities were running a total of 4,737 buses. Longer-distance routes were almost invariably privately operated. A rather different form of communication, which could also be represented as bringing the country closer together, was radio. A prime example of government willingness, since the experiences of the war, to intervene directly in the economy was the establishment in 1926 of the British Broadcasting Corporation. Actually, by 1930, the number of radio licences issued had not risen very much above two million, so radio, like the car, must at this time be regarded as a middle-class, rather than a national phenomenon.

Already, however, Stanley Baldwin had understood its potency. Unlike most of his contemporaries, he also realized that in broadcasting you are essentially addressing one family, or even one individual, certainly not a public meeting: he quickly developed a persuasive fireside manner, and it is entirely appropriate that Stanley Baldwin speaking into a BBC microphone should have been thought a worthy subject for photography (*Plate 47*).

## Corporatism and Crisis

Keith Middlemas, a foremost proponent of the idea that since the First World War Britain has steadily assumed the forms of the corporatist state, has written:

> The experience of 1914–18, and the widely disseminated industrial conflict before and after the war showed that the nineteenth-century British political system had broken down under the weight of antagonisms in industrial society. The wartime Coalition

government was, however, strong enough to resist the temptation to assume authoritarian powers taken, for example, in Germany in 1916 by Hindenburg and Ludendorff; and to fend off demands by the labour movement for what it considered wholly unacceptable changes in social and economic organisation. By 1922 it had become clear that a sufficient number of union and employers' leaders had accepted the need of formal political collaboration with the state. TUC and employers' organisations crossed a threshold which had not even existed before the war, and behaved thereafter in some degree as estates of the realm, to the detriment of more ancient obsolete estates, the municipalities, the churches, the 'colleges' of professional men, and the panoply of voluntary bodies, so important in the political system of the nineteenth century.[20]

Of course, institutions change, wax and wane; but, unlike Middlemas, I do not feel that there had been any qualitative change in the way in which pressure groups outside parliament attempted to influence decisions of government. Employers became better organized, but they had long had influence. At this stage, the real value of trade unions to their membership was in the workplace, rather than in central decision-making circles. Basic decisions, it seems to me, were essentially taken by a government and an administration largely monopolized by a cohesive upper class which was also dominant in finance and industry; these decisions, however, were moderated by a perceived need to maintain national unity, to carry the support of the people, and to respond to the pressures of the growing labour movement.

The Conservative government of Stanley Baldwin between 1924 and 1929 was in fact far from reactionary, or totally committed to the interests of the upper and middle classes. Its major achievements, for which Neville Chamberlain was the responsible minister, were the 1928 Pensions Act, and the 1929 Local Government Act, which brought to an end the local rule of the Poor Law guardians, transferring their functions to Public Assistance Committees of the local authorities, and also imposing many new responsibilities in regard to health upon local government.

Nevertheless, the growing strength of the political Labour movement was represented in the fact that from 1929 Ramsay MacDonald was able to form another minority government. Unfortunately, this government ran into worldwide economic crisis. In May 1931 there began a final series of bank collapses in central Europe, resulting in accelerated withdrawal of funds from London, and a loss of British assets deposited in central Europe. On the insistence of the more traditionalist Liberals in parliament (Lloyd George's group had actually presented ambitious Keynesian policies in the Liberal Yellow Book of 1928) a committee under the director of the Prudential Insurance Company, Sir George May, was appointed to investigate methods of pruning government expenditure, a high level of which, by traditional standards, was a cause of impaired foreign confidence. The moment parliament rose for the summer recess, the May report was published: it was couched in such gloomy terms that the outflow of funds was greatly aggravated. Had this trend been allowed to continue unresisted it would soon have led to a devaluation of the pound and an enforced abandonment of the gold standard, both of which would have been heavy blows to what remained of London's position as an international financial centre. The collapse of London as an international money market would mean the wiping out of a substantial portion of Britain's invisible exports (banking and insurance services) which for long had helped to keep the balance of payments just in equilibrium.

The first requirement was the restoration of foreign confidence, a difficult task for a minority Labour government. The Labour cabinet authorized its chief ministers to enter into discussions with the Opposition leaders over the nature of the emergency measures which would have to be introduced. In July the weekly journal of the ILP, whose tiny band of left-wingers in parliament had been more or less constantly at war with what it saw as the compromising policy of the Labour government, carried a front-page article headed 'Towards a National Government'. The final stages of the crisis began when on 11 August Ramsay MacDonald made a sudden return to London from holiday in his native Lossiemouth. Within the Cabinet, discussion was centred on the size and nature of the economies which would have to be made to effect the necessary restoration of confidence. Meanwhile, the Bank of England was endeavouring to raise loans from American and French banks. Provisionally, the Cabinet was prepared to approve economies of £76,000,000, though there was strong resistance to a suggested cut in benefits paid to the unemployed, reinforced when the General Council of the TUC came out strongly against any such attack on those who were already the worst-off members of the community. The Conservative leaders thought that greater economies would be necessary, and, in fact, on the evening of Sunday 23 August, news reached what proved to be the final meeting of the Labour Cabinet: the Federal Reserve Bank in New York would only grant a loan if the government proved its determination to face up to the problem of high government spending by imposing a 10 per cent cut in unemployment benefits. The Cabinet as an entity could not accept this cut, and so MacDonald received the resignation of each member.

MacDonald took the resignations of his government to the King, who next day persuaded him to continue as Prime Minister leading a National government of Conservatives, Liberals and three former Labour Cabinet ministers, Snowden, Thomas and Lord Sankey. The remainder of the Labour Cabinet and almost the entire Labour Party went into Opposition against this new National government led by the former Labour Prime Minister.

Traditionally, these events have been represented as 'betrayal' or 'treachery' to the Labour movement on the part of Ramsay MacDonald. The detailed biography, based on MacDonald's own private papers, by David Marquand, while not glorifying MacDonald, shows quite clearly that he had no advance plans, but simply did what he did because he was persuaded by the King that this was his national duty. In criticizing traditional accounts, Robert Skidelsky has taken a slightly different line. He has argued that the crisis has tended to be represented 'in terms of a struggle between socialism and capitalism'. He argues that 'the real cleavage of opinion occurred not across this divide, but another: between the economic radicals and the economic conservatives.' In rational terms Skidelsky is absolutely right, but historical events do not usually work out on a basis of rationality. He overestimates the actual possibilities of carrying out the policies of 'the economic radicals', as Ross McKibbin, in an important article, has shown.[21]

Yet the crisis was undoubtedly a matter of high drama, and of deep concern to millions of British people, who read ominous headlines about the perils facing the

48 'Psychology in a political crisis: scenes in London'. *The Illustrated London News* provided very fine coverage of the crisis. The particular caption for this photograph is: 'citizens of London gathered in their thousands to watch the coming and going of ministers at the Premier's official residence. A typical crowd outside No. 10, Downing Street'.

British economy and the livelihoods of everyone. *Plate 48* is a remarkably good example of a simple piece of visual evidence bringing out pungently the sense of general crisis attending the events taking place within the narrow political circle which I have just been describing.

In October, MacDonald led the National government into a General Election. The results (with 1929 results in brackets) were: Conservative 471 (261), Labour 52 (287). 'Labour Wiped Out' was the *Daily Express* headline, though in fact Labour's percentage of the total popular vote (1929 figure in brackets) held up remarkably well at 30.8 (37.1). The financial and economic crisis was actually resolved remarkably quickly. Recalling now the issues with which this chapter began, one might well feel that the ease with which the National government was created with members from all parties does suggest a very deep political stability. Labour's disastrous results in the 1931 election might well appear the signal for violent non-political action. But the really important (and too often neglected) feature is Labour's maintenance of almost a third of the total popular vote: in the country as a whole the Labour Party was still an important political force, and, in effect, a force for stability.

## Chapter Four

# The Thirties

## The Three Britains: Stability or Social Conflict?

The last sentence of my last chapter points to yet another controversy. In the aftermath of the great crisis, unemployment rose to over three million, and throughout the rest of the decade never dropped below one-and-a-half million; there were marches against unemployment, against hunger, against the means test; there were manifestations of fascist thuggery, and counter-protests; the Spanish Civil War brought about a further polarization of opinion. It is hardly surprising that the thirties has been represented as 'the devil's decade', as 'a low dishonest decade', as a time of a bitterly divided society on the brink of social revolution. But was it, any more than it had been at the end of the First World War? The older view is well presented by N. Branson and M. Heinemann in *Britain in the 1930s* (1971), a social history which makes important points about the appalling conditions affecting many areas in the 1930s. But the *coup de grâce* to the view that Britain was so deeply divided, and so unstable, as to be on the brink of social disintegration, was given by John Stevenson and Chris Cook in *The Slump: Society and Politics during the Depression* (1978).

The Jarrow March, or 'Crusade', of 1936 has become something of a symbol of the thirties: *Plate 49* shows the marchers arriving in Luton for the last stage of that march to London. Previous unemployed marchers had been organized by the Communist-front organization, the National Unemployed Workers Movement, and the Labour Party had kept aloof. The Jarrow Crusade had Labour Party support and that of many other individuals and groups. The final stage from Luton was led by Ellen Wilkinson, the local Labour MP who subsequently, in a classic book, encapsulated the tragedy of the closure of the Tyneside shipyards in the title *Jarrow; The Town that was Murdered*. In this photograph the weary but determined marchers, with their sashes and lapel badges, are portrayed as having something of that quality of the proud proletariat on the march which was in part, perhaps, borrowed from the Russian film director Eisenstein. But as the eye pans along to the left and we take in the British bobbie on his bike, this brave protest in the face of acts of great social and economic inhumanity assumes its place in the context of a British society, bitterly affronted but still essentially bound together by the bonds of secular anglicanism.

Four years earlier, in 1932, Wal Hannington, the NUWM leader, had been arrested 'for attempting to cause disaffection among the Metropolitan Police force'. But basically the aims even of the NUWM were limited and practical: to abolish the Family Means Test which had been introduced with the 1931

49 The Jarrow Marchers approaching Luton, 28 October 1936. News photo.

economy cuts; to improve the rates of benefits; and to resist the implementation of the new Unemployment Act of 1934 which, in creating a new form of Unemployment Assistance to be administered by local Public Assistance Committees (PACs), also involved a more stringent family means test and, in some areas, lower rates of benefit. *Plate 50* shows the massive demonstration in Hyde Park which followed the NUWM march on London in October 1934. There were some violent scuffles resulting in about sixty-five injured, but from the rather confused press accounts it does seem that most of the trouble was caused by a few specially-armed members of the London riff-raff, rather than by the main body of marchers. There is a good deal of visual evidence, including film evidence, but although it shows an episode of great seriousness nowhere do we find signs of extreme violence, or potential revolution.

It is important not to underplay the extremity of conditions in the thirties. In recent times the cotton industry had been notable for the tranquillity of its industrial relations: it was a sign of extremity that the cotton workers came out on strike in 1932, because of the attempt of the mill-owners to speed up the production lines. *Plate 51*, from the TUC Archives, was almost certainly set up to record the moment at which the workers poured out of the factory gates with the strike definitely declared. There is something positive about the demeanour of the strikers; while industrial relations in Lancashire were generally good, the speeding-up of the production lines was clearly more than the workers were prepared to take. Where management did not simply close down the plant, as, for example, in the north-east, the speeding-up of production schedules was a repeated phenomenon in the thirties. Later in the decade, a strike similar to that of the cotton workers was provoked among London busmen.

50 Hunger Marchers mass meeting in Hyde Park, 25 February 1934. News photo.

51 Lancashire cotton workers go on strike, August 1932. TUC photograph.

This England . . .

*St. Cross, Winchester, where the weary traveller may still ask and receive a crust of bread and a cup of beer.*

How easy it is in this England to step aside into some small pool of history, to be lapped awhile in the healing peace of a rich, still-living past. For this people — more perhaps than any other — carries tradition and old usage into its daily life . . . in places as in habits, in great things as in small. Thus do you have an ale such as Worthington remaining unchanged through the centuries—because it is brewed in a manner so long ago found worthy of continuance.

ISSUED BY WORTHINGTON AND CO. LTD., BURTON-ON-TRENT, ENGLAND

52 Wales, June 1931: 'Welsh Miners and Families in a Typical Street'. Social record photo (for the *Daily Herald*) of the type which came to be described as 'documentary'.

53 Advertisement from *Illustrated London News*, 13 February 1937.

If we look at *Plates 52, 53 and 54*, we have a graphic representation of what the novelist J. B. Priestley in his *English Journey* (1933) called the 'three Englands':

There was, first, Old England, the country of the cathedrals and minsters and manor houses and inns, of Parson and Squire; guide-book and quaint highways and byways England: 'visit ancient York with its 1,300-year-old Minster; and Durham where lies the Venerable Bede. Wander through the historic streets of Norwich, once the second city of England. Look down from the battlements of Conway Castle. Visit Lichfield Cathedral, renowed for its three beautiful spires, and put yourself back in the Middle Ages at Warwick. Every county of Great Britain speaks to you of your ancestors.' . . .

Then, I decided, there is nineteenth-century England, the industrial England of coal, iron, steel, cotton, wool, railways; of thousands of rows of little houses all alike, sham Gothic churches, square-faced chapels, Town Halls, Mechanics Institutes, mills, foundaries, ware-houses, refined watering-places. . . . Literary and Philosophical Societies, back-to-back houses, detached villas with monkey-trees, Grill Rooms, railway stations, slag-heaps and 'tips', dock roads, Refreshment Rooms, doss-houses, Unionist or Liberal Clubs, cindery waste grounds, mill chimneys, slums, fried-fish shops, public houses with red blinds, bethels in corrugated iron, good-class drapers' and confectioners' shops, a cynically devastated countryside, sooty dismal little towns, and still sootier grim fortress-like cities. . . .

The third England, I concluded, was the new post-war England, belonging far more to the age itself than to this particular island. America, I suppose, was its real birth-place. This is the England of arterial and by-pass roads, of filling stations and factories that look like exhibition buildings, of giant cinemas and dance-halls and cafés, bungalows with tiny garages, cocktail bars, Woolworths, motor-coaches, wireless, typing, factory girls looking like actresses, greyhound racing and dirt tracks, swimming-pools, and everything given away for cigarette coupons. . . .

The witting 'subject' of *Plate 52* is the miners and their families. But however much cheerfulness the photographer has coaxed from them, nothing can impede the testimony of the setting: decrepit, insanitary slums. This is not England, but south Wales: it could be the setting for A. J. Cronin's novel of protest *The Citadel* (1937), and could as well have been in my first chapter as in this one. *Plate 53* is not from a guidebook but an advertisement for Worthington's beer: thus was old England enlisted on behalf of commercial profit. Old England existed all right. Often in rural areas the squalor and poverty was at least as great as in the depressed industrial areas; but also there were established professional people and tradesmen drawing a good living and showing it.

The famous factory in the centre of *Plate 54* could indeed be an exhibition building, or even a cinema. This particular photograph is a document of considerable historical significance. We can see from the open spaces around the factory that Perivale was as yet scarcely built up as an industrial estate. The arterial road in front is the new Western Avenue, tribute to the growing power of the motor-car, though, as we can see, the humble bus is still carrying the day. Hoover was an American company catering for the fortunate majority whose living standards were rising and for the growing market in modern household conveniences which this created.

Many commentators, understandably enough, have followed Priestley in stressing the American influence on 'the third England'. Personally, I think the American influence has been exaggerated, and insufficient attention paid to the cultural distinctiveness of Britain, as compared with America. The cocktail habit was confined to a very tiny sector of society. Already large American towns had

54 The Hoover Factory, Western Avenue, London. Record photo.

55 USA: road-building in the thirities. Grand Central Parkway in Queens, New York, *c.*1937.

urban parkways and clover-leaf intersections (*Plate 55*); small and large towns had their drug-stores, performing functions analogous to that of café, pub, pharmacist and general shop combined; neither of these very different manifestations of American civilization appeared in the Britain of the thirties. A comparison between *Plates 54 and 55* helps to make this point. In fact, it is in this debate that the modernization thesis, for once, has utility: Britain, in its particular way, was sharing in a phenomenon whose roots lay in general industrial and technological history, rather than specifically in the United States. Though American movies and American movie stars were immensely popular (*Plate 61*), Britain had its own indigenous cinema featuring such genuine favourites as Gracie Fields and George Formby, and such films of genuine distinction – with which audiences clearly identified in a way in which they could not identify with the unreal world of affluent, or gangster-ridden USA – as *Hindle Wakes* and *South Riding*.[1]

Yet the very contrasts between the three Englands might well be seen as an incitement to revolutionary feeling. Marxist writers have blamed the Labour Party for failing to cash in on what they see as the radical potential of the British working class and, indeed, for never giving socialism a serious try. But an important work by Ben Pimlott has driven home some important truths:

> For the reality is not that Labour is bad or dilatory or half-hearted about radicalising the working class, or has not lived up to the high hopes once placed in it, or any similar formulation. It is simply that this never was a function the Labour Party intended to perform. Labour had never been a mass movement, still less a revolutionary vanguard. It was founded as, and remains, an electoral machine.[2]

Perhaps there is a little more than that to be said. Labour Party workers and Labour Party leaders believed profoundly in what they called 'socialism', though this was different from the socialism of Marxist-Leninism. Clement Attlee, leader of the Labour Party from 1935, who was always made by the newsreel companies to look awkward and ineffectual, made a most impressive radio broadcast in January 1939, attacking the Hitler régime, and explaining the socialism of the Labour Party:

> The Labour Party owes its inspiration not to some economic doctrine or to some theory of class domination. It has always based its propaganda on ethical principles. We believe that every individual should be afforded the fullest opportunity for developing his or her personality. The founder of our Party, Keir Hardie, always made his appeal on moral grounds. He believed that the evils of our society were due to the failure to put into practice the principles of the brotherhood of man.[3]

How, then, do we sum up the reasons for the manner in which Britain in the thirties, despite the appalling deprivation suffered by much of the working class, was actually remarkably free of violence and social conflict? First of all, depression was not universal and consistent throughout the country. Britain's newer industries actually did rather better than they had in the 1920s: there was a genuine, though limited, industrial recovery. There was a boom in the construction industry as housing of many types was built for the different social classes. *Plate 56* presents fine examples of the large detached houses, set in a deliberately rural landscape with garages at the side, built for the prosperous upper sections of the middle class: the first, third and last houses from the left, with their entirely phoney pretension of being partly or wholly constructed on wooden frames, were brilliantly described by the critic and cartoonist Osbert Lancaster as 'Stockbrokers' Tudor'. The slight economic upturn, then, and the slight improvement in real wages kept the majority relatively contented. For the unemployed, the dole did just keep them short of total desperation; when cuts were threatened, the actions of the NUWM and of Labour and Liberal groups usually succeeded in having the threat withdrawn.

Despite the attention attracted by Communist intellectuals and poets, the Communist Party was scarcely very popular. Till 1936 its membership remained below 10,000; its highest point was when it rose to 18,000 in the summer of 1939. It had strong support only in certain localized parts of Wales, Scotland and London.[4] The NUWM in any case, as we have seen, stuck to limited and practical objectives. On the other side, the body which might have provoked conflict, the National Union of Fascists, never had widespread support either. When the thuggery of their methods became only too plain, a middle-class pressure group came into existence, the National Council for Civil Liberties, and the government itself took action with the Public Order Act of 1936 which controlled processions and outlawed paramilitary organizations. As Stevenson and Cook put it, the debate over public order 'helped to articulate a consensus of opinion about what has been called "the threshold of violence" permitted in British society'.[5] Between these extremes, holding the middle ground, and the loyalty of a remarkable sector of the British people, stood the Labour Party, which both inspired general idealism and served as a common-sense pragmatic force in British society. Finally, there is that secular anglicanism in British society, of which I have already spoken. As I showed many years ago in an article in the *English Historical*

56 Modern houses at
Chislehurst, Kent,
February 1935. Photo by
Woodbine for the *Daily
Herald*.

*Review*, this took a particularly influential shape in the 1930s in the form of a
grouping of cross-party and non-party individuals who advocated genuinely
constructive policies against the failings of entrenched conservatism, these
groupings forming 'Middle Opinion'.[6]

## The Social Service State

Four streams fed into the 'social service state' (as the phrase was in the 1930s): the
long tradition, going back to the Elizabethan Poor Law, that the state must accept
some responsibility for its least fortunate members; the flurry of reforms of the
Edwardian era; the assumption by the state of great new responsibilities
necessitated by the war; and the further patient elaboration and rationalization
of the social services carried out in the inter-war years. We shall have to come
soon to the issue of how far the Welfare State was a matter of steady evolution,
and how far it was a product of the experiences of the Second World War: at any
rate we are not yet in the era of the Welfare State, a term best reserved for the
years after 1945. When Charles Loch Mowat, in his standard work *Britain
Between the Wars* (1955), offered the useful phrase 'the Welfare State in
scaffolding' for the 1930s he was thinking as much of the ideas which were then
being put forward for reform (in particular by 'Middle Opinion') as of actual
legislation enacted.[7] Social policy then affected four main areas: the provision of
some kind of income whenever ordinary earnings were interrupted or brought to

an end, whether because of unemployment, injury, bad health, or old age; health; housing; and education.

Mass unemployment was the great and terrible cause of interruption of earnings. Official figures almost certainly underestimated the magnitude of the problem, but at the highest point in January 1933 there were almost three million recorded as unemployed (over 20 per cent of the insured population); the figure did not go below two million till July 1935, and it was still at 1.6 million (12 per cent of the insured population) at the outbreak of war. By the beginning of the 1930s the system was that an unemployed man, in good standing as far as contributions were concerned, could claim 'of right' fifteen weeks of benefit at 17s (85p) a week (with further small sums for dependants); he then went on to 'Transitional Benefit' (christened the 'dole' by the right-wing press since it could be represented as a hand-out not covered by insurance contributions), which he would continue to receive provided he could demonstrate that he was genuinely looking for work and that he had formerly been in good standing as regards contributions.

By the Local Government Act of 1929 the old Poor Law had been taken over by the local authorities: men in danger of destitution because they had no Unemployment Insurance cover could apply for outdoor relief from the Public Assistance Committee (PAC) of the local authorities (Labour-controlled local authorities sometimes offered more generous rates than those provided by the national scheme). Though benefit rates were inadequate to the maintenance of minimum nutritional levels, the apparently uncontrollable cost of continuing to pay Transitional Benefits had been a factor in the financial and political crisis of August 1931. In the aftermath of this crisis, benefit rates were cut by 10 per cent (it was no consolation to recipients that in a time of general deflation prices also fell by at least that amount) and were to be paid for only twenty-six weeks; Transitional Benefits, now renamed Transitional Payments, were to be paid through the PACs and then only after the administration of a stringent Means Test. For the majority of the unemployed, their dependence on doles rather than insurance could not have been more forcefully or nastily driven home. The Means Test investigated all sources of family income and created further stresses between husbands and wives, parents and children, and parents and grandparents. Different local authorities paid different rates of benefit.

Harshly as it affected individuals, policy towards the unemployed was also administratively muddled. From 1934 onwards legislation was instituted which both brought order and uniformity and in effect ensured a social security system in prewar Britain more generous than that existing in any other major western country (I am excluding Australia and New Zealand): yet the changes were introduced in a manner and spirit which meant that even if the government had helped to preserve social stability it earned little credit. The 1934 Unemployment Act reasserted the sharp distinction between Unemployment Assistance and Unemployment Insurance, which was now extended to cover agricultural workers, with benefits (now restored to their pre-1931 level) strictly limited to twenty-six weeks: the scheme, to which employee, employer and state each contributed a third of the cost, was intended to be entirely independent and self-supporting. Unemployment Assistance was to be administered by a completely separate Unemployment Assistance Board (UAB) which now took over responsibility for unemployed workers receiving Transitional Payments from the PACs. The UAB in January 1935 announced new uniform rates and a standardized Means Test: there was an immediate outcry since the new uniform rates were below those being paid by some PACs. The government retreated and allowed the unemployed to claim either PAC rates or the new rates. Finally, in 1937 new higher uniform rates were established, and the Unemployment Assistance Board also took over responsibility for those in need due to other causes than unemployment – those who had hitherto had to apply to the Poor Law as now administered through the PACs. However, the new bureaucracy employed large numbers of young, untrained Means Test inspectors. The whole bitter subject of the Means Test and its application has figured prominently in the literature of the thirties, as for example in Walter Brierley's *Means Test Man*.

Insurance benefits, Transitional Payments, Unemployment Assistance, of course, were at best palliatives when what people wanted was work. Job security has come to seem as important a part of a Welfare State as income security; but in the 1930s there was little support in official circles for the idea of job creation. The one step taken in this direction was a small one: the 1934 Depressed Areas Act made a grant of £2,000,000 available for creating employment in specially designated 'Depressed Areas'.

The Widows, Orphans and Old Age Contributory Pensions Act of 1925 had provided pensions (of 10s – 50p – or £1.00 for a married couple) just as in the original 1908 Act, but to be payable from the age of sixty-five. In the thirties the scheme was developed so that widows could claim pensions at the age of fifty-five. In 1937 the 'black-coated' workers were brought in. Neville Chamberlain does not stand high in popular memory of the 1930s: he was, in fact, against considerable resistance from private interests, the creator of these pension schemes.

Since it ranked as a major issue in politics, unemployment provision, however inadequate, was slowly improved in the 1930s. In contrast there were no significant changes in the rather scrappy health insurance scheme. On the income security side, benefits for being off work due to sickness remained low: 15s a week throughout the inter-war years without any dependants' allowances. On the health side proper, provision was patchy and anomalous. Health insurance was not administered directly by the government, but through private companies, the 'approved societies', because of prevailing sentiments in support of private enterprise and because these companies constituted powerful pressure groups. All of the companies had to provide the standard benefit and also pay a capitation fee to a doctor, so that the insured person then became a 'panel patient', as distinct from a private fee-paying patient, of that doctor. Some of the approved societies were operated very efficiently and thus offered their members considerable benefits, such as dental or hospital treatment, over and above the minimum; others could manage no more than the minimum; and many were quite unscrupulous in using their favoured position to push 'industrial insurance' (i.e. burial insurance) on their working-class membership. There was no national hospital service: instead an absurd and damaging rivalry between voluntary hospitals, and hospitals run since 1929 by the local authorities. In both, the practice was to charge patients fees in accordance with their means. While genuine and important work on diet was accomplished by such figures as Sir John

57 '"The Daily Dozen": young children in their bathing costumes doing physical exercises in the shade of Brent Station (Middlesex) early this morning.' (12 August 1932)

Boyd Orr, the government tended to take refuge in a somewhat spurious emphasis on the value of physical jerks. *Plate 57* itself has a rather spurious quality. One cannot imagine children, some of whom are of pre-school age, regularly doing their exercises in the public highway. There are quite a number of photographs, and later some moving film, of scenes of this sort, all really part of an official propaganda campaign to publicize the virtues of fresh air and exercise. Ivor Montagu, the Communist film-maker, was quite right to satirize this part of the government's generally inadequate health policies, in his film *For Peace and Plenty*. However, if a comparison between this plate and *Plate 17*, the Edwardian school playground, suggests that the world of children had become less brutally disciplined, more relaxed, then that point would be a valid one.

*Plate 58* is a very stark presentation of one aspect of housing policy. Subsidies were provided from central government to local authorities to enable them (with further subvention from local rates) to build houses which could then be let at rents below the 'economic' cost. Since under this not brilliantly satisfactory system the bulk of the cost of the housing was raised through borrowing, even the subsidized rents were too high for the poorest sections of the working class. Leeds had returned a Labour council in 1933 (demonstrating, incidentally, Labour's potential strength on local authorities, if not in central government), and they appointed a city architect, R. A. H. Livett, to design the Quarry Hill flats,

considered a masterpiece at the time, the Leeds Labour council's answer to the famous workers' flats in Vienna. For the inhabitants, they offered amenities, baths, hot water, proper kitchens, not to be found in the type of housing seen in *Plate 52*. In Scotland, families had been living in flats for generations, though English working people found it difficult to overcome their predilection for the two-storey house as the perfect form of accommodation. At the outbreak of war such developments could still seem a model for the future. By the seventies, however, Quarry Hill was seriously vandalized and in 1975–6 this brave monument to the socialist planning of the thirties was demolished.

As with other plates (particularly *Plate 54*) there is an empty stillness about this scene which suggests how different the world of the thirties was from our own age. People's lives were still totally dominated by work, and outside of morning and evening rush hours, as we see, the bus station is very far from busy. We can note also the little Morris in the foreground, adapted for commercial purposes; and, of course, the ubiquitous apparatus of the electric tramways. The Leeds Corporation clearly believed that they were giving the workers a prestigious habitation. Elsewhere, class distinctions were very clear in the dwellings which arose out of the housing boom of the period (*Plate 56*). Aided by the expansion in mortgage business, there was a great growth of large private housing estates; at the same time, most local authorities built subsidized working-class housing of a

58 Quarry Hill Flats and Corporation Bus Station, Leeds, 1935 or 1936.

more traditional type. The classic instance of the class divide is the case of the Cutteslowe Wall in Oxford, where a wall was actually built to divide a working-class local authority housing estate from a middle-class private developers' estate.[8]

Education was very much part of the class structure. The public elementary schools were quintessentially working-class; the county and independent grammar schools largely middle-class; while the 'public schools' of various degrees, ranging from the lesser-known ones attended by the aspiring lower-middle class, to the highly prestigious 'Clarendon schools' where most of Britain's political and administrative élite were educated. Many working-class children had nothing beyond a limited and repetitious elementary education to the age of fourteen; quite a number managed to move on to some form of secondary education – despite the attempts of the government in the thirties to restrict such opportunities: very much depended on how local authorities interpreted, or indeed ignored, government directives. The Hadow Report of 1926, the Spens Report of 1938, and the Labour Party policy document *Secondary Education for All* (1923) evolved the ideas which became orthodox after 1944, but which have been much criticized since.

## Consumerism and Culture

*Plate 54* showed, in its elegant fashionable art deco forms, the more massive external manifestation of the consumer society. *Plate 59*, with the marvellously complacent little note underneath – 'advertising is the consumer's guarantee of merit' – breathes a myriad messages about other aspects of the consumer society, and many other facets of thirties' Britain as well. Note that these cookers have

59 Advertisement from *Good Housekeeping*, October 1936.

nothing to do with that modern miracle electricity, nor even that slightly older servant of mankind, gas. The Esse cooker itself, indeed, was a product of one of the country's traditional heavy industrial areas, the central lowlands of Scotland. The phobias of depression, the inward-looking protectionism, is apparent in the rubric 'this All-British cooker'. Even in the smaller residence envisaged in the lower picture, it is expected that there will be at least one servant, properly dressed up, though probably not a living-in servant. It does seem, though, that in the large residence it is the lady of the house who is taking up the challenge to provide 'the highest standard of cooking'. We are moving into the era of concern for smokeless fuel; but we are not yet into the era of the ubiquity of oil. Most significant of all in this visual document is the point I began with: we see here the important part played by skilful advertising in the equation between consumer demand and the production of new household conveniences.

*Plate 60* takes us to heart of one of the great success stories of the 1930s. Under the enlightened leadership of Israel M. Sieff, Vice-Chairman and Joint Managing Director, Marks and Spencer became one of the major retailing outlets in the country, with stores in almost every High Street. This 'in-house' photograph, taken by the company for its own uses, shows well the spacious and convenient layout. The central position, both in the picture and in the social role played by Marks and Spencer, is taken by clothing: the cheap but stylish women's wear played its part in that semi-revolution which led too many commentators to

60 Salesfloor, Marks and Spencers, Whitefriargate, Hull. In-house record photo.

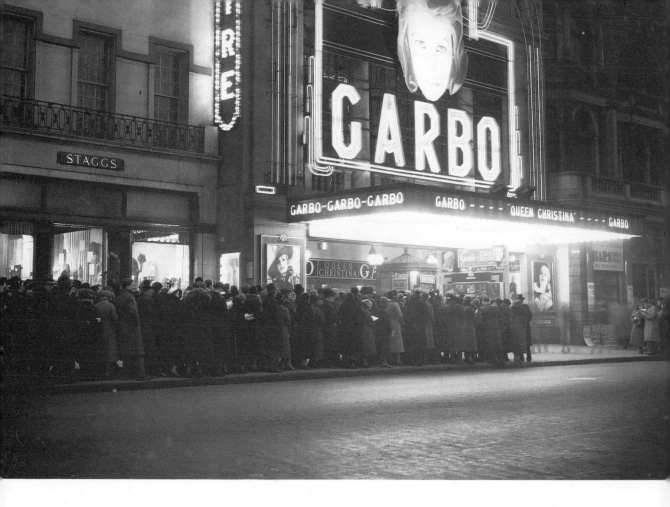

61 Queue at Empire Cinema, Leicester Square, London, for *Queen Christina*, 18 February 1934. Photo by Woodbine for the *Daily Herald*.

generalize about social classes becoming alike. There is a caution in the fact that the most prominent items for sale are overalls: work, as I have noted, was the imperative of the thirties – those without work were the country's *misérables*. The housing boom I have already mentioned carried with it a boom in gardening: for this, as we see from the bulbs on the right of the picture, Marks and Spencer also catered. We have, lastly, the boom in popular music, fostered by the dance halls, fostered by musical films, fostered, to a lesser degree, by the BBC, whose licences rose to nine million by the end of the decade, practically one wireless set for every family: a gramophone record (1/3d), we can see, cost almost two-thirds as much as a pair of overalls (1/11d).

*Plate 61* backs up what almost all the social surveys tell us, that Hollywood was master of leisure activity, and such great stars as Garbo the queens. Cinema admissions were running at twenty million a week, a thousand million a year. New and ever larger cinemas were being built. In 1921 there had been about four thousand cinemas, but almost all of them to the old-style, open-hall plan, seating no more than around five hundred. Most of these had fallen out of use, or been rebuilt, by 1934 when the total number was 4,300. But in 1934 28.3 per cent of all cinemas contained over 1,000 seats; the first 4,000-seat cinemas actually dated from 1925, in Glasgow, and from 1928, in Croydon.[9] Though there were still independent local cinemas, three big circuits, Gaumont British, the Associated British Picture Corporation, and Odeon, and one lesser one, Granada, were rapidly achieving control of the market. Although British domestic film production was to go into recession in the later thirties, because of the chronic problems of over-ambitiousness and failure to secure a steady capital flow into the industry, evidence was given to the 1936 Moyne Committee on Films that British pictures had demonstrated their 'superior attractiveness over foreign competitors' as far as British audiences were concerned. Most scholarly work on British cinema of the 1930s has concentrated on the documentary movement, associated in particular with John Grierson. I will simply state here that I believe this emphasis to have been totally misguided. The documentaries, whose influence in my view has been greatly overrated, were generally patronizing and tedious, while many of the commercial films, scorned for so long by intellectuals, can now be seen to have had genuinely life-enhancing qualities.

The better side of the documentary movement is to be seen in photojournalism, and photography as social comment. *Plate 62* brings that movement together with an area of leisure activity in which no one dreamed of foreign competition. The occasion was the Arsenal v Chelsea match at Highbury, on 10 December 1932. Insofar as the Prince of Wales had just opened Arsenal's new stand, this was not entirely an ordinary occasion. But this brilliant photograph, by Harold Tomlin, of the players at half-time gives us breathtaking insight into the condition of professional football at the time. The players, note, have not gone back into the dressing room: they are, on this December day, keeping themselves warm with sweaters, cups of tea, and by pacing restlessly around. Though a player's career, in these days, was usually over by his later twenties, these men have old faces. The professional footballer was simply a working-class man who had escaped to something precarious and not necessarily

62 Arsenal v Chelsea: players during interval, 10 December 1932. Photo by Tomlin for the *Daily Herald*.

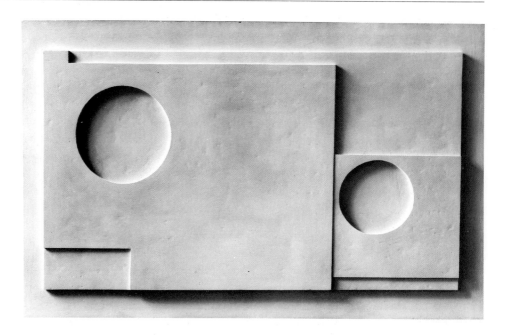

63 Ben Nicholson, *White Relief*, oil on mahogany, 1935.

a great deal better, in which both a maximum wage and a strict hierarchy of authority were rigidly enforced. But as a spectator sport, football was immensely popular: here, 60,000 watched Arsenal beat Chelsea 4-1.

So much for popular entertainment. Was Britain essentially a low-brow nation, or at best, a middle-brow one, rising at most to the unchallenging forms of the Hoover factory? I suggested that the canons of modernism had been encouraged by the disruptions of war. I mentioned, tangentially, the innovations of T. S. Eliot. There was indeed an *avant garde* throughout the inter-war years. Somehow, it was more visible in the thirties when some, though by no means all, of its practitioners became publically associated with left-wing and revolutionary politics. Among the painters, most austere, most detached from contemporary preoccupations, but most respected in the international art scene, was Ben Nicholson, one of a very tiny handful prepared to make a total break from the representationalism which was such a strong addiction in most domestic British art (*Plate 63*).

## Chapter Five

# World War Two

### Heroic and Unheroic Images

Photographers, cartoonists, illustrators and copywriters laboured under great difficulties during the war. From certain sensitive areas photographers were kept clear altogether; any photographs that they did take with the faintest connection with the war effort were submitted to the censorship, for newspapers, though not censored in advance, could be subject to very severe retribution if they did publish anything, photograph or cartoon, say, to which the authorities took exception. However, it is clear that the restrictions did not really bear terribly heavily on British photographers, journeymen rather than geniuses as most of them were. They shared the view that Britain had no choice but to wage victorious war against the German enemy; they had no wish to do anything which would disrupt the national effort; they had every wish to produce the kind of morale-boosting imagery with which most of us are still familiar. Much of the photography of the war is quite consciously 'heroic': portraying 'one of the "few"' (*Plate 64*), Churchill as the British bulldog (*Plate 65*), the bravery of the civilian firefighters (*Plate 66*), the resilience and cheerfulness of the British people in adversity (*Plates 67 and 78*).

However, many photographs did simply record events as they took place; and some actually give a remarkably unheroic view of the war experience. In, first, outlining the social history of the war, I want to bring out the contrast between the heroic, and by no means totally untrue, images, and the more banal, and sometimes revealing, unheroic ones. The domestic history of Britain at war falls into four phases: the period of the 'phoney war' or 'invisible war' in which not a lot happened; the period of the Battle of Britain and the Blitz, when invasion and defeat were real prospects; the long slog from late 1941, when for a further year the submarine menace to vital supplies was still desperate, but in which increasingly there was time to think of other issues than immediate survival; this merges into the fourth phase, when preoccupation with social reconstruction took the form of the preparation of a number of important government white papers, and when there was much public discussion of the prospects for substantial social change. Again, later in this chapter, I shall address the question of the relationship between war and social change rather as I did with respect to the First World War.

The declaration of war brought none of the 'ebullitions' (to quote *The Observer* of September 1939) of August 1914, but 'the sense of moral release was inexpressible'. Within hours the sounding of air-raid warnings over London

64 'Stafford Tuck at Martlesham Heath, 28.12.40'.

seemed to demonstrate that the long-held fears of a bombing war were only too justified: but that warning proved a false alarm, and for the time being there was no other. A complete black-out had been imposed from 1 September: road casualties doubled. Conscription, also introduced on the eve of the war, went ahead and a National Register was compiled: yet at the end of 1939 there were still about a million unemployed. Cinemas, theatres and football grounds closed, because of the fear of bombing raids: but all soon resumed save that, for obvious reasons, the standard of league football was greatly reduced.

The second phase of the war began with the German invasion of Scandinavia in April 1940, followed by the aborted attempt to land British troops at Narvik in Norway, the German invasion and conquest of France and the evacuation of British (and some French) troops from Dunkirk (29 May–3 June 1940). Since the beginning of 1940 the press had been referring openly to the 'creeping paralysis' affecting the British war effort under the direction of Neville Chamberlain. Less than a month before Dunkirk Chamberlain's Conservative government was replaced by a national coalition under Winston Churchill. After the fall of France and the rejection of Hitler's last peace offer there came his attempt to prepare the way for invasion by the destruction of British air power. Victory by the British fighter pilots, assisted by radar, in the Battle of Britain, helped to ensure that, whatever devastations British society might suffer, the centuries-old barrier of geography would not be directly breached. The Battle of Britain was essentially fought by an élite, 'the few' of whom Churchill spoke. *Plate 64* presents the ideal

65 Winston Churchill touring the City of London (with Mrs Churchill), 1940.

image of the solitary, noble, crusader: the tally of twenty-three swastikas indicates the number of German planes he believes he has shot down.

Defeated in his first objective, Hitler switched to the mass bombing of civilian centres: the intensive bombing of London began at 5 o'clock on a hot Saturday evening (7 September). The capital was bombed for seventy-six nights on end; then more sporadically for a further six months. On 14 November the entire centre of Coventry was destroyed, and in November and December other cities suffered severe bomb attacks. For *Plate 67*, the caption is scarcely necessary: whether spontaneously, or after some coaxing, the bombed-out citizens, together with men in uniform engaged in clearing-up operations, indeed give a marvellous show of 'British "grit"'. The caption, of course, is of interest in itself. The censors took photographs and proposed captions together as an entity, and newspapers or photographers wishing to get a photograph through had to choose their words carefully. Clearly it was better for morale if raids were presented as 'spasmodic' rather than, say, 'devastating': to those bombed, the raids may not have seemed

66 Firemen at work, Eastcheap, London, 1940.

quite so spasmodic. It is interesting to note that the prevalent sign is that of thumbs up; nowhere is the famous V sign which Churchill eventually popularized to be seen at this stage in the war.

Here we have the standard image, but in more recent years controversy has raged over whether bombing really did strengthen morale, consolidate support behind the British government, and increase a determined hostility towards Germany. Did not morale come close to disintegration? Was there not hostility to, and resentment against, government and authority everywhere? *Plate 68* presents a much more downbeat, unheroic perception of those bombed out of house and home. Whether the Union Jack was a deliberate piece of dressing, or whether it arrived spontaneously, one cannot know. But even if there was an attempt to set up this picture, dolefulness and personal tragedy (understandably enough) are what come through here. *Plate 69*, clearly a completely spontaneous news photo, shows two of the victims of Coventry squabbling with each other: in common with other photographs of the Coventry blitz, this photograph was not released by the censorship till February 1941. However, squabbling gloom, and indeed fear, do not equal collapse of morale. Only a few extroverts were responsible for the famous signs of chirpiness. It may be that had the bombing

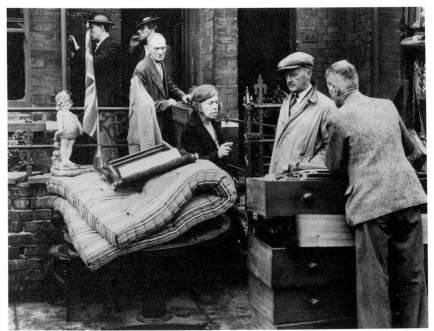

67 'SPASMODIC RAIDS ON LONDON DURING THE NIGHT. During the spasmodic raids on London last night some North London tenement houses were bombed. Photo shows –their houses are wrecked but the tenants of the tenement buildings in North London still showed the British "Grit".' (15 September 1940)

68 'Salvaging the Furniture. German aircraft again raided the London area during the night and more bombs were dropped on residential areas. Photo shows – the Union Jack among the salvaged furniture.' (24 September 1940)

69 'Sorting personal property after the German air-raid on Coventry' (14 November 1940). *Illustrated* photograph, not published until February 1941.

gone on much longer morale might have collapsed; as it was, the evidence favours the view that, without necessarily being overly cheerful about it, those sections of the British public which were affected stood up well. Churchill made a point of touring devastated areas, and the Ministry of Information made a point of releasing photographs of him doing this (*Plate 65*).

Hitler's invasion of Russia on 22 June 1941 meant an end to the continuous and persistent bombing of British cities, though there were to be further destructive raids, particularly the Baedeker raids of 1942 (so called after the famous German guidebook, since these raids were concentrated on historical English cathedral towns). Yet the Battle of the Atlantic intensified, and in mid-1941 the weekly ration of basic foods amounted to no more than what in a comfortable prewar household would have been thought sufficient for a single helping: a shilling's worth of meat (about ½ lb), 1 oz of cheese, 4 oz of bacon or ham, 8 oz of sugar, 2 oz of tea, 8 oz of fats (including not more than 2 oz of butter), 2 oz of jam or marmalade. The Japanese invasion of Pearl Harbor brought the United States into the war on 7 December, yet the long slog towards victory was not really clearly underway till General Montgomery's victory at Alamein in October 1942.

Montgomery himself sometimes addressed factory workers at home, and in filming one such occasion the Ministry of Information handled the matter with great care, though there is much unconscious humour for present-day eyes and ears.[1] However, in a period in which thoughts were beginning to turn towards postwar social reform, not all addresses from the military to civilians went down too well. *Plate 70* is an amazingly straightforward record of the boredom and resentment of workers on a building site being addressed by a British army colonel. One is reminded of a memo by the BBC's Director in Scotland, responding to a suggestion from London that perhaps selected workers should be given the opportunity to be heard on the air: 'The interests about which workers in the industrial areas would want to talk are – the war, home politics, industrial grievances, football, and the dogs. We believe that the kind of things they would want to say about the first three could not be broadcast.'[2] Looking at the photograph, one is perhaps most strongly struck by the crassness of the authorities who expected men to stand up in the most uncomfortable of positions during a 'morale-boosting' harangue. But war-weariness is also clearly etched on the faces.

70 'Colonel addresses workers on a building site'. One of a series of fifteen taken by a Keystone Press cameraman for the Ministry of Supply. Marked 'stopped' on reverse of print.

At the end of the war, Winston Churchill, refusing to be rancorous about his election defeat, said of the British people, 'They have had a hard time'. Already in 1942 a number of important committees concerned with possible social reforms after the war were established. During 1943 and 1944, when, first, the allies fought their way up through Italy, and then eventually in June 1944 invaded mainland Europe, important government white papers came out on *Employment Policy*, *A National Health Service*, and *Social Security*. On 4 May 1945 the German forces in north-western Europe surrendered to General Montgomery at Lüneburg Heath. On 7 May the German Supreme Command surrendered at Rheims, and 8 May was designated VE Day – Victory in Europe Day (the war against the Japanese continued). When Hitler invaded Russia, Churchill had declared that if Hitler invaded Hell, he would declare the devil an ally. On 9 May, Churchill drank a toast at the Russian Embassy in honour of the Russians and their great patriotic war, which had in fact served to turn the tide in Europe. The chirpy caption bears no relationship to the unheroic revelation of Churchill's true, gloomy feelings; and, as one can see, he is not with the Soviet Ambassador, but with the Russian Naval Attaché (*Plate 71*).

### Destruction – Disruption

The Second World War was longer and much more destructive than the First, yet it did not hit the country with anything like the shock of the earlier war. Events in Manchuria, Abyssinia and Spain had shown just what brutalities might be expected, though destruction of civilian life and property, greater by far than anything that had been hinted at in the First World War, proved in the end to be less than all prewar estimates suggested. British troops were at least spared the worst tortures of a tunnel war and the senseless slaughter of major set-piece battles: combatant casualties were half those of 1914–18, amounting finally to about 300,000 dead. Meantime 60,000 civilians and 35,000 merchant seamen were killed, so that there could be no bitter feeling of inequality of sacrifice this time.

Britain suffered some serious direct economic losses. To finance the war effort overseas investments, the return on which had for three-quarters of a century helped to bridge the gap between Britain's imports and exports, had been sold to the tune of £1,000 million; two-thirds of the small but vital gold reserve of 1939 was used up; domestic capital was run down by about £3,000 million, while new external debts were run up to about the same amount; exports, upon which more than ever before Britain's future economic survival would depend, dropped to one-third of the prewar level.

Total war involved the same sort of disruptions in domestic social life as had the conflict of 1914–18, underscored by the heavy bombing raids and the use of the island as a base from which Britain's overseas allies could participate in European military operations. Aerial bombardment and the threat of aerial bombardment produced very marked movements in population. The original national register compiled at the end of September 1939 indicated that $2\frac{1}{4}$ million people (5 per cent of the total population) had left their homes in Great Britain during the first month of war. Thereafter many millions of changes of address

71 'Winston Churchill, Prime Minister, visited the Soviet embassy where he and the Soviet Ambassador toasted the Soviet Union, the British Empire and Marshall Stalin in Russian(!) champagne with the utmost cordiality.' (9 May 1945)

were notified under the National Registration Act. Over the whole war, all changes of address totalled 60 million. Two out of every seven houses were affected more or less seriously by bomb damage.

Directly linked to bombing was the whole social experiment of evacuation of civilians from the most dangerous urban areas into the relatively safe countryside. Plans had been carefully laid in the prewar years, and the first evacuation began on Friday 1 September 1939, two days before the actual declaration of war. *Plate 72* gives a good direct view of the different emotions, and the different reactions stirred up by this first evacuation: the different expressions of the children, and the expressions of the adults repay close study. By the end of the year, however, most evacuees had drifted back. Then, with the coming of the Blitz, a second, hasty, evacuation had to be undertaken. There was a third wave of evacuation during the flying bomb and rocket attacks of the summer of 1944. There is controversy over the deeper social significance of evacuation. A volume of reminiscences edited by B. S. Johnson laid stress on the psychological damage caused by separation from home and parents, and it has authoritatively been argued that the disruption of the family bond was the single most traumatic factor for children living under air-raid conditions. Yet, others wrote of *Evacuation: A Social Revolution*, and there can be no doubt that the

72 Evacuees leaving
Chelmsford station,
7 September 1939.

revelation of the habits of children reared in the city slums to more prosperous
country dwellers had a considerable influence in directing middle-class opinion
towards support for social reform.[3] Maybe too much attention has been given to
evacuation in isolation: the revelations and reactions it produced are perhaps
better seen as part of an entire involvement of the worthy middle class with the
neglected multitudes brought about by the dislocations of war.

Throughout most of the war almost half a million foreign troops were
stationed on British soil, rising to $1\frac{1}{2}$ million at the time of the Normandy
landings. American soldiers brought a more direct encounter with American
customs than all the Hollywood movies could achieve. Black soldiers, and the
American's own treatment of them, together created a most complex disruptive
phenomenon. The Army Bureau of Current Affairs' journal advised:

> It may well be that occasional cases will occur which might arouse the resentment and
> even anger of British troops and civilians who witness them. On the other hand, it is
> obviously highly unsuitable for the British to try to interfere in those instances. . . .
> It can be seen therefore that any attempts to break down the various forms of social
> regulation accepted by the average American family, white or coloured, is not likely to
> achieve any good purpose, but on the contrary might well lead to trouble and even
> violence, especially where women are concerned.[4]

73 'Marking America's
participation in
England's "Salute the
Soldier" campaign,
American Negro troops,
part of a huge parade of
US troops and material,
march past Nelson's
column in Trafalgar
Square.' (30 March 1944)

In *Plate 73* we have a colourful Trafalgar Square as the scene for a 'Salute the
Soldier' campaign of March 1944. Black troops (with one white man in the
second battalion) can be seen taking a prominent part.

### Test and Participation

German bombers put British officialdom, national and local, to the test, and in many cases it was found desperately wanting. Mass Observation reported on the first blitz:

> Nobody foresaw the tidal wave of refugees spread all over the country after the first hideous week-end, inundating places like Oxford with homeless people, being decanted in peaceful Essex suburbs from lorries by desperate local authorities who hoped for the best that something would be done about them. Nobody foresaw that everybody would not know all about the official plans for them, that the rest centres would be overflowing, that people would stay there for weeks instead of hours, that people would not be able to be billeted in their own boroughs, that transport would not turn up, so that refugees were bombed to death in the rest centres, that people would flock to the tubes and unofficial deep shelters rather than use the official surface shelters which they regarded as deathtraps. In fact, there were rather too many things that nobody foresaw for official democracy to plume itself very much on its efficiency as a wager of war on the Home Front.[5]

Government did foresee that the rivalries between local authority and the endowed 'voluntary' hospitals would be a gratuitous handicap in dealing with civilian casualties. The Emergency Hospital Scheme, in effect, involved a kind of *ad hoc* nationalization of the majority of British hospitals. By 1942 the Ministry of Health was recognizing the significance of this development:

> In the last year or so the numerous organisations and authorities whose interests lie in the hospital world have been giving increasing thought to the future. All start from the accepted premise that there can be no return to the pre-war position of unrelated hospital units pursuing independent and often wastefully competitive courses. . . .[6]

The test and the participation dimensions of war come together in the great burst of social planning which characterizes the middle and later years. The consequences of participation showed in three different ways. Labour came straight into the Churchill coalition and the appointment of Ernest Bevin as Minister of Labour made it clear that Churchill recognized that he would have to carry with him the full support of the trade unions: it was because of direct pressure from the TUC that an inter-departmental committee of civil servants under the chairmanship of Sir William Beveridge was appointed in July 1941 'to undertake . . . a survey of the existing national schemes of social insurance and allied services . . . and to make recommendations'. Second, it was clear to all but the crustiest and most reactionary Tories that this war was indeed 'a people's war' and in many unexpected quarters the view was expressed that because of the people's participation in the war effort, so a better society must be created for them: 'So great a people', declared the Federation of British Industries, 'deserve the best. We must build again.'[7] José Harris, biographer of Beveridge, recognizes that there was a changing tide of opinion.[8] Thirdly, within the population at large, as Mass Observation surveys showed, there was a gradual shift in mood and expectation, building up towards a feeling that there ought to be serious social reform at the end of the war: a traditionalist nonconformist minister noted that men on leave were all preoccupied with the prospect of social change.[9]

The deliberations of the Beveridge Committee ought, according to their brief, to have been confined to social insurance. However, as I have just suggested, all matters of social policy were now a matter of general debate. Shortly after the members of the Beveridge Committee were appointed, the Minister of Health, Ernest Brown, referred in the House of Commons (9 October 1941) to future health policy: 'The question of post-war hospital policy and re-organisation, more particularly in relation to the Emergency Hospital Scheme, has for sometime been engaging the attention of the Government. . . . It is the objective of the government as soon as may be after the war to ensure that by means of a comprehensive hospital service appropriate treatment shall be readily available to every person in need of it. . . .' Nevertheless Brown made it clear that the government did not envisage a completely free hospital service.

The bulk of the Beveridge Report did indeed concentrate on social insurance. The major innovations recommended were that the insurance scheme should cover all classes in society, that it should cover all possible contingencies, and that it should provide uniform benefits which would guarantee minimum subsistence; as a good Liberal, Beveridge believed that it should be left to the individual to make additional provision through private insurance. What transformed the report into a truly historic document was the insistence that, 'Organisation of social insurance should be treated as one part only of a comprehensive policy of social progress': there must be attacks on ill health, inadequate education, bad housing and unemployment. The successful implementation of his social security proposals, Beveridge further insisted, depended on three assumptions: the institution of children's allowances, a comprehensive health service, and 'maintenance of employment, that is to say avoidance of mass unemployment'.[10]

Even while it was being drafted the Beveridge report ran into all kinds of difficulties. The files of the Beveridge Papers in the London School of Economics reveal clearly the powerful attacks which were mounted by the vested interests of the insurance and medical professions, and also from within the government itself. In his evidence to the Beveridge Committee, the Director of the Federation of British Industries expressed his hostility, though he said that he did not wish to make it public. He also unintentionally put his finger on the central irony of the war, that despite the views of him and his kind the war was bringing about social change: 'we did not start this war with Germany in order to improve our social services; the war was forced upon us by Germany and we entered it to preserve our freedom and to keep the Gestapo outside our houses, and that is what the war means.'[11] The moment the report was published the opposition was open and vociferous. There was much invocation of the British race and the British character, both of which, it was argued, would be destroyed by the Beveridge proposals. The Federation of British Industries now overtly dropped its former progressive stance of 1941, the *Daily Telegraph* was mainly hostile, and a leading figure in the insurance world declared that, 'If this scheme were to come to pass, truly might not Ribbentrop allege the Anglo-Saxon race was decadent.'[12]

It is now fashionable to point out that much of the Beveridge report, as was probably inevitable, was aimed at remedying the abuses of the 1930s and certainly contained nothing very revolutionary. It is also said, quite inaccurately, that the report had the support of all political and professional opinion. What the report does seem to have had is the support of the majority of the British people. Two weeks after publication, a national opinion poll found that 95 per cent of those interviewed showed some knowledge of the report; 88 per cent approved the idea of doctor and hospital services for all (showing how one of the

'assumptions' achieved central importance); 53 per cent believed the government would put the plan into operation, while 18 per cent doubted this. A year later it was reported that 256,000 copies of the full report had been sold and 369,000 copies of an abridged version (a further 40,000 copies were sold in the United States).

Churchill was unenthusiastic about the Beveridge report, and it was not published until 2 December 1942; there was no parliamentary debate on it until 16 February 1943. While the Ministry of Information seized on the report as a powerful propaganda weapon, Sir James Grigg at the War Office suppressed the attempt of the Army Bureau of Current Affairs (ABCA) to circulate a summary of its contents to the troops.[13] In the parliamentary debate two government spokesmen, Sir Kingsley Wood and Oliver Lyttelton (both Conservatives), were so feeble and hesitant in their support of the Beveridge report that they aroused the justifiable suspicion that the government had no serious intention of implementing it. The wartime shifts of opinion and formation of new alignments on social issues are strikingly represented in *Plate 74*, a cartoon published in the right-wing, though populist, *Daily Express*, the day after the big House of Commons debate on the Beveridge report. The cartoon also, of course, brings out the very uncertain future the Beveridge report seemed to have in face of the government attitude. Its two most noteworthy features (the reference to Beveridge as the architect of social security was fairly commonplace, the reference to the 'red white and blue' was all too predictable) are the indictment (from a paper usually a strong supporter of private enterprise) of the 'old economic confusion', and the phrase 'tenders invited', which could almost be read as an intimation of the takeover actually to materialize in 1945 of a Labour government committed to carrying out the Beveridge proposals.

Actually, the forces supporting Beveridge were stronger than this deliberately stark cartoon might suggest. From the records we can see the enormous efforts made by the Labour Party – particularly acting through its General Secretary, J. S. Middleton – by Attlee, who drafted a most pungent memorandum on the subject to Churchill, and by D. N. Chester, the former university lecturer who, as a wartime civil servant, was secretary to the Beveridge Committee.[14] These efforts bore fruit in the white papers of 1943 and 1944 which committed the government to the main lines of the Beveridge proposals and to a general policy of social planning and reform.

War again provided the opportunity for women's participation. I have not, in the brief space available to me in this book, discussed 'Dad's Army', the Home Guard on which much has been written elsewhere. Attention should perhaps now be focused on 'Mum's Army', the Women's Volunteer Service, without whom – it is as simple as that – the Home Front would not have kept going. During the devastating blitz of Coventry on 14 November 1940 the WVS headquarters there was practically destroyed. In leaving their bomb-damaged building, the WVS women on duty had to creep on all fours, soon taking cover amid the tombstones of a local cemetery. Only the tombstones saved their lives when a huge bomb fell a few yards away. But as soon as that wave of bombs had ceased normal duties resumed. At 5.00 am auxiliary fire servicemen came in for tea and sandwiches. One of them, mouth full, uttered the famous, but not unjustified line: 'I guess the WVS have won the battle of Coventry.'[15] This was in the heroic mould.

*Plate 75*, 'behind the scenes' as it were at Coventry the morning after, would in itself belong to my category of unheroic images: but set in the context I have just described it takes on rather a different character. *Plate 76* falls into the category not just of unheroic, but of downright dismal. Clearly this photograph survived because of what it objectively recorded: the King visiting a factory. Clearly, too, it was not possible for a photographer to coax royalty into the kind of heroic, or dramatic, posture which would better have served the official imagery of war. What we are left with is a direct image of a quite unglamorous woman clearly engaged in skilled engineering work. *Plate 77* offers the more familiar, standard, heroic image, with perhaps just a touch of glamour (for these austere and prudish times) in the exposed calf: radio location work was, in fact, highly responsible and in the whole air campaign the role of women on the ground was crucial.

Feminists have questioned how far the roles taken on by women during the war can be equated with emancipation, or, and more important, how far there really were any long-lasting effects. Undoubtedly there was no complete abandonment of traditional roles. One poster calling for recruits to the Women's Land Army made a special appeal to those 'who liked doing housework'. Yet again I would wish to stress the further self-confidence and assertiveness engendered by the war experience, even if some of that continued to be overlaid by women's natural tendency to self-sacrifice and self-effacement.

Perhaps the most penetrating account to emerge from the Second World War is the one recently published as *Nella Last's War: A Mother's Diary 1939–45*. Nella Last gained her opportunity through the appeal of the Mass Observation organization for ordinary people to keep a day-by-day record of their war experiences. In this diary we have the classic instance of a woman explicitly, in the circumstances of war, coming to realize what perhaps she had sensed implicitly in time of peace, that she is by far the tougher partner in her marriage,

75 '"Queen's messengers". Food convoys making sandwiches by the million at Coventry on "the morning after".' (15 November 1940)

76 'H.M. the King talking to workers [*sic*] during a visit to a factory.' Originally marked 'stopped', though eventually published.

77 'RADIOLOCATION: By means of the information cables, this girl reports to the guncrew the position of the aeroplanes.'

that her powers of organization and her resilience are far greater than those of her husband; that above all, women's work, vital at all times, and now crucial in time of crisis, has for too long passed without proper recognition. The detail of menus planned, scraps saved, clothes cut up and restyled, while toys are made and meals cooked for the WVS, makes fascinating reading: as clear an account of woman as triumphant organizer in face of adversity as one could find. One is led relentlessly to this reflection of 1 August 1943:

> I suddenly thought tonight, 'I know why a lot of women have gone into pants – it's a sign that they are asserting themselves in some way.' I feel pants are more of a sign of the times than I realised. A growing contempt for man in general creeps over me. For a craftsman, whether a sweep or Prime Minister – 'hats off'. But why this 'Lords of Creation' attitude on men's part? I am beginning to see I'm a really clever woman in my own line, and not the 'odd' or 'uneducated' woman that I've had dinned into me. . . . I feel that, in the world of tomorrow, marriage will be – will *have* to be – more of a partnership, less of this '*I* have spoken' attitude. They will talk things over – talking *does* do good, if only to clear the air. I run my house like a business: I have had to, to get all done properly, everything fitted in. Why, then, should women not be looked on as partners, as 'business women'?

Against that we have the 1945 testimony of a young Wolverhampton war worker:

> No one asked us to leave work, and we dared not ask to leave, so in awe were we of the Works. But, as the men filtered home there were weddings and homes to set up. There were weddings, such as my own, where the man had to return afterwards, back to base to finish his service time. We had managed to find a house to rent, although in a run-down condition, and with my man away, it was left to me to get it in shape. Although I had not been given my cards, I asked for a week off – but I never did go back. I'd had enough, and in any case, by now I had my Navy wife's pay book, which gave me £2 5s od a week.[16]

The slow but steady expansion in women's employment after the war may be attributed to long-term technological change, rather than to the war itself; such attitudes as the one just cited may be attributed to ever-present social pressures; but the changing consciousness of Nella Last (and others like her) clearly bears a direct relationship to the war experience. Two specific issues, furthermore, were looked at afresh because of the war: equal pay, and the employment of married women. On equal pay only very minor advances were made, though a majority in the House of Commons supported an equal pay amendment to the 1944 Education Bill. Before the war it was common practice in many professions to sack women as soon as they married. During the war a scarcity of labour inevitably meant that married women were given employment, and the old myths about their unreliability as employees were clearly exposed for what they were. More than this, in a few cases, employers, encouraged by the Government, experimented with the setting up of nurseries which permitted the employment of women with young children. This pointed to an irreversible trend: a government survey conducted among private business at the end of the war showed a remarkable swing round in opinion with regard to the question of the employment of married women.[17]

Before we turn from participation to a final brief comment on the test effect of war, let us take a close look at *Plate 78*, a good example of the richness and density of photography as an historical 'text'. In intention this photograph forms

78 'Woman at work the morning after an air raid', 28 September 1940.

part of the heroic imagery of the war, showing an East End clothing worker carrying on unflappably the morning after a destructive raid. The two exterior figures (policeman and warden?) look extremely 'normal', save for the tin hats, into which are concentrated the quintessence of abnormality. In the archaeology of the picture are jagged chunks of painted-over glass and swathes of black-out material. Contradicting the propagandist intention of the photograph, there appear to be a couple of absentees inside. And what of women's work?: what has changed, and what has not changed? (compare *Plate 11* with *Plates 25 and 27*).

There were some moves in the thirties, we have seen, towards a more scientific and technological orientation for British industry. The demands of war necessarily made this a more wholehearted process. One of the foremost authorities on contemporary British economic history, Professor Sidney Pollard, has stated that, in contrast with the inter-war years, Britain by the end of the war 'had acquired great strength in some of the most promising sectors like vehicles, aircraft and electronics'.[18] This, at least, was something to put in the balance against the substantial economic losses caused by the war.

## The Psychological Dimension: The Overall Impact of the War

The calculating invocation in the 1960s of the 'Dunkirk spirit' by Harold Wilson, followed, fifteen years later, by the less calculating but naive appeals to the 'spirit of 1945' by Michael Foot have been enough to sink the credibility of any notion that there was in wartime some genuine reconstruction of the national psyche. Cynics now stress censorship and propaganda rather than unity and altruism. I want to suggest that, given always the class inequality and traditionalism of British society, there were genuine changes in attitude throughout the

79 Catford Central School for Girls. Picture dated 21 January 1943 and marked 'banned'.

population, which arose from within society rather than being imposed from above by the state.

In essence the organization of British censorship and propaganda was based on the unvoiced assumption that proprietors and editors of newspapers, controllers and programme planners in the BBC, filmmakers, senior military personnel, ministers and top civil servants, coming from the same social class background, shared the same attitudes, and would co-operate easily in the cause espoused by all, the proper prosecution of the war effort. There was a convention that dead bodies were not shown; pictures of extreme devastation, we have noted, were not usually released till sometime after the event. One of the worst late raids in the war, prior to the V1s and V2s, came on south-east London on 20 January 1943. Catford Girls School, whose pupils had long since filtered back from evacuation, took a direct hit, thirty-eight children and six adults being killed. Although some pictures were printed in the press at the time, *Plate 79*, with the bodies in sacking, was banned by the censorship.

There was talk of the government taking over the BBC, but in effect that body continued to operate autonomously, even if constrained by formal links with the Ministry of Information which in practice steadily weakened as the war proceeded; the government, however, always had its reserve powers and ultimate sanctions. The release of footage of military operations was strictly controlled, but although the Ministry of Information took some initiatives of its own, and in one case put up finance for a feature film, the making of films was left in the hands of the private companies; the actual filmmaking, however, could be closely, and often irritatingly, supervised, and the Ministry could exercise further influence through the powers it had over the distribution of film stock and other necessary supplies and over the exemption of staff for military service.[19]

The single most significant item in the press history of the war is the triumph of the *Daily Mirror*. Before the war the *Mirror* had, without any firm political or social stance, cast around for means of attracting readers and groups generally neglected by the press, particularly women, and the better-off working class. During the war the *Mirror* employed colloquialisms, working-class idiom, parodies of upper-class speech to stress its identification with its readers. While other newspapers were generally respectful towards the government, and detached in their criticism of errors and misjudgments, the *Mirror* enthusiastically enrolled itself on the side of 'us' the people in face of a government which was often secretive, authoritarian, and uncomprehending of individual grievances. Through its ordinary letter columns the *Mirror* kept in the closest touch with its readership.[20]

British cinemas quickly returned to the boom conditions of prewar days. Now, in addition to the normal cinema programme of two feature films and a newsreel, ten minutes were set aside for showing official documentaries related to the war effort. There were other 'non-theatrical' outlets for informational (or propaganda) films, and the Ministry of Information had its own cinema vans touring the country (*Plate 80*): these could reach big audiences right where it counted, in the factory canteen. War conditions actually provided the opportunity for the full achievement of some of the possibilities in the British cinema industry, which had only been hinted at in prewar days. In particular,

80 'CINEMA IN A CHURCH: Ministry of Information van outside a church. These vans travelled the country, showing mainly documentary films.'

production at last went ahead with a film of Walter Greenwood's novel *Love on the Dole*. Not only was this film of the inescapable tragedy of working-class life in the Depression produced and released, it concluded with a message from A. V. Alexander, a Labour minister in the Churchill government, declaring that such evil conditions must never be allowed to return again. Most films, certainly, had their propaganda overtones. *Millions Like Us* showed young women from different social backgrounds adapting to factory life: yet the spirit it represented of pulling together was far from false. But the more potent form for purporting to convey to civilians what the war, fought in the skies, fought in the Atlantic, fought in North Africa and in Italy, and, finally, fought in Western Europe, was really like, was the newsreel (though there was much unauthentic material, and many deliberate deceptions – British soldiers being dressed in Italian uniforms to represent an Italian surrender, for instance).

Yet, without any doubt whatsoever, the medium which was central to the British war effort in all its aspects was sound radio. The two most significant developments were the revolution in the presentation of news broadcasts, and an acceptance that if the loyalty of listeners was to be preserved, more attention to their tastes, particularly in the realm of popular music, would have to be conceded. For much of the world overseas, the BBC was the voice of integrity; for people at home it was a basic, and almost ritualistic, link with the war and the world outside. The condition (essential, too, to the importance of television) of receiving news and entertainment direct in one's own home by the turning of a knob had clearly been reached in the years of war.[21]

For particular messages which the government wished to get over – the need to buy savings stamps and war bonds, how the different rationing schemes worked, what to do with incendiary bombs, fifth columnists or powdered eggs, how to 'make do and mend' – the full range of resources were deployed. At the height of the war as much as 20 per cent of newspaper advertising was directly sponsored by the government. Ministry of Information posters dominated the hoardings. *Plate 81* shows one of them: 'careless talk costs lives' is a resonant message, redolent of the atmosphere of tension, of the threat of invasion, and of spy scares, of the early years of the war.

What did it all add up to? Two questions are relevant: was the welfare legislation of the postwar Labour government of a different order from the social legislation obtaining in the prewar period; and, if it was, can this qualitative change be convincingly linked to the war? The essential point in regard to the first question is that postwar legislation was informed by the principle of *universality* – that is to say welfare provisions were available to rich and poor alike, so that there could be no risk of a second-rate service for the poor; social provision in the thirties had been dominated by the notion of *selectivity* – state welfare, essentially, was for the working class alone, and medical provision for this class, without any doubt, *was* second-rate. More: compared with the thirties, the forties were a time of high levels of demand, economic activity, employment and earnings.

With regard to the second question, José Harris has argued that it cannot be answered till much more research has been undertaken, though she does in fact herself recognize that the 'growing desire for some kind of major reform of the social welfare system' emerging in the thirties was 'strongly reinforced by the

81 Ministry of
Information poster.

outbreak of war' and she does give explicit attention to the new wartime 'surge of interest in social questions'.[22] Taking the particular question of family allowances, an assumption of the Beveridge report, actually implemented by the caretaker Conservative government which held the fort between the dissolution of the national government and the General Election of 1945, John Macnicol explicitly rejects the 'war and social change' theory.[23]

Yet, in common with many others who *assert* that there is nothing in this theory, Dr Macnicol actually presents at least four good arguments for supporting the view that the war experience had a great deal to do with the enactment of Family Allowances in 1945. Now, one of the pioneer writers on war and social change, the late Richard Titmuss, undoubtedly did provide a somewhat naive analysis of the relationship between war and social change. Titmuss wrote that 'the mood of the people changed, and in sympathetic response values changed as well'; that Dunkirk 'summoned forth a note of self-criticism, of national introspection, and . . . set in motion ideas and talk of principles and plans'.[24] To criticize Titmuss as Dr Macnicol very properly does is not, however, to dispose of the rather more complex analysis of the relationship between war and social change which, for example, I have presented. Macnicol deploys the 'certainly . . . undoubtedly' technique: he actually shows where the war did affect social policy but somehow, for reasons which are never made clear, we are expected to discount these points in favour of the blunt assertion that the war had no real effects. What really happens with Macnicol and others like him is that they get caught up in the wrong argument. They want to show that politicians were a bad lot and opposed to social reform. Actually, if one concedes this, it strengthens the case for war's influence in overcoming their opposition. Old-fashioned political historians believed that by tracing out what politicians wrote to each other you could work out the influences on, and motivations for, their actions. This methodology leaves out of account the fact that pressures on politicians are multivariant and that frequently they have to take actions which, if free to operate on the basis of their own prejudices, they never would take. Here is a passage from Macnicol, with a few parentheses of my own:

> It is hardly likely that the events described in this chapter fit a 'war and social change' explanation. *Certainly* [my italics], the Second World War brought about a change-over in the technique of government, from the *laissez-faire* approach that had dominated in the interwar years to the liberal–reformists' 'middle way' interventionism that had been slowly developing in the 1930s – a change-over that took place most rapidly in May 1940 with the entry into government of Labour Party leaders and previous political heretics like Churchill, Macmillan and Amery [I would describe this as the *test* effect]. In addition, there *undoubtedly* [my italics] was great public interest throughout the war in what sort of Britain the people were fighting for, as the events surrounding the Beveridge Report showed [I would see this as a product of the *participation* and *psychological* effects]. The movement for Family Allowances benefited enormously from this, and ministers and civil servants realised that they had to concede to popular pressure to some extent. However, this is not the same thing as saying that they necessarily accepted the *arguments* of social reformers [I do not see this point as relevant to the main issue]. In the case of Family Allowances, ministers (Amery, Greenwood, Dalton and Morrison) accepted and civil servants generally did not. As this chapter has shown, the two crucial stages in the development of Family Allowances occurred during the Stamp Survey and the Beveridge Committee's work. In the former, Family Allowances were seen primarily as a means of holding down wages and combating inflation [again, motivation is not important: this was a reaction to a *war* problem – inflation – an example, therefore, of the *test* dimension]; in the latter, as a means of ensuring less eligibility, work-incentives and labour mobility. In both cases it was the needs of the economy rather than the children that dominated discussion.[25]

If this statement is accurate, it is still admitting the influence of the needs of war; actually it is not accurate, as Macnicol himself revealed in an earlier sentence: 'By this time [April 1941] the Treasury seems to have realised that public and political pressure was growing at such a rate as would make it very hard to resist demands for Family Allowances in the long run . . .'.[26] A few pages later Macnicol makes a couple of statements which again seem slightly to contradict the conclusion he is determined to come to. The Second World War he writes, 'Undoubtedly speeded up trends that were in evidence in the late 1930s'. To my taste this is a simplistic cliché, but it is certainly recognizing some influence attributable to the war. More significantly, Macnicol writes: 'The opposition of the trade unions was an immense obstacle . . . until the Second World War, which brought about certain conditions conducive to trade union co-operation . . .'. Basically, these were trade union *participation* in government, and a full-employment, high-wage economy, product of the test effect of war. My conclusion, then, is that the effects of war were so pervasive and self-evident, that even those historians who, for whatever reasons, are unwilling to recognize the fact cannot help in the course of their discussion revealing the very real effects that the war did have.

How one assesses the changes of the Second World War seems, in the end, to depend on ideological point of view. Those who believe in a classless society, or a society in which everywhere women and men fulfil the same roles, will tend to assess the war's impact negatively: those who are content to make direct comparisons with the inadequacies of the thirties may, like me, feel that limited, unsatisfactory, and contradictory as it undoubtedly was, recognizable social change did take place in Britain between 1939 and 1945.

## Chapter Six

# Postwar Britain: 1945–1951

### The Legacies of War: Aspiration and Austerity

The General Election of 5 July 1945 is one of the most famous in Britain's history: the Labour Party won 393 seats against 213 for the Conservatives, and 31 for the various other parties. One can never be absolutely sure about these things, of course, but it seems as certain as anything ever is that this striking victory owed much to the experiences and upheavals of war. Certainly, there was no electoral trend in favour of Labour in the late thirties, and it seems unlikely that had the normal election been held in 1940, Labour would have won it.[1] Having said that, the point has to be made that in regard to actual votes cast, Labour's victory was by no means as sweeping as textbook accounts often suggest. Of those who took the trouble to vote, 47.8 per cent voted Labour; but 39.8 per cent voted Conservative, with 9 per cent voting Liberal; and 20 per cent did not bother to vote at all. The results were delayed by a couple of weeks to make sure that they included the servicemen's vote (unfairly excluded, for the most part, in the previous 'khaki' election of 1918); overwhelmingly, the servicemen voted Labour.[2]

Demobilization photographs from the previous war tend to stress the turning in of weapons. *Plate 82* is very characteristic of 1945 (though from a *Picture Post* story of January 1946), very redolent of the spirit of the citizen, having done his duty, now returning to civilian life and civilian dress (however ill-fitting) and headgear (unfortunately not seen in the photograph). J. B. Priestley attempted to capture the spirit in his short novel *Three Men in New Suits* (1945). Priestley was a committed socialist of the 'brotherhood of man' type and in linking him with the young officer in *Plate 82*, whose opinions of course we do not know, we must not put more weight on his words than they will bear. Yet Priestley's immense popularity during the war as broadcaster, novelist and film writer, and his position as one of those leftish figures to whom the war gave new opportunity and new influence, invest his inventions with special value at this juncture in British social history. The novel discusses the appearance and attitudes of three young men from very different social backgrounds: 'There was a distinct likeness between them, as if all three had come from the same place, and had been doing the same things there.' One of them declares their credo:

> We don't want the same kind of men looking after our affairs. We act as if we've learnt something. We don't keep shouting 'That's mine – clear off!' We don't try to make our little corner safe – and to hell with anybody else! We don't talk about liberty when what we really mean is a chance to fleece the public. We don't go back on all we said

82 'The Problem of the Demobbed Officer, 1945: At the Clothing Depot in Olympia the Major goes through the last stage of the demobilisation procedure – the issue of civilian clothing', *Picture Post*, 26 January 1946.

when the country was in danger. We do an honest job of work for the community for what the community thinks we are worth. We stop being lazy, stupid and callous. . . . Instead of guessing and grabbing, we plan. Instead of competing, we co-operate. We come out of the nursery – and begin to grow up![3]

Idealistic aspiration, of course, would have to adapt to the economic realities. The bleak situation created by the direct destructiveness and cost of the war has already been noted. It was made suddenly worse when the end of the war against Japan forced the American government to implement a previous resolution of Congress and bring to an end Lend-Lease Agreements; throughout the war these had enabled Britain to lay hands on the supplies she needed to keep the war effort going. Britain's chief negotiator, J. M. Keynes, did secure the necessary basic credits from the US and from Canada, but the Americans insisted that the pound be restored to full convertibility as quickly as possible. When in the autumn of 1947 convertibility was restored there was an immediate flight from the pound as holders of sterling rushed to seize the opportunity to convert their holdings into scarce dollars. The crisis was severe and convertibility had again to be suspended: the glorious age of the pound had clearly gone for good. Meantime, the original loan was being used up too rapidly. However, from 1948 the British economy was able to draw upon a new American reconstruction plan; between the end of 1948 and the beginning of 1951 Britain received a total of £2,400 million in 'Marshall Aid'.

The nation's difficulties were aggravated by a number of worldwide economic trends. Throughout the world in the postwar years there was a persistent upward movement in prices, which, as a natural consequence of the disruptions of war and the return everywhere to civilian production, was particularly marked in the primary materials which Britain had to import. Because of the destruction of capital during the war and need to rebuild industry after it, and because of the movement everywhere towards new technologies requiring high levels of investment, there was a worldwide shortage of capital. Against this, Britain did stand to profit from the expansion in world trade which took place in the postwar years: in 1939 world trade in manufactures was little higher than it had been in 1913; by 1950 it was already 50 per cent higher. Britain, with a proportion of her 'invisible income' of prewar days gone, must, to make her way in the postwar world, not only regain her lost export markets, but increase exports to 75 per cent above their prewar figure. The seriousness of this challenge was mitigated by some of the consequences of the test effect of war, the expansion in the newer, more technological industries, already noted. For all that, Britain's power supplies still depended overwhelmingly upon coal. After the appalling tale of callous neglect in the inter-war years, the new strains imposed on the coal industry by the Second World War brought the industry to a very serious pass: in 1945 coal production was at the very low level of 175 million tons. Not even prompt nationalization, the miners' battlecry in the 1920s, could win over workers who had been left to rot in the inter-war years, and output per manshift remained low, matching the prewar level only in 1950. In the meantime came the desperately cold winter of 1946–7. The enfeebled coal industry simply could not meet the extra demand, and massive cuts in power supplies spread a wave of temporary unemployment throughout British industry which reached a peak of 800,000.

In its 1945 election manifesto, *Let Us Face the Future*, the Labour Party stated its ultimate purpose as: 'The establishment of a Socialist Commonwealth of Great Britain – free, democratic, efficient, progressive, public-spirited, its material resources organised in the service of the British people.' The basic model for Labour's nationalization programme was the establishment of public corporations. Thus, the coal industry was entrusted to the National Coal Board, the railways to the British Railways Board, road haulage to the British Transport Commission, and the two major public utilities to an Electricity Board and a Gas Board, with an infrastructure of area boards. Cable and Wireless Ltd became a public corporation; British European Airways and British South American Airways joined with the British Overseas Airways Corporation in running British civil aviation. Formal nationalization of the Bank of England was carried through. Planning, both of the Socialist Commonwealth, and, more immediately, of the export drive, was to be achieved partly through the 'commanding heights' controlled by the nationalized industries, partly through direction of investment, particularly towards the 'development areas' and partly by various controls and quotas, designed, for example, to encourage successful exporters. Foreign exchange control was continued from the war period.

Fearing the return of unemployment, Labour followed a 'cheap money' policy, a bank rate of 2 per cent. In what turned out to be a time of full employment and inflationary pressure, this may well not have been exactly the right policy. Certainly, the government was not successful in restraining inflation (a worldwide phenomenon): there was modest success for a brief period in the later forties when the government secured trade union co-operation in a voluntary 'wage restraint'. However, the target of raising exports to 75 per cent above the prewar level was achieved by 1950.

The pound remained weak, and some devaluation was probably inevitable in 1949; it seems, however, that in reducing the pound from $4.03 to $2.80 Sir Stafford Cripps rather overdid things. The upshot in any event was that while exports, by being rendered cheaper to overseas buyers, did receive a temporary boost, the cost of British imports rose, thus, in value terms, offsetting the gains.

*Plate 83* (also from that great product of the thirties documentary movement, *Picture Post*), a photograph taken nearly four years after the ending of the war, presents a sharp image of some aspects of the mixed legacy with which the country was contending. The considerable amount of bomb damage is apparent on the right side of the picture, as also the vast hoardings advertising the fact that, no longer unemployment, but shortage of labour was the problem. The old urban transport systems are still operating. The jaunty contemporary caption, inevitably, shows no awareness of any deeper historical significance in this photograph. *We* know, of course, that this entire area has become an ugly mess of characterless concrete boxes. Bomb damage, together with the genuine desire to rebuild society, to provide decent housing on the model of the Quarry Hill experiment, combined eventually to produce the redevelopment of the fifties and sixties. That is looking ahead from the immediate postwar world, but from this piece of evidence we can note what a relatively small proportion of the destruction of Britain's older urban fabric was actually directly due to Hitler. For the immediate postwar period, the history is of the gaps left by bombs remaining unfilled because of the shortages of materials and labour.

In many inner-city slum areas where jerry-built houses had collapsed under the effects of bomb blast like houses of cards, it must be said, bomb devastation was more widespread. This can be seen in *Plate 84*, as also can the prefabricated houses which were the government's response to the immediate appalling housing shortage. Many couples became attached to their 'prefabs', mainly because they were self-contained, and had gardens. But their cramped and provisional nature should be taken into account in any final assessment of the high-rise housing boom which was yet to come.

If *Plate 85* joins with *Plates 82–4* in driving home that we are indeed in a postwar, not a peacetime world, *Plate 86* – in many ways the most stunning picture in this entire collection – brings out how much of the nineteenth century there still was in this postwar Britain. With its productivity and labour-shortage problems, the government was very happy to have the labour of German prisoners-of-war (mainly on farms) and of 'pit-brew girls' in its collieries. *Plate 85* is from a characteristic *Picture Post* story (21 August 1948) on the last German prisoners-of-war finally returning to Germany. This is obviously not a set-up picture (look at the girl cut in half on the left) and it radiates a cheerfulness not always to be associated with the population dislocations involved in modern war. Altogether there had been 417,130 German prisoners-of-war in Britain. In his article, Lionel Birch reported:

> Nearly all the prisoners liked England . . . How many of them learned to like 'English democracy?' You can take your choice of two clues to the answer. Two young Englishmen who had spent many months with German P.O.W.s, passionately believed that 90 per cent of the prisoners had been 'converted to democracy.' 'These chaps

83 'Life in the Elephant:
View of the meeting
place of six traffic
arteries of London',
*Picture Post*, 8 January
1949.

84 Prefabs in the East
End, *Picture Post*, March
1946.

85 'THE GERMAN
PRISONERS ARRIVE IN
CIVVY STREET: Last
German prisoners
repatriated from Britain
leave Bury St. Edmunds
Transit Camp. On Bury
station they say goodbye
to girl friends. 270 of
them have married
English girls.' *Picture
Post*, 21 August 1948.

really feel that we've shown them the way to live. They know that we and they are really the most akin of all Europeans. They'll never fight us again. And nor will we.' On the other hand, two middle-aged Englishmen, who'd 'had' the Germans, and the German prisoners, during, and after, both world wars said: 'We wouldn't put it as high as 90 per cent of "converts". We'd put it somewhere between 3 per cent and 5 per cent. The rest may be very polite about democracy and all that; but they'll slip back, all right – you'll see.'

Perhaps what the two clues together convey most strikingly today is the patronizing chauvinism which was still very evident in the 1940s. The caption tells us of the 270 German POWs who have already married English girls and indicates that here they are saying goodbye to girlfriends. Actually, only one girlfriend is in evidence (or one-and-three-quarters to be puristic) and the scene is scarcely charged with intimate personal emotion. With the British soldier looking on and the POW on the right having lost his cap, it suggests, what had become true, that the Germans in a pleasantly human and informal way had become integrated into local British society. The deeper sadness, if there was one, was that they were going back to a Germany suffering an economic deprivation far beyond anything still existing in Britain.

*Plate 86* is one of those documents which, however unambiguous the direct testimony it offers, must arouse quite different reactions in different viewers. Does one say, 'how horrific, how archaic, women still working at coal pits a hundred years after the campaigns of Lord Shaftesbury'?; does one say, 'good, women occupying their rightful place in the industrial world'? Today, American women work underground in the mines of Kentucky and West Virginia, and take

86 'Women working on the picking belt of a colliery's screening plant shortly after the Second World War.' National Coal Board record photo.

time off to fight cases against sexual harassment. Where then do we place this photograph, and all it implies: at the end of an old story which involved the evil exploitation of women and children, or as part of a new story of women's emancipation? Probably I over-dramatize. What these women are doing is sorting out the coal on a screening-belt: it is relatively light, though very dirty, surface work. By the early fifties, women were no longer employed on this work: those who did not voluntarily leave the pits altogether, were employed in the canteens gradually established by the National Coal Board.[4] There is perhaps no great sign of emancipation here. These women are segregated, doing 'women's work'; women were certainly not working with men at the coal-face. The picture looks archaic principally because of what the women are wearing: skirts to their feet, jackets, and scarves round their heads. Latter-day American women pit workers look different because they have modern pit showers to get the dirt out: the women here portrayed had to do their best to keep the dirt from getting in. So, a classic document of the old Britain that survived into the postwar years.

Most women, of course, were not working in quite the conditions represented in *Plate 86*. Yet the years under review undoubtedly brought harassment for the ordinary housewife coping with shortages and juggling with the various forms of rationing. Basic food stuffs were on 'coupons', clothing on 'clothing coupons', tinned fruits and dried fruits on one kind of 'points', and chocolate and sweets on another, popularly known as 'sweetie coupons'. Rations fluctuated, but in 1948 they worked out at a weekly allowance per person of 13 oz of meat, $1\frac{1}{3}$ oz of cheese, 6 oz of butter and margarine, 1 oz of cooking fat, 8 oz of sugar, 2 pints of milk and 1 egg. In neither world war, although the whole gamut of adulteration had been run in 1918, had it proved necessary to institute bread rationing: but in 1946 the Minister of Food, John Strachey, introduced this ultimate symbol of belt-tightening, which lasted from July 1946 to July 1948. The big freeze-up associated with the fuel policies of Emanuel Shinwell brought forth the anti-slogan in the Tory press: 'Shiver with Shinwell and Starve with Strachey.' Already-modest rations had to be further reduced in the aftermath of the convertibility crisis of 1947, when there was at no time great popular enthusiasm for the various delicacies offered by the Ministry of Food such as whale meat, and the mysterious but aptly-named canned fish, snoek. Officially meals in restaurants were restricted to three courses costing not more than 5s (the majority of British people did not, in any case, at this time eat meals on that scale in restaurants; the minority who did, though irritated by the restrictions, often were able to find ways round them). Controls were greatly reduced in 1948 and again in 1950, with the abolition of milk rationing in January 1950, of points and of restrictions on restaurant meals in 1950, and of controls on flour, eggs and soap in the autumn of 1950.

Clothes rationing, which did not end till March 1949, was a particular bane. The journalist J. L. Hodson remarked that the rich were distinguished by their ability to bring a bit of colour into their clothing.[5] To the rich, too, was confined the unadulterated version of the Parisienne 'New Look' which arrived in 1947 (*Plate 87*). Since the New Look featured curvaceous lines, long and loosely pleated skirts and, in sum, conspicuous consumption of materials, it never really reached the bulk of the female population in the way perhaps suggested by the popular press, with whom the term became something of a catch-phrase.

Coventry, as the first provincial city to be blitzed, held a special interest for journalists. *Illustrated* did a feature on 'The Future of Coventry' in 1949, from

87 'NEW LOOK: After the fasion kings of Paris decided that longer skirts would be the dominating feature of their new designs, women in countries that are influenced by the French fashion centre found themselves buying the "new look" models in their local shops. "Picture Post" sends a cameraman on a tour of London to record some of the women who are wearing the latest styles.' (1949)

88 'THE FUTURE OF COVENTRY. Arcade roof has gone and rain may come in, but shops near Broadgate are well stocked and housewives smile their way until days of rebuilding are well advanced.' *Illustrated*, 29 October 1949.

which *Plate 88* is reproduced. Coventry has an even greater interest in that, despite the destruction of November 1940, it became a very prosperous industrial centre during the war as a growth area for engineering, motor manufacturing and other light industry. This scene forms a good visual metaphor for a prospering part of Britain in 1949. The arcade roof has not yet been repaired, and is still open to the elements. The people look purposeful and reasonably well-off, as they go about their shopping. The women's fashions are square, rather dowdy, showing little of the influence of the New Look, save perhaps in the length of skirt.

A much more fundamental fashion issue concerns the absence, or presence, of male headgear. Neither the man in the foreground left, nor the one in the middle distance right is wearing a hat; nor are the boys in the foreground right. Now quite a lot of hats are missing in the bombed-out group (*Plate 67*), though hats are much in evidence in *Plate 70*. As we have noted, with each demob suit was issued also a hat. We only have to compare the mass of pre-Second World War photographs, with the mass of more recent photographs to draw the conclusion: at some point the custom whereby all males habitually wore a hat came to an end. There is an interesting clue in John Braine's novel *Room at the Top*, which was published in 1957, written rather earlier in the 1950s, but actually *set* (this is the crucial point) in the late forties. Joe Lampton, the narrator who successfully ends up at the top, critically scrutinizes a young man who 'had a navy-blue overcoat, gloves, and scarf, but no hat; he was following the odd working-class fashion which seemed to me now, after Alice's tuition, as queer as going out without trousers.'[6] If a working-class fashion, it was, as all the photographic evidence makes clear, a pretty recent one.    From a study of the main trade magazine, *Hatters Gazette*, it is clear that a swing away from hat-wearing by men had first appeared in the 1930s; a phenomenon, I would surmise, basically related to long-term economic depression. Then 'the long years of the Second World War gave hat-wearing a body blow', and although the trade tried to convince itself that hat-wearing in the services led to the formerly hatless contracting a habit which would continue into civilian life, this – although there were obviously exceptions within the main trend – did not in general prove to be the case. A survey published in October 1948 showed that while among the over forties, 70 or 80 per cent still always, or usually, wore hats, of the under-forties 60–70 per cent were generally hatless, though some would wear hats on special occasions; but the real rub, and the essential basis for the trend now established (whatever the temporary fluctuations might be) was that among under-twenty-fives and teenagers hardly more than 15 per cent ever wore hats.

Nonetheless, things still did not look too bad for the industry in November 1952, when another survey, broken up geographically but not by age group, put the hat wearers at 56.7 per cent of the whole population. But it was clear from this survey that the habit was strongest in the remoter rural, and more traditional industrial, areas: thus hats were more generally worn in Scotland than in the rest of the United Kingdom, and the single city with most men wearing hats was Newcastle, with a figure of 70 per cent. On the other hand, two of the boom towns of the postwar era, Birmingham and Bristol, had a 60 per cent majority not wearing hats. By 1954 the *Hatters Gazette* itself was coming out only once every two months instead of once a month. Throughout 1956 there is open recognition of declining sales among hats for men, though gross figures keep up reasonably well because millinery sales were prospering. The straits of the men's headwear industry in the middle-fifties can be summed up in the resort to aggressive sloganizing, the best being: 'Get ahead, get a hat'. At the end of 1958 the *Hatters Gazette* ceased publication.

The statistics give some help

**Hats, Caps and Millinery**

| Year | Gross Output (£ millions) | Total Employment (thousands) |
|---|---|---|
| 1907 | 5.6 | 33.1 |
| 1912 | 8.0 | 39.0 |
| 1924 | 14.2 | 32.0 |
| 1930 | 13.3 | 33.1 |
| 1935 | 13.9 | 40.0 |
| 1948 | 18.3 | 20.5 |
| 1949 | 18.3 | 19.9 |
| 1950 | 19.4 | 19.8 |
| 1951 | 21.7 | 19.9 |
| 1954 | 25.4 | 21.1 |
| 1958 | 21.9 | 15.2 |
| 1963 | 21.8 | 13.0 |
| 1968 | 19.2 | 8.9 |
| 1970 | 19.8 | 7.6 |

In interpreting these statistics we have to remember that women's hats, a major element in the actual value of the gross output, are included, that working-class expenditure on caps could be a relatively minor element, since caps were intended to last, and we must allow for inflation both over the First World War period, and, more relevantly, in the period since the Second World War. Taking all of these points together, the large-scale abandonment of hat-wearing by men would have a relatively small effect on the global figures. What we are looking for is a definite, if small, sign of down-turn, and it is perfectly clear that this comes between 1954 and 1958. Figures from 1948 onwards are not as high as one would expect, taking inflation only into account. Thus, there obviously was a diminution in hat-wearing as a result of the disruptions of war, and the austerity of postwar years. But the deliberate change, resulting, I have suggested, from decisions first made by younger men, appears in the middle to later fifties. Nonetheless the war, with all its scarcities and shortages and informalities and disruptions, seems to be the turning point. After the war, the hat remained a formal requirement, but no longer a normal one. In the fifties, as we shall see, working-class freedom was to be taken over by other classes.

## Aspiration and Achievement

If the Labour government had an achievement less tarnished than any other, it was the Welfare State. As I have already suggested, the universalist quality of this Welfare State made it more than just the culmination of a steady evolution, though, without doubt, many of its forms were determined by the preoccupations of the war period. Actually, the first major piece of postwar social legislation was enacted by the caretaker Conservative government: family allowances represented the fullest expression of the universalist idea, in that they were paid to all families, rich or poor, were financed from general taxation, and were themselves subject to tax. The first major act of the Labour government, the National Insurance Act (1946), which amalgamated all the main forms of interruption of earnings, also applied to all classes, though it retained the principle of the insurance contribution: benefits were, as Beveridge had insisted, on a flat rate, though at a higher level than envisaged by Beveridge. Since the insurance principle was maintained there had to be another system to provide for those who did not have the necessary contributions. While, therefore, the 1948 National Assistance Act formally abolished the old Poor Law, it did retain a revised form of the Unemployment Assistance Board of the thirties (renamed the Assistance Board in 1940) as the National Assistance Board.

In the main the new National Health Service (based on the act of 1946, coming into effect in 1948) embodied the universalist principle: it was entirely open to everyone and, save in the case of certain specified extra services, it was entirely free. Treatment in no way depended upon insurance contributions, and there was indeed a complete separation between the question of income need (now dealt with by National Insurance and National Assistance) and health need. Against the opposition of the Conservatives, but building upon the Emergency Hospitals Scheme experiment of the war years, Aneurin Bevan, the responsible minister, was able to create a nationalized hospital service. Between 1946 and 1948 there were many battles between the doctors and the government, before the

**HERE HE COMES, BOYS!**

7th August, 1945. Mr. Aneurin Bevan's appointment as Minister of Health is not welcome in certain circles.

overwhelming majority of doctors decided to come into the scheme, on the understanding, however, that they would be paid on a capitation fee basis, not as members of a salaried service. The remarkably early *News Chronicle* cartoon by Vicky (*Plate 89*) is characterized both by simplification and prescience. Many, possibly a majority, of ordinary GPs were, till around this time at least, in favour of the principle of a National Health Service. True, this cartoon centres on Harley Street, home of the very highly-paid specialists. Yet, in the end, through making big concessions to them in the form of the retention of their private practices, Bevan on the whole won the support of the specialists. The putative support of the ordinary doctors was lost mainly because of their, not totally unjustified, fear of being put under the control of the local authorities.

The National Health Service, and the Welfare State generally, were subject to much criticism at the time, and in the years which followed. To Conservatives, who, it should always be remembered, voted against the second reading of the National Health Service Bill (while supporting the idea of a comprehensive health service)[7] the Service went too far in the direction of state control of medicine. To advanced medical opinion the Service was a 'sickness service' not a 'health service'. To a variety of critics the 'tripartite' administrative division of the NHS was clumsy and inefficient: new regional hospital boards for the hospitals; new local executive councils for the general practitioner services; old-established local authorities for the many other services. But whether in a nation addicted to white bread and sweets, or indeed in any other nation in the world, the establishment of a service directing all citizens towards healthy living from the cradle to the grave was a practical reality may be doubted.

When attempts were made in the 1970s to alter the tripartite structure, criticism, if anything, became even more vociferous. In the early years, because of economic difficulties and shortages, there were certainly great deficiencies in physical facilities. The demand for medicine of all kinds, as also for dentures and spectacles, proved to be enormous, and while this was in large part a measure of the woeful neglect during the 1930s, it also drew attention to the fact that the human capacity to consume free medicine is practically inexhaustible. In 1951, with the Korean War as the excuse, the Labour government itself introduced certain health service charges. But in all major respects the NHS, at point of service, remained free; in this, it was superior to those continental schemes in which patients had first to pay for treatment, then reclaim it – a deterrent from which the British were spared.

Labour politicians liked to boast of the mosaic of the Welfare State; in fact, it was more of a crazy-paving. The flat-rate National Insurance benefits quickly fell well behind the cost of living; it soon became clear that many entitled to apply to the separate National Assistance scheme did not do so, because to them it still carried the stigma of the old Poor Law, or of the dole. Really, the major feature of the later forties was full employment, and a level of incomes comparable with, or higher than, that of the war and, therefore, considerably higher than that of the thirties. How much full employment really owed to deliberate government policies, as distinct from worldwide trends issuing from the war, is debatable. One neglected measure, which genuinely looked forward to more constructive attitudes towards employment, was the Employment and Training Act of 1948, which created the first comprehensive and efficient Youth Employment Service throughout the country. The Children's Act of 1948, which firmly defined the responsibilities of local authorities towards homeless children, should also be noted as an important innovation.

But in the end, social policies are at the mercy of economic trends. Churchill denounced the Labour government for concentrating too much on social welfare, when the prime task was to get the economy right. As the deep structural weaknesses in the British economy have steadily been revealed, it is perhaps less easy to write Churchill off as a jingoistic reactionary than it was at the time, though it has also to be said that Churchill, in common with most of the upper class, almost all publicists, and many politicians (including Labour ones) continued to have quite exaggerated ideas about the continued significance to Britain of the Empire.

The nationalization and economic planning policies of the Attlee government were successful neither in creating a Socialist Commonwealth (as understood by Attlee and his colleagues) nor in laying the basis for an efficient mixed economy. The latter judgment is perhaps a little harsh since the major failings are really to be found in governments after 1951. In the 1983 British film *Ploughman's Lunch*, Ann, the veteran Marxist historian, laments that the Labour government took over the most clapped-out 20 per cent of industry and then put the same fuddy-duddies in to run it. There is much truth in this. Nationalization certainly did practically nothing to alter the social class composition of those running major industries. By shilly-shallying the Labour government lost the opportunity to take over the prospering steel industry (the Conservatives denationalized it before Labour's belated nationalization had time to take effect). On the other hand, from the point of view of economic success, it is not the fact of nationalization which counts, but the business policies which are pursued. One has to conclude that nationalized (as currently understood) or denationalized, it would not have made a great deal of difference to the steel industry or, indeed, to the workers in it.

Putting undue faith in its ability to control the commanding heights of the economy through its nationalization of one-fifth of all industry, the government devoted little thought to the 80 per cent left in private hands: it neither developed efficient mechanisms for encouraging desirable investment within the private sector, nor, on the other hand, did it provide much but discouragement to small business enterprises anxious to pursue profits and productivity in their own way. Operating on lower baselines of expectation, continental governments were able to exact from their citizens higher productivity for lower earnings, and could site new industry in the most favourable locations secure in the knowledge that hungry populations would follow.

Carrying through its social engineering for a people who had 'won the war' the British government sought to take jobs to the people, and was never able to establish a due relationship between earnings and productivity. As they moved into recovery, continental countries planned road systems anew, integrated road, rail and canal. In Britain, too much of the old survived; too much faith was put in words like 'socialism' and 'planning'; too many committees were established, but too little direct thought was given to working out what from a rational economic point of view were the areas needing immediate heavy investment. Many of the most important initiatives had their origins in the war, rather than in socialist planning. Developments in the remoter areas of Scotland also owed much to the personal vision of the Scottish socialist Secretary of State for Scotland during the war, Tom Johnston, who saw the Hydro-electric Development (Scotland) Act through parliament in 1943 and the establishment of the North of Scotland Hydro-electric Board. The building of giant hydro-electric schemes in the later forties (*Plate 90*) symbolizes some of the greater achievements of the Attlee government, but then, of course, such areas as Loch Sloy were virgin territory, with only the traditionalism of the sheep to be overcome.

At the very beginning of this book I raised the question of how far Britain's industrial decline was already determined by the beginning of our century. The particular attributes of the British upper class, which continued, to a remarkable degree, to exercise sway after 1945, cannot be gainsaid. However, the British record up till the Second World War was not notably worse than that of its European competitors. At the end of the war, Britain really had considerable advantages over these competitors. Attention, therefore, has been directed by Professor Sidney Pollard towards top civil servants, particularly those at the Treasury, and towards the economists who provided them with advice. Pollard concluded that the Treasury was consistently narrow and traditionalist in outlook (and I would, myself, relate this to the inadequacies of British upper-class education compared with, say, the system of *grandes écoles* in France) and that British economists, while in the top rank as far as theory was concerned, fell down when it came to the practicalities of guiding productive investment into the most fruitful and essential areas.[8] But there must be criticism, too, of the great financial institutions, making up the City – which the Labour government, despite its token nationalization of the Bank of England signally failed to control – for continuing to look overseas, towards purely financial transactions and quick returns, rather than towards steady investment in British industry. Nor can British industrialists escape censure; like the British working people they believed they had earned the right to have it easy once the war was over.

90 Loch Sloy Dam. Werner Bischof photo for *Illustrated*, 5 August 1950.

The Attlee government missed some opportunities and avoided some fiendishly difficult decisions; but, on the whole, as things stood the economy was off to not a bad start at the beginning of the fifties. One other debilitating cloud, however, was already hanging over it. Although the Labour government was proud to see itself as anti-imperialist, and regarded the acceptance of Indian independence as one of its greatest achievements, the country was still embroiled in many parts of Africa, in the Middle East, and in Malaysia: preserving the pretences of Empire used up monies needed for the restructuring and retooling of British industry.

Attlee himself looked and sounded a traditionalist, and indeed came from that old middle class which by the end of the nineteenth century was joining itself to the bottom part of the upper class. In wartime, much had been done to reorientate public policy in directions favourable to both the arts and the sciences. The wartime Council for the Encouragement of Music and the Arts (CEMA) became the Arts Council; yet traditionalism and parochialism had a firm hold. When, in April 1945, Francis Bacon exhibited his *Three Figures at the*

91 Francis Bacon, *Pope Shouting*, oil on canvas, 1951.

*Base of a Crucifixion*, which contained the elements for which he was eventually to become well known – malignant, ominous, twisted figures, part-human, part-animal – the response was one of outrage and ridicule at what were described as being obsessive, ferocious distortions. By 1951, which was when *Pope Shouting* (*Plate 91*) was painted, Bacon was well on the way to critical acceptance, though that section of the British public which had any interest at all in painting tended to prefer the romanticism, even lushness, which was the characteristic of the artistic and literary establishment of the time. John Piper was a painter of great native genius, who had been commissioned by a government-sponsored scheme to paint wartime scenes. Once again Coventry (*Plate 92*) emerges as a symbolic city in Britain's recent history. Piper paintings of this *genre* were reproduced in

92 John Piper, *Bombed Ruins of Coventry Cathedral*, watercolour, 1940 or 1941.

their thousands for a British society which had not yet really opened to the powerful artistic and literary influences which were even then germinating in the United States and on the continent of Europe.

The wartime golden age of science dimmed, though wartime developments had many important civilian spin-offs, particularly in the realm of medical sciences. Even so, a spirit of dejection took over in, for instance, Medical Research Council (MRC) reports, where references were made to 'conditions often of frustrating difficulty' and to 'grave shortages of accommodation, of equipment and also of trained men'.[9] The closing days of war had been overshadowed by the dropping of the first atomic bombs. Secretly, the Attlee government initiated developments towards the production of Britain's own

atomic weapons. Low's cartoon (*Plate 93*) really says it all. Not quite all, however: the Development of Inventions Act of 1948 did lead to the establishment in 1949 of the National Research Development Corporation, one of whose major tasks was to be the provision of 'financial and other support' for the development of electronic computers, a sphere in which Britain, though far behind the United States, was able to establish a commanding lead over the other West European countries.

In 1851, on the initiative of Prince Albert, the nation had celebrated its triumphant emergence from the stresses and strains of early industrialization to a position of relative prosperity for the majority, and international dominance in technology, industry and trade. There was just enough of a parallel in 1951 for the government to plan a Festival of Britain to take place on the south bank of the Thames. *Plate 94* includes Waterloo Bridge and the railway bridge into Charing Cross Station. Working from the foreground backwards, can be seen: the Dome of Discovery, designed by Ralph Tubbs; the Skylon, designed by J. H. Moya; the Royal Festival Hall, which was really a London County Council project, designed by their Chief Architect, Robert Matthew, and would have been built anyway, festival or no festival; and the 1826 Shot Tower which, at first, the festival planners thought would have to be dismantled – in the end, as can be seen, it had a lighthouse and a radar telescope added to the top. Shot was still being made in the Shot Tower in the traditional way in December 1948, when it was visited by the Director General of the Festival, Gerald Barry, who provided this description:

> The process had all the charm of the antique. At the top of the tower – or at a platform below if a smaller size shot was required – was a platform holding on which stood a large cauldron of molten metal, warmed from below by a glowing brazier. Beside it stood a vessel perforated at the base with a large number of holes almost too small for the naked eye to see. The scene was a John Piper burlesque. Over the cauldron loomed

94 Aerial view of
Festival of Britain, 1951.

95 Festival of Britain:
interior design.

the gigantic figure of a man, sleeves rolled and forearms covered in long leather gloves, casting grotesque shadows up the wall who, armed with a ladle long enough for supping with the Devil, scooped up huge spoonfuls of leaden soup and emptied them into the monster colander. . . . Next time you are on the grouse moors remember Mephistopheles at the top of the Shot Tower.[10]

The precise significance of the Festival of Britain has been much argued over. It seems clear that it did have a powerful effect in spreading what was conceived to be a 'modern' style in architecture; whether this was good or bad, and whether because too modern, or not modern enough, has formed the basis of debate. Equally, thanks to the opportunity the festival offered to the Council for Industrial Design, interior design was greatly influenced (*Plate 95*). Though there was a travelling festival exhibition which visited Manchester, Leeds, Birmingham and Nottingham, and quite a number of smaller individual festival efforts, as well as some larger ones, such as the Exhibition of Industrial Power in Glasgow, the Festival of Britain in reality, if not in intention, came over as very much a metropolitan affair. However, Reyner Banham has stressed the coincident expansion in the mass media. 'If the Festival was not a "turning point in taste" itself,' he wrote, 'it was part of the raw material that fed the influence that did help to modernise public taste: the media'.[11]

Yet, even that would seem an optimistic assessment to those who see the festival as a product of British postwar weakness, and as a signal pointing to further decline. At the time, the fashionable joke about the Skylon was that like Britain it had no visible means of support. Subsequently, Charles Plouviez has written of the Festival that: 'It might be said to mark the beginning of our "English disease" – the moment at which we stopped trying to lead the world as an industrial power, and started being the world's entertainers, coaxing tourists to laugh at our eccentricities, marvel at our traditions and wallow in our nostalgia'.[12] This is harsh, and, as will become clear in Chapter Eight misrepresents the cultural changes of the 1960s.

Probably, the Festival of Britain is of most interest for the way in which it cuts a slice into the assumptions, attitudes and conceptions of style of the time. Gerald Barry's reference to grouse moors will not have escaped the vigilant reader. The Festival of Britain was sponsored by a Labour government, but as with most other major ventures of that government it was essentially run by the upper class. The Chairman of the Festival Council was General Lord Ismay, and Bevis Hillier has rightly remarked that 'There was a certain upper-drawerness about most of the Festival organisers'.[13]

## Chapter Seven

# The Early and Middle Fifties

## Tory Freedom

In the General Election of 1950 Labour's massive majority in the House of Commons was reduced to nine. The ageing Labour leadership soldiered on, then seemed to give up the ghost. In a second General Election in 1951, the Conservatives were returned with a majority of twenty. Yet, any idea of massive popular discontent with Labour must be ruled out by the figures. Labour actually polled more votes than the Conservatives, and more votes than it had itself obtained in the glorious year of 1945. Only the peculiarities of the British electoral system gave the reins of government to the Conservatives in 1951. I do not myself regard general elections as forming watersheds in social history; more often they indicate continuity rather than change. The Korean War (1950–53) prolonged the sense of uneasy insecurity characteristic of the postwar years, diverted resources away from social investment, and further made life difficult for the Labour government.

Conservative economic policy did not at bottom differ greatly from Labour. True to the adversarial public quality of British politics, the Conservatives had to start off with important gestures in the direction of free enterprise: steel and road haulage were denationalized. Thus a factor which in the sixties and seventies became quite significant in Britain's economic decline made its early appearance: the uncertainty created in the business and investment worlds by the habit of incoming governments of sharply reversing important policies of their predecessors. After the Korean War international terms of trade swung in Britain's favour: primary products cost less, manufactured products commanded higher prices. The postwar growth in international trade continued. The Conservatives were able to end rationing in 1954, and although there were recessions in 1952–3 and 1957–8, which showed that revival in the older depressed areas was far from secure, wage levels in general slowly rose. But more than ever the British economy was simply floating with the international tide, rather than making any effort to sail ahead of the competition: there was no concerted attempt to place investment where investment was needed; there was no urgency over capturing new markets.

The achievements and the failings of the motor-car industry are instructive. By 1947 the industry had almost recovered the 1937 peak output of well over half-a-million vehicles. By 1950 production had reached 903,000 vehicles, 52 per cent of the total European output. But the European countries had not yet had time to rebuild their own productive capacity; for the time being they had no wish to

96 'BABY AUSTIN IS BORN AGAIN: the empty assembly line at the Longbridge Works awaits full scale production of the new Austin 7.' *Picture Post*, 20 October 1951.

97 London trams. *Picture Post*, 26 May 1951. (The last trams ran in London on 5 July 1952.)

98 'London Transport bus Inspector leading a bus by aid of a flare through the fog over a crossing at Aldgate, London E.' *Picture Post*, 8 December 1952.

spend dollars on American cars. In this situation the British manufacturers carried on the old tradition, producing too wide a range of different models, generally built with British rather than foreign needs in mind, and failing to give adequate attention to the problem of providing after-sales service and spare parts. The producers of luxury and specialist cars, which could have been an almost permanent export success, actually took a quaint pride in boasting of how long the waiting time was for delivery of their cars – eventually customers got fed up with waiting. *Plate 96* offers a clue. The Austin Seven, the new version of the old 'Baby Austin' much loved between 1922 and 1938, had just been launched, yet, though the ships might be waiting, the assembly line is empty, since there had been a hitch over moving into full-scale production. At the 1951 Motor Show the Austin Seven was exhibited side-by-side with the Volkswagen, which was to prove a devastating rival.

The government gave primacy to defending the position of the pound. Hence the stop-go economic policies which so gravely handicapped those industrialists who did wish to work out long-term investment programmes. Overactivity in the economy sucked in exports, and put the pound under pressure; thus, the government would raise interest rates and cut credit programmes in order to impose a sudden damper on the economy. These policies were as harmful as was the continuing effort to maintain the overseas commitments of a world empire.

The Britain of the early fifties was still a tight, parochial little island, wedded to the old ways. Trams lorded over city streets, Bisto, Ty-Phoo and the good old British products stood pre-eminent, trains ran on steam, London was still often brought to a walking pace by smog; Liverpool was a city of which the rest of the country knew little (*Plates 97, 98 and 99*). However, it was in the fifties that the

99 'Scenes at Lime Street Station, Liverpool'. *Picture Post*, 1954.

effects of wartime educational reform began to work through. The Butler Education Act of 1944 had made 'secondary education for all' a genuine reality, though it left largely intact the class basis of British education: in grammar schools the more diligent working-class kids could join with the middle classes, but there were (secondary) modern schools for the rest; the private public schools for the rich remained untouched. Under the Labour government, state funding for university students was greatly extended. Thus there were coming into prominence in the fifties, significant numbers of working-class products who had been through grammar schools, and lower-middle-class products who had been through universities.

A rather different institution affected almost all of the male youth of the country: National Service, subject of one of the last big *Picture Post* photo-investigations (*Plate 100*). Under the terms of the National Service Act of 1948 (not repealed till 1960) something around 160,000 young men were each year called up to undergo basic military training and military service for a period of

100 'THOSE FIRST DAYS OF NATIONAL SERVICE: *Picture Post* visits the Royal West Kent Depot at Maidstone to see what happens to an 18 year old youth conscripted for National Service. Sten Gun practice.' (November 1954)

two years, sometimes in such hot spots as Malaya or Korea. For most men National Service implied boredom and waste, though few denied to it any personal benefit at all. A young factory worker whose personal experience is given in the collection *Called Up* (1955), edited by Peter Chambers and Amy Landreth, noted: 'When I was back in Civvy Street and looked back on all the good times I'd had with my friends, my National Service didn't seem so bad after all. But I do think that a lot of time is wasted in the Army just hanging around.' While it is probably true that once a Teddy boy had been called up he probably ceased forever to be a Teddy boy, it is hard to say whether National Service really served as a force for social control (as latter-day right-wing advocates of its restoration have maintained) or whether, by breaking family links, disrupting apprenticeships, opening new horizons, imposing new, and sometimes brutal, stresses it was a potential agent of social dislocation. The editors of *Called Up* found it

> difficult to estimate to what extent National Servicemen take advantage of the freedom from parental control to gain sexual experience. Certainly a young man unversed in the 'facts of life' will very soon learn the repertoire of sexual possibilities from the conversation of his comrades. If he is posted abroad, he may visit a brothel for the first time in his life, but that does not mean he will avail himself of the opportunities provided by the establishment. . . . On the other hand, the moral climate of Service life tends to impel the soldier towards sexual adventures, and if he leaves the Army unexperienced in this field, then it is likely to be for moral or psychological reasons, not for lack of opportunity.[1]

A survey by the King George's Jubilee Trust took a more pessimistic view. National Service, it concluded,

> has profoundly affected the outlook of the boy who leaves school at 15 years of age. . . . For him it is more than a break away from education; it cuts his life into two almost

unrelated parts – before and after National Service; it creates an artificial interlude in which the high hurdles still ahead of him obscure the need to plan and work for his future. Often the years of the gap are a time of 'wait and see', a time in which irresponsibility can become a fixed habit of mind, a time even of deterioration, in which some boys forget so much of what they knew when they left school that those who receive them into National Service are discomfitted to find that some of these new recruits are barely literate.[2]

Probably National Service did help to preserve that slightly archaic quality which one still finds in British life well into the 1950s.

The Teddy boy of the early 1950s was no doubt a sign of reaction against that archaism and complacency. Previously, styles had tended to filter down from above, or from the cinema: the advent of the Teddy boy was a genuine indication that a more prosperous, more independent, working-class youth was now able to take initiatives of its own. Higher up the social scale, there was a sort of criticism from the literary group known as 'The Movement'. The Movement, certainly, was critical of the romanticism and the lushness of accepted high culture in the postwar period, and also of established social conventions and hypocrisies. For a wider public the message had to be transmitted in novels rather than poetry. Kingsley Amis's *Lucky Jim* (1954) was extremely funny, in the way in which ordinary observation among intelligent middle-class people can be extremely funny, about phoney culture and the brutal realities of sexual attractiveness and unattractiveness. In 1956 John Osborne's *Look Back in Anger* was presented at the Royal Court Theatre by the newly established English Stage Company: in the newspapers it attracted the attention of more than just the professional theatre critics, and it successfully toured the country. The phrase 'Angry Young Men' was coined to describe an unco-ordinated group of writers (mostly in their late twenties and early thirties) whose common target seemed to be the behaviour and attitudes of the established upper-middle class. John Braine's *Room at the Top* (1957) was the story (not unfamiliar to connoisseurs of world literature) of the working-class lad, prospects greatly boosted by the war, who unscrupulously plays the marriage game to take him from lower-middle-class employment to the top. Playwrights and novelists extended their subject matter in a manner summed up in the press as 'kitchen sink'.

Aspects of working-class life became a matter of attention in an altogether different way from the social surveys of the inter-war years. In his seminal *The Uses of Literacy* (1957) Richard Hoggart described the traditional, confined, working-class culture of back-to-back housing, identified the dilemma of the youths educated out of their culture, and analysed the potential, negative and positive, of the mass media. Leeds City Council took some deliberately propagandist photos of the old housing, of a type which still existed in many areas, and in which the phrase 'kitchen sink' takes on quite a new dimension (*Plate 101*), and of the way in which such houses could be, and were being, modernized (*Plate 102*). The tragedy for much of the working class was to be that modernization of old properties generally lost out to the mania for 'redevelopment'.

Again, we are reminded not to make too sharp a split between the late forties and early fifties. The establishment of new towns was one of the proud achievements of the Labour government, but in the nature of things, the actual

101 Back-to-back housing, Leeds in the 1950s. City Council photograph designed to demonstrate appalling conditions.

102 Similar house modernized. City Council photograph designed to demonstrate triumphant modernization.

103 Beverley Way shops, Peterlee New Town, c.1955.

building of the towns only came anywhere near fruition in the 1950s. By strict economic criteria Peterlee (*Plate 103*) may not have been the best chosen of sites; at the same time, there was an understandable desire to do everything possible to regenerate the north-east of England. Many of the buildings, too, proved to be much less well designed than they appeared, and in recent years have given rise to many complaints about water inlets. Where successful, though, the new towns were very successful and undoubtedly a token of much that was best and most forward-looking in the period of reconstruction.

Our favourite city of Coventry was itself, because of the attentions of Hitler's airforce, ready for redevelopment. One issue had aroused much contention: that of the rebuilding of Coventry Cathedral (*Plate 104*). It was announced in August 1951 that Basil Spence had won the competition for a new Cathedral, the money for which was to come from the government's War Damage Commission and from public subscription. The Local Reconstruction Committee was very enthusiastic about Spence's design, very much in the Festival of Britain idiom, but the Coventry City Council was strongly opposed.[3] However after a six months' controversy over whether the initial design was too 'modern', and would anyway

interfere with other building priorities, the Council withdrew its opposition. On 6 May 1954, the Ministry of Works issued the necessary building licence. At about the same time, the Minister (David Eccles) wrote to the Lord Mayor of Coventry:

> The Cathedral is not a building which concerns Coventry and Coventry alone. The echo of the bombs which destroyed your City was heard round the world. We cannot tell how many people are waiting in this country and abroad for this church to rise and prove that English traditions live again after the Blitz. The threat of far worse destruction is with us today demoralising and corrupting our thoughts. We have never had a greater need for acts of faith.

The terms of the building licence were somewhat more prosaic: 'One responsible person must be appointed to complete information on the progress of the job, on Ministry of Works form C.P.S.23, which is sent out each month, and should be returned to Regional Programmes and Statistics Officer as soon as possible after the last pay day of each month.' In July, *Illustrated* ran a story on the whole episode, from which the carefully set-up picture, with the plans nicely exposed, reproduced in *Plate 104*, is taken. The Cathedral was completed in 1962.

157

## Suez, Skiffle, and CND

In 1954 the Conservatives did bring about some serious reductions in British overseas commitments, more in keeping with the realities of the world situation. In 1951 the European Coal and Steel Community had been founded, but Labour and Conservative politicians were united (with only Liberals dissenting) in wishing to keep Britain well clear of Europe. The British knew 'in their bones', said Sir Anthony Eden, who, in 1955, was to succeed Churchill as Prime Minister and win another election for the Conservatives, that they could never join a European federation.

The great unhappy event which encapsulated Britain's painful readjustment to a changed world, and the powerful psychological reactions to this readjustment, was the Suez War of 1956 when Britain, in consort with the French and the Israelis, and in flagrant violation of her obligations under the United Nations Charter, attacked the Egyptian Republic. The 'armed conflict' (as Eden called his war) lasted for a week, long enough to demonstrate that Britain no longer had the logistic power to mount an efficient seaborne operation in the Middle East, and for Britain to be branded by the United Nations as an aggressor, before American opposition, Russian threats, and the inevitable run on the pound brought an ignoble venture to a humiliating conclusion.

The Suez Crisis aroused passionate argument, and more (*Plate 105*) throughout the country. The caption provided by the *Glasgow Herald* for its own photograph is not necessarily fully illuminating. Undoubtedly, opinion was sharply divided in the student body, and the action of some Scottish Nationalist students in burning the Union Jack provoked a very strong reaction from ex-National Service students. In this picture, it can be seen that the 'Eden must go' banner has received the most violent attention. The other banners, by today's standards, seem rather undramatic. Two figures in the bottom-left (the African student, and the student in the roll-neck sweater) show traces of the flour bombs which were the most potent weapons used in this engagement.[4] The shortish figure in the right-centre of the picture, engaging with a rather taller opponent, is actually a young history lecturer, John P. Mackintosh, subsequently a distinguished Professor of Politics and much respected, if individualistic, Labour MP till his tragic early death in 1978.

The storm over Suez was intense, but it passed away quickly, and the issue was little mentioned in the General Election campaign of 1959, which in any event was won by the Conservatives led by Harold Macmillan, a determined supporter of Eden's policy. At the time the division of opinion followed party lines very closely. Opinion polls gave little support to the widely-held contention that a substantial section of Labour supporters found their patriotic senses agreeably titillated by this venture in gun-boat diplomacy. The one Labour MP to support the government, Stanley Evans, was shortly forced to resign by his constituency party. On the other side those Conservatives who could not support their government were treated with similar roughness by their local organizations. That Labour voters in the main opposed the Suez venture does not, of course, preclude the possibility that substantial sections of the working class, who might in any event be Conservative voters, approved of it. Equally many of the most influential organs of Conservative opinion came down in opposition to Eden.[5]

105 'Edinburgh University students demonstration over government's action in the Middle East. Women students carrying protest banners are surrounded by government backers.' *Glasgow Herald*, 4 November 1956.

The loss of imperial power, finally signalled by Suez, ought, in the eyes of many theoreticians, to have had a profound effect on British society. Many of the upper classes, of course, lost the jobs, and the sources of income, which Empire had offered to them. There does (as I shall shortly be suggesting) seem to have been a new release of energies as Britain opened herself to other influences; the Suez episode strengthened the critiques of government and establishment which were being formulated: but beyond that, I cannot find that the loss of Empire affected ordinary people as seriously as perhaps it ought to have done.

Some of the new influences I am thinking of simply bypassed the old centres of power in British society. American rock 'n' roll music first hit Britain in the middle fifties. The film *Rock Around the Clock* crossed the Atlantic in 1956; Bill Haley went on his epochal tour in 1957. The first British response was very much do-it-yourself, cheap, local, and to a considerable degree working-class. A skiffle group could be created out of washing-board and cymbal, 'double bass' created from a broom-stick, and one or more guitars (the only really expensive items) (*Plate 106*). Skiffle made news. Two early practitioners who quickly rose to the heights were Tommy Steele and Lonnie Donegan. Two others whose ascent was slower but, in a slightly different musical form, much greater, were John Lennon and Paul McCartney, two working-class lads in Liverpool, who in 1956 formed the Quarrymen. *Plate 106* is testimony to the publicity value of skiffle. No doubt this particular scene is a contrived set-up, but the group itself, its working-class composition, and its popularity in public houses are facts. The combination of steam train on the right, and classic middle-fifties hairstyle on the left, is irresistible.

Apart from American rock, the other important foreign influence on Britain of the fifties was Italian. As with rock, the Italian idiom was populist, accessible: Italian *couture* very definitely was not *haut*; the famous Zeffirelli production at Covent Garden was of the most popular, not to say vulgar, duo of Italian operas, *Cav* and *Pag*; the sentimental popular song *Volare* reached the top of the British hit parade. In addition, most British cities already had something of an Italian population, mainly engaged in some branch of the catering trade. Thus the Italian influence manifested itself in a highly visible way, the coffee bar (*Plate 107*), which itself became the centre point of a youthful culture.

It would be wrong to imagine anything like a sharp divide in British society between, say, youth – and to a considerable degree working-class youth at that – on the one side, and the middle-aged, upper-middle class on the other. When what was in effect the last statement of the Angry Young Men appeared in 1957 in the form of *Declaration*, edited by Tom Maschler, its own middle-class tone was all too apparent, or, in the case of the contribution by left-wing film director Lindsay Anderson, upper-class. Coming back to Britain, Anderson wrote, is

106 '"WORKERS' PLAYTIME": four British
Railways employees, all members of the
staff at Hornsey Sidings (N. London) have
formed their own Skiffle Group, calling
themselves, appropriately enough "The
Main Liners".' (11 March 1957)

107 London 'Expresso' coffee bar, with its
distinctive Italian coffee machine (September
1955).

> in many respects like going back to the nursery. The outside world, the dangerous
> world, is shut away: its sounds are muffled. . . . Nanny lights the fire, as she sits herself
> down with a nice cup of tea and yesterday's *Daily Express*; but she keeps half an eye on
> us too. . . .[6]

Few of the skifflers or coffee-bar devotees had had a nursery or a nanny; but they
were already escaping from the eye of conformist authority. Shortly after Suez,
Eden gave place to Harold Macmillan, and Macmillan, aristocrat though he was
himself, quite enthusiastically identified himself with growing affluence and the
free-wheeling behaviour which that encouraged among the young. Suez might
have been the crisis in British society which so many on the left still wished that it
had been; but again I must invoke that deeper secular anglicanism which kept
British society together and meant that quarrels were fought out in limited arenas
(such as the Old Quadrangle at Edinburgh University), not across society as a
whole.

There was still much pride that Britain could lead the world in peaceful social
adaptation, as in, for instance, the peaceful use of atomic energy. It was still a

108 Calder Hall. (Photograph actually taken in January 1967, to recall opening by the Queen on 17 October 1956.)

quiet assumption that British technology, though perhaps not always exploited as effectively as Americans exploited theirs, really led the world. Curiously, it was within the month before Suez that the Queen opened Britain's first nuclear power station, and the first in the world to produce electricity on a full commercial scale. It was fondly believed that Britain was well on the way to solving all of her basic energy problems (*Plate 108*).

The left did not demur, for at that time it still held to the view that science and social engineering marched forward together hand-in-hand. The left, however, was changing. The Labour Party, torn by bitter disputes throughout the fifties, had, left wing and right wing, its own indigenous form of socialism; the Communist Party was dull and committed to an outmoded Marxist–Leninism. But from the middle fifties certain British intellectuals became influenced by new continental and American approaches to Marx. 'The New Left' was born. The *Universities and Left Review* was founded in 1957 (merging in 1960 into the *New Left Review*).

Yet it was very much figures from the old left, and from nowhere in the left, who staffed the great movement which in its own way marks the transition between the middle fifties and the Cultural Revolution of the sixties: the Campaign for Nuclear Disarmament (CND) founded in 1958. As *Plate 111* in Chapter 8 shows, we have here very much a middle-class organization, rather in the hiking, open-air radical tradition of the thirties, though too young to have direct memories of that time. Yet this was a serious movement with a serious cause. It aroused the enthusiasm of ordinary housewives: it too was a part of a stirring deep in the middle depths of British society.

## Chapter Eight

# The Cultural Revolution:
# 1959–1973

### Points of Change

Many will dispute the title of this chapter, and the implications which lie behind it. Derisively, in some cases: China yes, Britain no. In my view, the evidence – visual, written, oral, on film, in painting, in private memoirs, in public records and gramophone records – is indisputable that some time between the mid-fifties, which we have just been discussing, and the world recession of 1973 changes so important in major aspects of British society took place as to establish the phrase 'cultural revolution' in the legitimate realm of hyperbole rather than the illegitimate one of bathos.

The ingredients, compounded in the fifties, we have just studied; but the crucial year of breakthrough, in my view, was 1959. The Angry Young Men had foreshadowed the radical criticism, and the satire boom, of the early sixties; skiffle had been a prelude to revolution, but was not the revolution itself. It was in 1959 that three vitally significant British films, *Room at the Top*, *I'm All Right Jack* and *Sapphire*, were released. It was also the year in which Hugh Carlton Greene was appointed Director General of the BBC; he was to take it upon himself to encourage snooks to be cocked at established morality. In 1959 occurred the trial for obscenity of the publishers of *Lady Chatterley's Lover*. The prosecuting counsel made an ass of himself in a peculiarly noteworthy way by asking the jury whether the book was one they would wish their servants to read, but the acquittal of the publishers was the forecast – overtaken as forecasts usually are – of the arrival of a new moral frontal system. The characteristics of the Cultural Revolution I take to be: self-expression, participation, joy and release from the social controls which had held British society in thrall since Victorian times; more directly, this meant dislocation, though not destruction or transformation, of class, of race, of relations between the sexes, and between the youthful and the middle-aged; above all it meant a new style in which Britain genuinely led the world in many aspects of creative endeavour.

*Plate 109* is from the film *Room at the Top*. It is of the utmost relevance to what I have said about style and creative endeavour that films themselves should form a central part of a movement of historical change. That is not to say that the conventional wisdom that British films of previous decades were of utter insignificance (and, indeed, that the films I am about to discuss were an over-rated flash-in-the-pan) is correct. The successes of '59 and the sixties, and of many individual years since, were based in a tradition of highly competent filmmaking, always, however, aborted by the egregious incompetence of the industry's financial management.

The film of *Room at the Top* condensed, and therefore sharpened up, the elements of social criticism of the original novel; it also presented Joe Lampton as a less introspectively complex, and much more straightforwardly predatory character, and therefore one with whom cinema audiences could more readily identify. The accents and dialogue were not flawless (the dialect phrase 'dear kipper', meaning someone with expensive tastes, became converted into a simple term of endearment; Laurence Harvey's West Riding accent, however, stood up remarkably well). But the provinces were made visible, a working-class figure was shown to have individuality and determination, but little respect for the 'anglican' decencies of British life, social inequalities were openly commented on, and, above all, the nature of sexuality, particularly female sexuality, was given an exposure hitherto seen only in imported continental films. *Plate 109*, though stunningly tame by post-sixties' standards (much of what was most shocking in the film was in fact contained in the blunt use of language), must be seen in that context. It shows Joe with Alice Aisgill, wife of a local businessman; Simone Signoret was brought in for this crucial role, since it was felt that no British actress of the time could have coped.

*I'm All Right Jack* was something totally different, though equally subversive. *Room at the Top* was disliked by the *Daily Worker*: the wicked rich, it thought, were faithfully portrayed, but a wicked working man was a travesty. The entire left, and many Liberals, hated *I'm All Right Jack*. But only because of that blinkered habit of certain British intellectuals of thinking in narrow political categories, could it be seen as a right-wing film. Usually previous British films – I make exceptions of the magnificent *Love on the Dole* (1940) and *The Shipbuilders* (1943) – while quite careful in delineating the nuances of class distinction, had suggested that in the end classes would come together, making their own special contribution to the public welfare. *I'm All Right Jack* ruthlessly, rudely and hilariously painted a picture of a snobbish, arrogant and corrupt upper class and a pig-headed, work-shy working class, perfectly secure in its own *mores* and folkways, with some rather uneasy middle-class elements in between: at bottom, the two major classes, the upper class deliberately, the working class through ignorance and prejudice, were together doing the nation down.

*I'm All Right Jack* was a highly deliberate and historically sensitive social satire: there was a very self-conscious pre-credit sequence sketching the history of the decline of the old upper class since 1945, when it had been rooted in the world of finance ('The City and Threadneedle Trust', 'Capital Gains Unlimited'), to the present, when its representatives are, somewhat shadily, involved in industry. Ian Carmichael plays Stanley, an earnest and gormless young man, who has been 'brought up a gentleman'. At his university appointments board he is told that what is required above all is 'an air of confidence'. We see the elegant, aristocratic household of Stanley's great aunt (Margaret Rutherford), where the maid is addressed curtly as 'Spencer'. Stanley fails to get a string of 'suitable' appointments, and finally his uncle (Dennis Price), unknown to Stanley, fiddles him into a manual job in the factory he owns. The great aunt's comment is: 'I expect you just supervise, dear'. But Stanley goes to work with a fork-lift truck

109 Film still from *Room at the Top*.

(the uncle, for nefarious reasons, to do with a shady arms deal with a shady Arab, intends that Stanley should create a strike).

The atmosphere on the factory floor, the working-class accents and attitudes, are beautifully established, with only the necessary minimum of satirical exaggeration. Left-wing commentators at the time were particularly outraged by the character of Kite (Peter Sellers), the Communist shop-steward. Kite has high intellectual aspirations: he speaks in a stilted, polysyllabic and, in the end, ill-educated fashion: and that surely was the point – Kite with his immensely laudable aspirations has, in fact, been educationally stunted by the class society in which he grew up. He refers proudly to the week he spent at summer school at Balliol (which he mispronounces beautifully – 'bah—' instead of 'bay—'). Balliol, one of the poshest, most academically demanding, and liberal in entry policy of the Oxford colleges, is an important factor in the British class structure. A Labour leader of the sixties, George Brown, has referred in his autobiography to his days at a Balliol summer school.[1] In the earlier Ealing comedy *His Excellency* (1951) the upper-class ladies who are so upset at the prospect of a docker as governor general remark on an upper-class socialist of their acquaintance: he 'came out of the right stable', he had been at Balliol.

Kite takes Stanley home to tea, and offers him lodgings. Compared with the austere working-class house of the Ealing tragedy *It Always Rains on Sunday* (1948), the Kite household betrays some signs of affluence. Stanley is a little taken aback by the tea, even more by the Australian burgundy which is brought out in special celebration, and utterly appalled by Kite's verbosity. But he is captivated by Kite's daughter Cynthia (Liz Fraser), a spindle-polisher: he takes the lodgings. The contrast between upper-class twit and working-class dumb blonde is cruelly done: 'Are them your own teeth?', she asks: 'You keep them so nice and white'.

Personnel Manager at the factory is Major Hitchcock, played by Terry-Thomas with that matchless plummy accent and manner which makes one suspect that the major either has not quite made it into the upper class or else has come down slightly in the world. In the best of many memorable lines, Hitchcock describes Kite, to whom in public he has to show the utmost friendliness, as 'the sort of chap who sleeps in his vest'. Kite calls the inevitable strike. Stanley is sent back to work on his own by his great aunt: 'unheard of that a gentleman should go on strike. Officers don't mutiny', she says. In the kind of scene beloved of British filmmakers, the mildly obsequious, but totally plain-speaking and self-assured Mrs Kite (Irene Handl) gets on famously with the condescending, but patently human, great aunt. Stanley breaks the picket lines (both police and pickets are shown as behaving in a most restrained 'anglican' way) and is sent to Coventry by Kite and his fellow-workers. The shady deal planned by Stanley's uncle and the ghastly Mr de Vere Cox (Richard Attenborough), whose accent, at a moment of crisis, reveals his lower-class origins, progresses.

The film's climax comes in a television programme (sign of the times!) in which Stanley, the scales having dropped from his eyes, denounces both his uncle ('you're a bounder') and Kite. But virtue does not triumph. Bosses and workers are exonerated and continue in their dishonest, work-shy ways. Realistically, the film recognizes the barrier of class in not having Stanley marry Cynthia: he is bundled off to the terrors of a nudist camp (nudist films had just come into fashion a year or two earlier – the sadder side of the British film industry).

The third significant film of 1959 was *Sapphire*. This, apart from giving employment to an unprecedented number of black actors, used the classic whodunnit formula in offering a sensitive and subtly nuanced presentation of the liberal, anglican reaction to the eruption on the British scene of the race problem.

The novel *Saturday Night and Sunday Morning*, by Alan Sillitoe, was published in 1958. It was more immoral, and more sexually uninhibited than *Room at the Top*, the film. But successful films have a public impact generally denied to novels. The film reduced the loose, almost poetic, content and structure of the novel to a tightly constructed account of a young factory worker (we actually see him at work at his lathe, *Plate 110*) who rebels against everything, including older members of the working class, and the laws of alcoholic consumption. Sillitoe's original novel was set in the period of the Korean War, but director Karel Reisz took the opportunity of setting the scene in the early stages of the Cultural Revolution: for example, a pop group plays in the pub in which Arthur Seaton (Albert Finney) gets gigantically drunk. In the novel, Arthur Seaton moves on the fringes of the feckless working class, given to thieving and violence. In the film, he is made more universal, representative of the ordinary hardworking young worker, though, of course, with thoughts and a fecklessness

of his own. The film is realistic in recognizing that there is little real possibility of escape from the working class. Sunday morning in the film is acceptance of marriage with Doreen (Shirley Ann Fields), who works in a hairnet factory, symbolically represented by a fish caught on Arthur's own fishing line. But Doreen's aspirations in regard to their future house were a reasonable one for the age: 'I want a new one with a bathroom and everything'.

The point of change is in culture and life-styles, but, of course, it was rooted in economic changes. Between 1955 and 1960 weekly wage *rates* rose 25 per cent; taking overtime into account, average weekly *earnings* rose 34 per cent. By 1969 wage rates had risen by 88 per cent, and earnings by 130 per cent. This last figure was almost exactly matched by the average earnings of middle-class salaried employees, which rose 127 per cent between 1955 and 1969. These rises completely swallowed up the effects of inflation: retail prices rose by 15 per cent between 1955 and 1960, and 63 per cent between 1955 and 1969. Still more to the point, almost all products of modern technology, from motorbikes to electronic amplifiers, were costing much less in real terms, and some actually less in money terms, than they had at the beginning of the fifties. To look at the matter in actual money terms: back in 1951 the average weekly earnings of men over twenty-one stood at £8.30 per week; a decade later the figure had almost doubled to £15.35; in 1966 it was £20.30, in 1968 £23.00, and in 1971 £30.93.

Despite the continuing structural weaknesses in the British economy and the misguided policies of the Treasury and the City of London, to almost everyone living through them the late fifties and the sixties seemed like a time of boom, of affluence. In 1954 Britain provided 20 per cent of the world's manufactured exports; by the early sixties she was providing only 15 per cent. Meantime Germany's share had gone up from 15 per cent to over 19 per cent, and Japan's from 5 per cent to nearly 7.5 per cent; France was increasing her exports three times as fast, Germany and Italy six times as fast, as Britain. Taking 1950 as 100, British productivity per worker stood in 1960 at 125; the German and French figures for 1960 were 159 and 177 respectively. By the sixties Britain seemed to have moved definitively into the situation where her annual increase in productivity, good by prewar standards, lagged behind that of all her competitors (2 per cent compared with an average among the industrialized countries of 3.5 per cent). While there was consistency in the basic failure to channel investment where it was needed, the return of a Labour government in 1964, and of a Conservative government in 1970, created all the stupid short-term disruptions of Tweedledum and Tweedledee politics. However, from the point of view of the Cultural Revolution the real presence of affluence, particularly among working-class youth, was the thing; deeper failures in the economy were simply fuel for the satire industry.

### Deliverance from Victorianism

The Angry Young Men had not really been all that young. Nonetheless the publicity which surrounded them encouraged the notion of a culture whose intellectual leaders were rather younger than the sages of a previous era (J. B. Priestley, for example). There was what one might call a 'shunting' effect – such figures now seemed to be fifteen or twenty years younger than they used to be, so the age of popular entertainers and fashion-setters, too, was shunted back by fifteen or twenty years. But it is important to stress how much the new visibility of youth came genuinely from below.

This visibility was apparent in many ways. I have already defined CND as part of the transition from the fifties into the Cultural Revolution. *Plate 111*, featuring the CND youth group from Norwood, a lower-middle-class suburb in south London, brings out the political activism of one section of the country's youth. College scarves are much in evidence, but the appearance is very different from that of the smartly-suited Oxbridge young Communist League demonstrators of the late thirties. Youthful activism was also apparent in less honourable causes. From the mid-thirties to the mid-fifties offences of violence against the person had risen by about 6 per cent a year. From the mid-fifties onwards they were going up by about 11 per cent a year. In 1955 the total figures for crimes of violence were 5,869; in 1960 they were 11,592; in 1964, 15,976; and in 1968, 21,046. The increase in criminality was a feature of the population as a whole, but it was most significant in the seventeen to twenty-one, the fourteen to seventeen, and even the eight to fourteen age groups.

The Committee on Children and Young Persons, appointed in October 1956 and reporting in October 1960, brought out how during the very period in which it was deliberating the whole scene had changed for the worse. By 1958 a great increase in crime in the population at large was apparent, but it was most significant in the seventeen to twenty-one and fourteen to seventeen age groups, where crime rates reached the highest ever known; among the eight to fourteen group, too, there was a rise from 924 criminal offences per 100,000 in 1955 to

111 Aldermaston March, 1961.

1,176 per 100,000 in 1958.[2] The Committee recognized the importance of the upheavals of war, in both their immediate and delayed consequences, but they argued cogently that an equally potent factor in the recent increases in juvenile crime was the process of unguided economic change:

> During the past fifty years there has been a tremendous material, social and moral revolution in addition to the upheaval of two wars. While life has in many ways become easier and more secure, the whole future of mankind may seem frighteningly uncertain. Everyday life may be less of a struggle, boredom and lack of challenge more of a danger, but the fundamental insecurity remains with little that the individual can do about it. The material revolution is plain to see. At one and the same time it has provided more desirable objects, greater opportunity for acquiring them illegally, and considerable chances of immunity from the undesirable consequences of so doing. It is not always so clearly recognised what a complete change there has been in social and personal relationships (between classes, between sexes and between individuals) and also in the basic assumptions which regulate behaviour. These major changes in the cultural background may well have replaced the disturbances of war as factors which contribute in themselves to instability within the family.[3]

Within the same time-span the Christian Economic and Social Research Foundation detected a sharp increase in drunkenness among the under twenty-ones.[4] It is to the first of these reports that the cartoon reproduced in *Plate 112* refers. Despite all the screaming from the hysterical wing of the Conservative Party for the restoration of judicial flogging and birching (abolished by the Labour government only in 1948) this committee came out very strongly against

169

"Bad luck, Sir! Never mind – if I catch the scoundrels, I'll give them a sharp tap on the head with this report!"

any such measures. The escaping youths on the right have Italian haircuts (cf the skiffler singled out in *Plate 106*), winkle-picker shoes, cosh, chain and open razor. The police constable is R. A. Butler, one of the great moderate and reforming Conservative statesmen of the twentieth century, at that time Home Secretary in the Macmillan government. The cartoon is a salutary reminder that however appropriate it is to stress liberalization and change, the punitive viciousness of the Victorian era still had strong roots in British society.

However, the political tides very definitely were moving the other way. In October 1965 an Act was passed by parliament abolishing capital punishment as a five-year experiment. Before the five years were up, James Callaghan, Home Secretary in the Labour government which had been elected in 1964, and reconfirmed in power in 1966, made the abolition of hanging permanent. The first three years of the experiment had demonstrated convincingly, as was well known in any case to all authorities on the subject, and had been demonstrated from foreign experience, that there was no clear connection between the number of murders committed and the existence of the death penalty.

Three matters which, till very recently, had been taboo, were dealt with in Acts passed in 1967. First, the Abortion Act, put forward by the Liberal MP, David Steel, but supported by the Labour government, and also by several Conservatives. It had been possible in the fifties and early sixties for the well-off to secure abortions through private clinics, where doctors and psychiatrists were able to steer through the uncertainties of the existing law dating back (of course) to Victorian times. However, penalties for the well-intentioned medical man or woman could still be extremely severe. More critically, for the less well-off woman suffering from an unwanted pregnancy the choices were two: to go through with the birth, or to seek a back-street abortion, with all its attendant horror and danger. That classic film of the affluent working-class swinger, *Alfie* (1966), brought the situation out well enough. Under the new Abortion Act, it was merely required that two doctors should be satisfied that an abortion was necessary on medical or psychological grounds: the number of private nursing homes providing this service now greatly expanded, but at least their fees were much reduced; it was now possible, though often with the prospect of having to go on a waiting-list, to get an abortion on the National Health Service. The National Health Service (Family Planning) Act of the same year (1967) made it possible for local authorities to provide contraceptives and contraceptive advice. Thirdly, thanks to the efforts of the backbench Labour MP, Leo Abse, the Sexual Offences Act made legal homosexual acts between two consenting adults in private.

As part of the same trend of liberalization in (mainly) sexual matters, came the abolition of theatrical censorship in 1968. The censorship system remained for the cinema but there was a noticeable relaxation in what was regarded as acceptable. More central to the real misery of many unfortunates was the Divorce Reform Act of 1969. Right on into the sixties the pejorative concept of 'matrimonial offence' had remained; without such an offence being committed (or fabricated) by one or other party no divorce could be obtained. Although Dr Shirley Summerskill, representing an older feminist tradition, described the act as a 'Casanova's charter' most people saw it as offering freedom to both sexes from an irksome and unjust social control. Clause 1 of the Act, with one sharp blow, ended the religious mumbo-jumbo of centuries: 'After the commencement of this Act the sole ground on which a petition for divorce may be presented to the court by either party to a marriage shall be that the marriage had broken down irretrievably'.

The Matrimonial Property Act of 1970 established that a wife's work, whether as a housewife within the home or as a money-earner outside it, should be considered as an equal contribution towards creating the family home, if, as a result of a divorce, that had to be divided. In the same year was passed the Equal Pay Act. The Act was not to come fully into effect for another five years, and even then there were, regrettably, exceptions and loopholes. Still in law, if not always in custom and practice, much had been done to recognize women as equal individuals in their own right.

By the end of the sixties a new word had come into widespread use: 'permissiveness'. The word covered uninhibited theatrical performances, displays of nudity in magazines, fashions which stressed sex appeal, and, of course, personal sexual behaviour. Probably the main factors affecting sexual behaviour in general, and that of women in particular, are: religious and social restraints; the threat to transgressors of punishments ranging from eternal damnation to social ostracism; fear of physical consequences, such as venereal disease or pregnancy – the latter, obviously affecting women more than men; and, most important, what is taken to be 'normal' behaviour. From around 1959 onwards there was a conjunction of circumstances which removed old restraints and fears, created new opportunity – the world of coffee bars and rock groups playing in cellars was a world of free mixing of young people – and positively encouraged the active sexual life as normal. The pill was not the sole factor – many of the sexually active never touched it – but its advent contributed to a situation in which contraception (something no respectable girl would have dreamt of mentioning ten years before) could be spoken of openly.

The height of sexiness in women's fashion came when mini-skirts swept London and the provinces in 1965 and 1966: as the Victorians had always known, it was a good deal easier to seduce a girl if, in the horizontal position, she had no

113 London Christmas decorations: Carnaby Street, 1967.

skirts which she could keep pulling down. Mini-skirts were followed by the equally short, though slightly more protective hot pants – in any case the notion of seduction, if it had ever meant much, was wilting in the face of girls' assertion of the right to make their own choices. However, a vital part of the whole movement was that fashion was for young men as well as for young women. Once, fashion had been a means of covering up the imperfections of the human body: pleats in trousers, for example, helped to conceal pot-bellies, and wide trousers scrawny legs. The fundamental characteristic now was the emphasis on youthful sex appeal: the new fashions were not kind to the old and the ungainly.

Actually the origins of pop fashion go back to 1955 when Mary Quant and Alexander Plunkett-Greene opened their first Bazaar in the King's Road, Chelsea; within a year or two John Stephen had opened his first menswear shop in Carnaby Street, at that time a rather run-down street in the least fashionable part of Soho, near Oxford Circus. *Plate 113* conveys well the colour and exuberance which made Carnaby Street in the sixties at least as famous as the King's Road. Amid the congestion of vans and cars we can see that the young man from Glasgow, John Stephen, has made quite a name for himself; we can also see that the street really did have a genuine thriving life of its own, not having yet been

114 'MARY QUANT'S GINGER GROUP – SPRING
COLLECTION 1969

FLYING TRAPEZE. . . .a show-stopping dress with the
wildest sleeves in town. . . . . .Trimmed with vividly
contrasting ric-rac.

Take to the air in your FLYING TRAPEZE!!!

FLYING TRAPEZE   Retail Price £10.2s.0d.   Sizes: 5–13
Colours:

| | |
|---|---|
| Navy/Yellow | Ric-Rac |
| Black/Yellow | Ric-Rac |
| Mustard/Red | Ric-Rac |
| Terracotta/White | Ric-Rac |
| Sludge/Red | Ric-Rac |

The increase in fashion images with movement was due
to the increasing use of electronic flash equipment,
which superseded the tungsten lighting of earlier years.

converted into a pedestrian precinct (see Chapter Nine). The Union Jack motifs
are worth noting. This is a time in which old conventions are shattered; it is a
time, not so much of direct criticism of authority, but of bypassing of authority.
There was also a complacency among many of those who saw themselves as in
the van of the Cultural Revolution, and that complacency, as the flags suggest,
became a kind of chauvinism – people spoke of 'swinging Britain' almost as a
rather different lot of people had spoken of 'British parliamentary institutions'.

Of single firms in the sixties fashion world, perhaps the most important was
Biba, founded by Barbara Hulanicki and her husband Stephen FitzSimon in 1965.
But the name of Mary Quant remained a dominant one throughout the period:
*Plate 114* is taken from the 1969 Spring Collection of Mary Quant's Ginger
Group Ltd. Most important was the way that boutiques selling the fashionable,
sexy gear spread to every town in the country, so that the Quant and Biba styles
could be seen everywhere.

However, the central cultural form of the revolution was the new phase of rock
music which had developed on from skiffle. The Quarrymen were transformed
into the Silver Beatles, a beat group playing in such Liverpool clubs as the Cavern
and Jacaranda. As the Beatles, this group returned from visits to West Germany's

115 David Hockney, *Picture Emphasizing Stillness*, paint on canvas, 1962–3.

116 Elisabeth Frink, *First Man*, sculpture, 1964.

sin city, Hamburg, equipped with new hairstyles and a new cosmopolitan image and exuberance exactly matching the expansiveness of the dawning age. Decca, Pye, Columbia, HMV and EMI all refused to record them but in May 1962 they were taken on by George Martin of Parlophone. Consisting now of Paul McCartney, John Lennon, George Harrison and a new drummer, Ringo Starr, they recorded and released their first record 'Love Me Do', which reached the top twenty. The Beatles' publicity success reached its peak, and was sustained for several years thereafter, with their American tour of 1964. For national and international fame their only possible rivals were the London-based rhythm-and-blues group the Rolling Stones, who had a stronger pro-youth, anti-establishment, and altogether wilder image than the Beatles. They also came from a social class above the totally Liverpool working-class ambience of the Beatles: Mick Jagger, lead singer, was a student at the London School of Economics and two other members were at the Sidcup Art School.

That the Beatles received the attention of serious music critics does not mean that the old distinctions between high and popular culture were abolished. But, partly because of the pressures of commercialism and the needs of the blossoming advertising industry (a lucrative refuge for many members of the upper class), posh critics and quality papers now gave more attention than ever before to such art forms as film and photography. In photography, the upper-class Tony Armstrong-Jones led the way, but he was quickly followed by three upwardly mobile products of the London working class, David Bailey, Terence Donovan and Brian Duffy.

The link between art school and the Rolling Stones was symbolic. Young products of Britain's art schools, fully open to the latest international influences, particularly that of American pop art, but highly sceptical of the solemn reverence for modernism, suddenly threw off the cosy nationalism or banal imitativeness that dominated British art (Francis Bacon being a striking exception). David Hockney, a lower-middle-class boy from Bradford, vegetarian and conscientious objector, took to etching at college because he could not afford the materials for painting, visited New York on £100 he had managed to save, and produced the series of etchings, *The Rake's Progress*, which made him £5,000 while still a student. Showing an eclecticism and inventiveness worthy, at times, of Picasso (*Plate 115*) he went on to fabulous success, another of the youthful standard-bearers of the age. But perhaps the most original and appealing of the new artists of the time was Elisabeth Frink, toughly and uncompromisingly female (rather than feminine) in her powerfully realized male nudes (*Plate 116*).

## Class and Work

An important part of the liberalization of society was the expansion in higher education. Many colleges, particularly colleges of art and design, were upgraded, as were teacher training colleges. Quasi-university status was given to leading colleges of technology: they were rechristened polytechnics, and their degrees were to be awarded by one *national* body (a sharp break with British educational tradition, this), a Council for National Academic Awards (CNAA), founded in 1964. Seven colleges of higher technology became full universities. Most important, 'new universities' were established. First in the field, and foremost in social prestige, was the University of Sussex. *Plate 117* shows some of the first students arriving in October 1962 in the elegant buildings designed by the hero of

117 The University of Sussex opens, 18 October 1962.

175

Coventry Cathedral, Sir Basil Spence. Curiously, though the new universities were to play a significant part in increasing higher education possibilities for women, not one female student is to be seen in this photograph. Sussex was followed by York, Kent, Warwick, Lancaster, East Anglia, Essex, and Stirling.

There were profound changes in other sectors of education as well. Criticism of the eleven-plus examination, whereby some children (they usually turned out to come from relatively comfortable backgrounds) went on to grammar schools, while others (often from deprived backgrounds) went to secondary modern schools, had been steadily mounting. In July 1965 the Labour government issued Circular 10/65 calling upon all local authorities to submit proposals for establishing comprehensive schools. But five years later the incoming Conservative government issued Circular 10/70 which stressed that the reorganization of secondary education was entirely a matter for the local authorities. Thus secondary education was an arena of some controversy and bitterness, still rather closely related to the realities of class on the one hand, and to the, often inaccurate, theories of class of Labour educationists on the other.

If Britain led the world in pop fashion and pop music, it certainly did not do so in student protest. British universities were on the whole pleasanter and more humane places than their continental and American counterparts – proper practitioners of secular anglicanism, as it were. There were not the mass teaching methods which had such alienating effects abroad; there were not the gulfs between established professors and insecure, radical, junior staff, identifying themselves with students. However, there were local grievances at, for example, the cramped urban quarters of the London School of Economics or the austere environment of the University of Essex. More than this a general revulsion against American policies in Vietnam provided a kind of unifying blanket which could cover also somewhat inconsistent reactions against commercialism and the affluent society. On 17 March 1968 there took place in Grosvenor Square, location of the American Embassy in London, an anti-US demonstration organized by the Vietnam Solidarity Campaign. *Plate 118* conveys some of the quality of the violence which attended the demonstration. Still more of the mood comes through in the Independent Television News reporter's account, which accompanied some vivid television pictures that very evening:

It's going, it's going, the police are being pushed backwards. The police are just holding, but they can't hold anymore. They're all down on the floor now.

Well, I've just broken through the police lines, the column has just come down the road there. Unfortunately I've just been hit in the face. The column I gather is about a mile long. They pushed through the barrier but didn't quite make it. There were about three lines of policemen three or four deep. The police are just about managing to hold it. There're several smoke bombs. They're through, they're through, the first are through now, the first are through.

The horses are moving in. They're in, the horses are in now, the horses are moving in now, they must – the horses tried to hit – they're screaming now, absolute hysteria, the horses are moving them back now. Since they reached the Square, the police haven't as yet drawn – the only *real* force the police have shown is with the horses. Now the fire crackers are being thrown at the police horses now. There's a horse down there I see with stain all up his legs. Yes, there goes another one right in front of the police horses, but they're standing their ground, they're not backing off.

Now you can see the banners are being used as clubs. The clubs, the banners and flags hurled at the police and the horses and the police are being hit with the banners now. Off goes another hat, another policeman's helmet sails through the air.[5]

118 'Police remove one of the demonstrators during violent clashes in Grosvenor Square, 17th March 1968.'

119 'Battle of Grosvenor Square: violence near the Embassy.' *The Times*, 28 March 1968.

Had a new spirit of confrontation, a new violence, crept into British society? Since 1965 the Metropolitan Police had equipped itself with a new arm, the Special Patrol Group (SPG), modelled on the riot-control groups of continental Europe. Yet, exactly a week later, the image of violence was replaced by a rather different one. On 24 March, the Campaign for Nuclear Disarmament held its anti-Vietnam demonstration in London. CND, for all its particular qualities, did fall into the older British tradition of peaceful demonstration. In fact, this march became a model exposition of secular anglicanism in practice. As the same ITN news reporter confirmed:

> Well this is nothing of course compared with last week. The police cordon is holding really firm, gently pushing back the crowds into the centre of Whitehall, taking the pressure off the inner cordon in Downing Street itself. Six demonstrators are being allowed into Downing Street to hand in their petition at the front door of No 10.[6]

The third of the Vietnam demonstrations took place on 28 March. This, the most violent yet, was the one which became known as 'the Battle of Grosvenor Square'. The photograph (*Plate 119*) makes clear the violence of police reactions. But there was yet another demonstration in the autumn (27 October 1968) and this, to complete the seesaw motion between violence and non-violence, was remarkably peaceful. Although 30,000 demonstrators took part, it brought from the Home Secretary, James Callaghan, this self-congratulatory comment: 'I doubt if this kind of demonstration could have taken place so peacefully in any other part of the world'. And, setting the seal on what seems like the re-establishment of the anglican tradition, Bernard Nossiter, the main *Washington Post* man in London wrote:

> What did not happen, quite simply, was something that has occurred in every other major Western country this year, a truly violent confrontation between angry students and sadistic police. . . . British experience in building a non-violent relatively gentle society seems of paramount importance to a world beset by police brutality and student nihilism.[7]

While Britain in the sixties was certainly not classless – though the word was bandied around, it really meant no more than that much of pop had sprung genuinely out of working-class antecedents, that some working-class individuals had achieved great success, and that provincial and working-class accents were no longer a source of outrage in smart circles – it was certainly not marked by anything which could be seriously described as class conflict. True, there was a marked change in the pattern of strike activity in 1968. Hitherto, most days lost had been due to unofficial strikes. From 1968 onwards there was a significant growth in the number of days lost due to strikes, and an increasing proportion of strikes were now 'official' and led by the large unions. After 1970 there was a general hostility to the political philosophy of the Heath Conservative government, yet careful study of the actions of union leaders shows them continuing to act with great caution and restraint.

However, race provided a new source of open social conflict. Immigrants from India, Pakistan and the West Indies had begun arriving in numbers in the 1950s, settling in the poorer parts of London (almost a third of all immigrants), in the West Midlands, in Bradford, and in other run-down urban areas. In August 1958 violent race rioting broke out between local whites and the heavy concentration

120 West Indian immigrants disembarking. *The Times*, 25 July 1962.

of West Indian immigrants in Notting Hill, west London (177 people were arrested). Attempts to control immigration began with the Immigration Act of February 1962, which ironically touched off an accelerated influx of Commonwealth citizens rushing to get in before the Act took effect: *Plate 120* accompanied a *Times* news story entitled 'Immigrants beat the Act'. Attempts to deal by law with race discrimination began with the Race Relations Acts of 1966 and 1968. Deep popular hostility to immigrant communities, and, above all, to further immigration seems to have gone along with considerable popular support for legislation against racial discrimination. Race, as a political issue, led to the establishment, through a fusion in 1966 of existing groups, of the National Front, as a minority party of the extreme right.

The immigrant communities were not themselves homogeneous. The most energetic and aggressive group, the West Indians, were in some ways the most assimilable, while the Indians and the Pakistanis, generally industrious, sometimes prosperous, and whose children were often dedicated pupils at school,

121 The Mosque in Peel Street, Cardiff, September 1964. British Official photograph for British Information Services.

more obviously displayed the alien ways which aroused British xenophobia. But new ways and new religions were undoubtedly here to stay. *Plate 121*, an official Central Office of Information record photograph taken in September 1964 shows the mosque in Peel Street, Cardiff. The flags (one of them the Union Jack) are flying for the celebration of the end of Ramadan. Most significantly (here my phrase 'secular anglicanism' takes on a quaint twist) the mosque was actually erected by the Cardiff City Corporation. It continued to stand as the rest of the city's dockland area was demolished. At this point in time there were approximately 2,000 Muslims in the Cardiff area, supporting two other smaller mosques, and a school where Mohammedan children were taught the Koran after normal school hours.

There were academics in the 1960s who argued the thesis of *embourgeoisement*, the thesis that as workers became more affluent they were becoming part of the middle class.[8] Actually, workers could only indulge in middle-class tastes if they performed extra hours of work in what, and this is the critical point, remained working-class conditions. The character of work is a central phenomenon dividing the social classes. Work is the curse (a bigger or lesser one depending on class) by which almost all human beings are afflicted; yet it is the activity through which most people establish their identity, feel pride, and, perhaps, find fulfilment; at the very least, it is the activity which fills the largest slice of any person's time between birth and death. *Plate 122* shows the conditions of work, in May 1968, in the modernized factory of John Smedley Ltd, manufacturers of high-quality knitwear. In general aspect, the photograph is not dissimilar to *Plate 7* in Chapter One; here, though, the work force is entirely female. (As already suggested it can also be compared to *Plates 25 and 27*.) Here is

an account (published, as it happens, in 1968) by a machine minder in a knitwear factory of the agonies of repetitive, yet also high stressful, work:

122 Textile factory, May 1968.

> Watching the cones, checking the fabric, attending the machines which constantly break down, you're on the go all the time. If a machine stops, it must be started, and when it is going the cones are running out and have to be replaced. Hour after hour without break, from one machine to another and back, putting up ends, changing cones, starting the machines and trying to watch the fabric. The machines aren't designed for the operator. You bend low to see the fabric, and climb up on the machine to reach the arms holding the thread. To see all the cones you have to walk twenty-five feet round. Usually an operative has three machines with a total of 150 cones – many of which you can't see immediately because they're on the other side of the machines; you have to memorize which cones are going to run out. With bad yarn the machines snag constantly; it's gruelling keeping everything running. . .
>
> Hey, the machine's stopped. A top red light? Find a stick, disentangle the thread – break off the balled-up yarn, put the end up, check the thread is not caught, press the button, throw the handle. Peer at the fabric – needles? lines from tight yarn? Feel the yarn as it runs, alter the tension; we're not supposed to, it's the supervisor's job but he's too busy. Change a tight cone. A red light above droppers – cone run out? press-off? A yellow light – the stop motion has come up, maybe something is out of position on the needles, a build-up of thread or a broken needle. Clear the build-up, change the needle, start the machine again. And the other machines, are they all right? One of them stops every other minute on average. Can't spend more than thirty seconds looking at one, leave it for the two others, make sure they're all right, come back to the first. May take five or ten minutes to clear. By the time the trouble's clear, another one's stopped. Break off the bad yarn, disentangle the cone, restart the machine – a few seconds later do the same again.[9]

Repetitive, stressful, or just plain dirty, work. Whatever the great changes of the sixties, and they were great changes, the basic lot of the majority did not qualitatively change. And many of the most vaunted changes in their living

123  Kirkby New Town.
New shops situated near
blocks of skyscraper flats
in Kirkby New Town,
near Liverpool (15 June
1967)

124, 125  Before and
after: City of Norwich
Planning Division
photographs to
demonstrate the effects
of pedestrianization on
London Street, Norwich.
The scheme was
implemented in July
1967.

conditions proved empty ones. When Kirkby New Town, near Liverpool, was opened in 1952, a leading local socialist, Barbara Castle, told the local Labour Party: 'This is your chance to build a new Jerusalem'. *Plate 123* shows part of Kirkby as it was on 15 June 1967. It still looks spruce and fairly prosperous, and the caption supplied with this Fox photo is optimistic:

> Since the beginning of its development, in 1952, when it had a population of 3,000, Kirkby New Town, near Liverpool, has become a bustling township of 60,000 people, and it is still growing.
>
> It now possesses the finest schools in the North – 30 Junior and Primary, 4 comprehensive, a college of further education and a teachers training college, which attract education officials from all over the country who come to make inspections.
>
> Employment is provided for about 25,000 local inhabitants at the Kirkby Industrial Estate which houses about 140 firms, and which is separated from the housing estate by large parks.

But the bubble was about to burst: literally when in 1968 a gas explosion brought the collapse of Ronan Point, a system-built tower-block in east London. Much else collapsed as well; and architects and planners must be given some credit for realizing that they had a crisis on their hands which cast doubt on the supremacy of the architect and the validity of his alliance with the planners. There was, at the same time, a concern for the environment and, in middle-class areas at least, a real participation which broke through the standard apathy of British political culture. Protest groups took action against motorways urban and rural, the siting of new airports, and the invasion of suburban streets by heavy goods vehicles. In go-ahead areas pedestrian precincts were established: London Street, in Norwich, opened in July 1967, was one of the first (*Plates 124 and 125*). Nevertheless low-cost housing estates of dubious popularity went on being built, and thousands of people were to continue on into the present, unhappily marooned in flats hundreds of feet above the ground. Kirkby New Town itself became a paradigm of dereliction and vandalism.

Yet overall British society digested well – without the disruptions and violence apparent on the continent, in the United States, and in Japan – the very real social changes which had moved into high gear in 1959. Accommodation to the claims of youth, for example, was recognized in the lowering of the voting age in 1971 to eighteen. As I hinted at the beginning of this chapter, many serious commentators would seize on the material of my last paragraph to argue that no real cultural revolution took place, that, for example, *Room at the Top* and *Saturday Night and Sunday Morning* are essentially traditionalist in outlook.[10] Often this viewpoint, on examination, turns out to depend upon feminist assumptions. It is true that the modern feminist movement had scarcely got going in the period I have been examining. Germaine Greer's *The Female Eunuch* was published only in 1970. There was none of the violent activism or extreme anti-male hostility which had already appeared in the United States. It is absolutely true that most of the developments of the sixties were male-dominated. Women were emancipated in various ways, not least in their role on the dance floor; but full independent equality was not achieved. Most of the pop groups were totally male. Even the great female cult figures of the time, Mary Quant, the model Twiggy, Barbara Hulanicki of Biba, were very dependent on their male partners. But cultural change can be judged from other perspectives than that of the purely feminist, or, for that matter, socialist one.

## Chapter Nine

# Recession: 1973–1980

### 'Is Britain Ungovernable?'

To parcel this book up into chapters I have had to construct turning points, between the twenties and the thirties, say, or between the late forties and the early fifties. It is hard to argue with 1914, or, say, perhaps 1945. But of all suggested turning points 1973 is one of the least open to debate. Since the war the nations of the industrial world had enjoyed a long spell of economic boom; in 1973 the oil producers doubled their prices, and the world moved into a cycle of economic recession. By most outward signs, Britain continued to be a prosperous country, but just as previously she had rather floated along on the world boom, as though engineless, now she began to flounder seriously in the trough of depression: this was seen in business failures, growing inflation, high unemployment, and a general sense – by no means fully justified – of a lowering of living standards and a decline in the amenities of life.

There were other matters of grave concern. So much so that the question featured at the head of this section was actually being seriously posed in 1974. One might suggest that the rapid and complete way in which that question actually receded from consciousness indicates an enduring cohesion and stability in British society. Still the facts of confrontation and violence on a new scale are incontrovertible. Actually, the most bitter confrontation between government and unions since the war had come in 1972, mainly, but not entirely, because of the determination of Edward Heath's Conservative government to implement its new industrial relations legislation and because the miners, under Joe Gormley, were determined to improve their living standards. The Yorkshire miners' leader Arthur Scargill pioneered the technique of 'flying pickets'. In February 1972 at the Saltley Coke Depot, Birmingham, a picket died under the wheels of a lorry in what was really a most unfortunate accident.

There was more violence during the building workers' strike in the summer of 1972, arising out of the primitive sub-contracting conditions in that industry, known as 'the lump: the menacing intimidation carried through by pickets at Shrewsbury resulted in three prison sentences. Also there took place in 1972 the IRA bomb attack near the Aldershot barracks, in which five civilians died. But 1974 was the year of the really horrific IRA bombings. In July 1974 one woman was killed in the Tower of London and 41 children badly injured. In October and November there were pub bombings near Army barracks in Guildford and Woolwich: 7 were killed. Then at Birmingham in November, 21 were killed and 162 injured in a pub holocaust. In June a march of mainly Trotskyist 'liberation

126 Red Lion Square, June 1974. *Sunday Times* Focus photograph, with Kevin Gateley ringed. *Sunday Times*, 23 June 1974.

demonstrators' was organized to oppose the holding of a National Front meeting in the Conway Hall, Red Lion Square, London. The liberation demonstrators arrived first and it was actually in their encounter with the police that the student Kevin Gateley fell to the ground and was found to be dead. The police kept the rival groups apart, finally permitting the National Front marchers to hold their meeting as planned. The *Sunday Times* was at this time establishing an enviable reputation for its investigative journalism, and *Plate 126*, with Kevin Gateley ringed, is taken from the brilliant illustrated reconstruction of the episode which it published on 23 June 1974.

The years of the Heath government had been marked by a boom in share dealing and property speculation; businesses were acquired, not in order to put productive investment into them, but in order to make a quick profit out of reselling their most valuable holdings – 'asset-stripping' as it was called. In late 1973 this spurious boom collapsed; with it went one of the great institutions of the sixties, Biba. Much more seriously, at this time the world oil-producing nations were deciding to double the cost of this fuel upon which the industrialized world had come to depend so heavily. Yet, ironically, it was exactly at this point in time that Britain herself was about to become a major oil producer. Seismic prospecting for natural gas and oil in the North Sea had been going on since 1962, and full-scale exploration activities began in 1964, following the enactment of the Continental Shelf Act in that year, and the subsequent award of the first round of licences. Further licences were awarded in 1965, 1969–70 and 1971–2. The first oil find was made in 1969, and in 1970 it was clear that oil was present in significant quantities. The first North Sea oil came ashore in 1975, and in 1976 and 1977

production began to expand rapidly. Most of the oil fields faced the east coast of Scotland, and the formerly staid and bourgeois city of Aberdeen became something of an oil boom town. By the end of the decade about 80 per cent of the oil was coming ashore through 750 miles of submarine pipeline. But from many fields oil had to be brought ashore by tanker, so that new ocean terminals, capable of taking giant tankers, had to be built. *Plate 127* shows BP's terminal at Finnart, which is actually on the west coast of Scotland. Tankers berth there, then the crude oil travels by inland pipeline to the refinery at Grangemouth in central Scotland. Grangemouth also receives oil from the smaller terminal at Dalmeny, in the Firth of Forth. *Plate 127* gives a marvellous representation of one of the facets of late twentieth-century civilization, the intrusion of an advanced industrial-technological complex upon an area of wild and beautiful landscape. Similar terminals, with pipeline connections to refineries, were built at Amlwch and Angle Bay in Wales. British Petroleum (a British multinational conglomerate, in which the government at that time had a 46 per cent stake) was one of the two leading British companies in the field, the other being Shell Transport and

127 Aerial view of British Petroleum's Finnart ocean terminal, Loch Long, Scotland, 1976. Record photo by British Petroleum Oil Ltd.

128 Aerial view of National Exhibition Centre, Birmingham. Publicity photo.

Trading (part of the Dutch and British multi-national conglomerate). Many other, mainly American-owned, companies were operating in the North Sea. In 1976 the government set up, as a public corporation, the British National Oil Corporation to operate both as an oil trader, by virtue of its right to purchase from the other oil companies 51 per cent of their product, and as an enterprise directly engaged in oil production. In 1979, for the first time, Britain's own production of oil exceeded its imports.

The advent of North Sea oil could not conceal the fact that, in a harsh world, Britain's industrial base was shrinking drastically. The total numbers in manufacturing employment declined by 2.2 per cent between 1972 and 1974, and by a further 6.1 per cent between 1974 and 1977. Nor could the revival by the Labour government of more active interventionist policies in industry (the National Enterprise Board, BNOC, the nationalization of British Leyland) conceal some major developments in modern capitalism. In the years after 1945 it had seemed that the state and the big municipal authorities would assume more and more responsibility, not just for health and the environment, but for cultural, sporting, and other leisure activities. Then, of course, broadcasting had been a government monopoly, broken in 1954 with the establishment of commercial television, somewhat against the instincts of the senior Conservatives of the day. Now, private sponsorship of everything from opera to darts was widely in evidence, and commercial radio stations competed with both the BBC local and national radio. There was a rapid expansion in 'business services', advertising, market research, public relations, consultancy, private employment agencies (including the highly exclusive ones charged with finding executives in the six-figure income bracket), and conference centres. Advertising expenditure rose by 16 per cent in 1979, even though it was not one of Britain's happiest years.

*Plate 128* presents us with a giant symbol of the new internationally-oriented business services (and also, it should be said, of a determination in the west Midlands to resist the metropolitan hegemony of London). At the top-right are the buildings of Birmingham International Airport; to the left is the specially-built National Exhibition Centre Railway Station, stopping-point for even the fastest Intercity trains. To the right of that are the flat, functional, exhibition buildings. Then the neat bit of landscaping, with the lake and its wooded island and peninsulas, the latter caressing the 750-bed Birmingham Metropole Hotel, a banal classic of the international hotel style. In the immediate foreground is the link to Britain's motorway network. The international trading situation was not kind to the National Exhibition Centre; it could rely on the biennial motor industry show of the Society of Motor Manufacturers and Traders; meantime other conference centres were under construction at the Barbican in London and at Harrogate in north Yorkshire. At the same time a greater sector of the British economy was occupied by multinational corporations than was the case in any other European country. The dominance of the multinationals aggravated basic weaknesses: with a range of countries to choose from, the multinationals preferred not to invest where productivity was low and labour relations bad, hence they were said to be 'exporting jobs'.

With the same *folie de grandeur* which was so debilitating for British economic growth, Britain's governors, we have seen, had stood aloof from Europe in the 1950s. In the 1960s, the government of Harold Macmillan tried to join the European Economic Community, but was spurned by President de Gaulle of France. The government of Edward Heath renewed the attempt, and Britain became a member of the Common Market in 1973; a referendum subsequently held by the Labour government seemed to suggest that that was where the country's destiny lay.

This positive opening towards Europe, combined with technological developments which replaced the traditional muscular skills of the docker by containerization, changed the configuration of Britain's ports. Between 1970 and 1979 container and roll-on traffic trebled and by the latter year was accounting for almost one-third of non-fuel traffic. Down the Thames from London, the world's largest terminal for refrigerated containers was built at Tilbury; the other main ports for this type of traffic were Liverpool, Southampton, Dover and Felixstowe (*Plate 129*), on the Suffolk coast, near the old European train ferry port of Harwich, and not far from Constable's Vale of Dedham. At the end of the seventies a £32 million scheme was under way to provide two deep-water container berths at Felixstowe. The photograph in *Plate 129*, taken in 1981,

129 The port of Felixstowe's new Dooley terminal. Port of Felixstowe record photograph, also used for public relations purposes.

shows the completed Dooley container terminal, and gives a good impression of the technology involved: the two rail-mounted quayside cranes in the background; and in the foreground a rubber-tyred gantry crane in operation, loading one of the port's tugmaster and trailer units. Such developments spelt the death of the traditional dockland areas in London, Liverpool and Glasgow. Taking oil into account, Britain's top eleven ports in 1979 were: London (including Tilbury), Milford Haven, Tees and Hartlepool, Forth, Grimsby and Immingham, Southampton, Shetland (the ocean terminal of Sullom Voe), Medway, Orkney (the oil port at Flotta), Liverpool, and Manchester (standing on the only canal from the classical Industrial Revolution still in effective commercial use).

*Plate 130*, showing the Queen opening the Humber Bridge on 17 July 1981, has many resonances. South of the Humber at Scunthorpe was one of the country's largest steel plants, run by the British Steel Corporation, which had been created by the renationalization of the industry in 1967. North of the Humber, and somewhat isolated by the facts of geography, was the principal industrial town in Humberside: Hull. Most important, as the government's Official Handbook for 1981 put it, 'The Humber ports are strategically situated for direct access to Western Europe', adding in the same sentence, 'while the Humber Bridge will improve domestic communications'.[1] With a span of 1,410 metres (4,626 feet) this new bridge had a span longer than any other in the world.

However, pride in this triumph of British technology is somewhat tempered if one goes back to the Official Handbook of 1974. There one reads: 'A £26 million bridge across the River Humber, with a span of 4,626 feet (1,410 metres) – longer

130 'QUEEN OPENS HUMBER BRIDGE July 17th 1981'. . . 'The Queen wearing spectacles to read her speech formally declaring the new £91 million Humber Bridge open today from a rostrum on the Hull side. She and the Duke of Edinburgh then became the 302,930th and 302,931st passengers across the structure, the longest suspension bridge in the world which was open to traffic 22 days ago.' Picture by Press Association Court photographer Ron Bell.

than any existing bridge span in the world – is to be completed in 1976–77'.[2] The bridge, after many mishaps and a violent escalation of costs (the actual cost was £91 million), was just five years late. By the time it was opened, the steel industry was suffering from severe cutbacks and the bridge no longer seemed quite such a vital part of Britain's communications network. Royalty being involved, the photograph was taken by the Press Association court photographer. The flags are bravely in evidence, the brass band, and members of the public genuinely concerned to get a view of the Queen. The caption to the photograph concentrates on the fact that the Queen is wearing spectacles to read her speech. Such are the pressures on the Royal Diary that the bridge had actually been opened to traffic for over three weeks.

Britain's record in science and technology is indeed a paradoxical one. Much had been done in the sixties to develop science teaching in all types of secondary schools, yet in the seventies there was a swing back in student choices from science to arts subjects. There was still a strong élitist atmosphere about university science, yet, despite economic stringency, British scientists retained their enviable eminence in the international community. Developments were particularly arresting in 'the life sciences', in micro-biology, molecular biology and immunology. Basically it was the achievements in immunology which made possible the transplant surgery which attracted so much attention in the press. Most attention of all was focused on the arrival, early in 1979, of the world's first 'test-tube' baby, resulting from the partnership of Robert Edwards, physiologist at Cambridge University, and Patrick Steptoe, gynaecologist at Oldham General Hospital.

In the world of technology the arrival of the silicon chip was of crucial significance; developed in the United States, it made possible very complex computerization within a small space. Slightly surprisingly, perhaps, an area of lowland Scotland emerged as (there was some exaggeration) Britain's 'silicon valley'. In the 1960s, research into robot technology at Hawker-Siddeley and Guest, Keen and Nettlefold had been as far ahead as any in the world, and significant advances were made at the University of Nottingham in the early 1970s. Yet, while from the very beginning of the seventies the Japanese, and in lesser degree other west European countries, had exploited the possibilities of automated 'robot' factories, in Britain appreciable developments came only at the very end of the decade. In September 1980, there was a press showing, complete with publicity photographs (*Plate 131*), of British Leyland's automatic Mini Metro factory at Longbridge, Birmingham. *Plate 131* repays study. There are no robots in evidence, and indeed none of the robots at Longbridge were of British manufacture. What is most in evidence is the good old manual worker. Somehow this vision of a 'computer-controlled Mini Metro trim track' fails to convey any sense of speed, efficiency, or high productivity.

Just at this time, nonetheless, several firms began to announce lay-offs due to automation based on micro-electronic robot technology. And unemployment is the doleful ground bass to all the other developments we have been looking at. Actually it was only in 1976 that it became absolutely clear that unemployment was on the up and up, though the psychological barrier of two million unemployed had been broken in August 1975. The percentage unemployed out of the total number of employees stood at 2.6 per cent in 1970, rising to 3.5 per cent and 3.8 per cent in 1971 and 1972 respectively, with a fall back to 2.7 per cent in 1973 and 2.6 per cent in 1974; in 1975 it rose to 4.1 per cent, in 1976 to 5.7 per cent, in 1977 to 6.2 per cent, with a slight remission in 1978 to 6.1 per cent, then up again in 1979, and on catastrophically upwards into the 1980s, and above the three million mark.

The central device of Labour social and economic policy in the later seventies was the 'Social Contract', which had many similarities to the wage restraint implemented by the Attlee government after the war. In return for promises of social legislation beneficial to the mass of the people, the trade unions co-operated in keeping wage rises, and therefore, in some degree, inflation under strict control. Personal incomes actually fell by 0.2 per cent in 1976, and by a further 1 per cent in 1977. However, later in the decade real incomes began to move upwards again. People tended to think they were worse off, but this was largely because they had been conditioned to expect continual betterment. The situation can perhaps be put into perspective if it is realized that a manual worker with average earnings would have had to work thirty-four minutes to buy a pint of beer in 1950, but only eighteen minutes in 1977. He would not necessarily have had more money to spare, because he probably drank more beer in 1977. The success of the Social Contract suggested that the spirit of co-operation and civic loyalty was still strong in Britain.

For all the stresses and economic failings, that question about the governability of Britain with which I began this chapter really could be set aside as much of the deeper stability of society reasserted itself. However, James Callaghan, who had succeeded Harold Wilson as Labour Prime Minister in 1976, persisted too

131 One of the three computer-controlled Mini Metro trim tracks. British Leyland publicity photograph.

inflexibly with the statutory wages policy. He also stubbornly refused to seek a mandate in the spring or autumn of 1978 when the Social Contract was still holding up. 1978 was a year of drastic cuts in public expenditure, demanded by the International Monetary Fund upon whom Britain was dependent for loans. So the country moved into what was quickly dubbed 'the winter of discontent' of 1978–9. In 1979 the number of days lost due to strike action exceeded those of the General Strike year of 1926. As the date by which the Callaghan government had to have a general election approached, it was attacked from the right for its failure to control the unions, and from the left for its public spending cuts and attempts to hold down wages.

In the Conservative Party meantime, Mrs Margaret Thatcher, advocating more cuts in public expenditure and a much greater role for private enterprise, had replaced Edward Heath as leader. In the 1979 general election her party received 43.9 per cent of the votes of those who voted; but 36.9 per cent still voted Labour; and nearly 30 per cent did not vote at all. Even by the early months of 1981, when further drastic cuts on public expenditure had been carried through, and substantial sections of government-owned industry had been sold off to private interests, it was impossible to say that an irreversible shift in British social and economic policy, as distinct from an acceleration of trends already apparent in the seventies, had taken place. Conservative supporters of the old reformist and consensual politics seemed in a strong position as Mrs Thatcher's own popularity was low. Predictions were that in any future general election votes would be fairly evenly split between Conservatives, Labour and the newly-formed Social Democratic Party and its allies the Liberals (see next chapter). Already in this book I have stressed the great social significance of two total wars; a very little, and a very distant, war was to change all that.

## The Media and Social Values

While (as noted in connection with the death of Kevin Gateley) there were matters to admire in the British quality press, the overall story of the press since 1945 had not been an inspiring one. In May 1974 a Royal Commission (the third since the war) was set up. Its *Final Report* (July 1977) noted that sales of national dailies had fallen from 15.8 million per day in 1961 to 14.0 million in 1976; while the provincial press generally prospered the national press was in a condition of chronic financial crisis. Different categories were considered in turn. First came the 'qualities': *Daily Telegraph, Sunday Telegraph, Financial Times, Guardian, The Times, Sunday Times* and *Observer*. Second were the 'populars': the *Daily Mirror, Sunday Mirror, Daily Express, Sunday Express, Sunday People, Daily Mail, Sun,* and *News of the World* (later there was to appear the *Daily Star*); the Commission found it difficult to fit the *Morning Star* (the Communist Party newspaper) into either of these first two classifications. Third came the weekly 'journals of opinion': *Economist, Spectator, New Statesman, Tribune* and *New Society*. Fourth was the 'alternative press', creation of the sixties, expanded in the seventies: *Gay News* (which, first published in 1962, now had a bigger circulation than either the *Spectator* or *Tribune*), *Private Eye*, product of the sixties' satire boom, and *Time Out*. Fifth and sixth were the 'provincial mornings', of which there were now only twelve in England and Wales, compared with eighteen in 1948 (Scotland still had four), and the 'evenings', of which nine had closed since 1961, leaving no single provincial city with more than one evening paper (London still had two, though they were to be amalgamated in November 1980). Lastly the Commission came to a series of categories, some of considerable antiquity, some either launched, or substantially developed, in the seventies: 'free sheets', product of participation and consumerism; ethnic newspapers; 'general periodicals', including traditional lower-class products like *Reveille* and *Titbits*; the newer specialist magazines orientated towards do-it-yourself or, say, pop music; the increasingly explicit sex magazines; and the 'women's press' made up of the more conservative weeklies and monthlies such as *Woman* and *Good Housekeeping*, the newer 'emancipated' monthlies such as *Cosmopolitan* (founded in 1972), the firmly feminist organs such as *Spare Rib* (also founded in 1972), and the mass of girls' magazines.

Apart from the menace of mergers and consolidation of ownership (the British press was in effect owned by ten large companies, four of which were not even British-owned), the Commission identified four other major problems: the invasion of privacy by reporters; the weakness of the Press Council in maintaining high journalistic standards; the growing control of the major alternative source of information, television, by the newspaper combines; and poor industrial relations:

> One debilitating legacy to national newspapers from the post-war days of easy profits and weak management has been the exceptionally high earnings of print workers and a disposition among publishers to yield easily to threats of unofficial action. Industrial relations in Fleet Street have been notoriously bad for a generation and their improvement has been the regularly falsified hope of everyone who has attempted to set the industry on the path of modernisation.[3]

132 'A National Graphical Association picket offering a leaflet to Mr. M. J. Hussey, chief executive and managing director of Times Newspapers as he arrived yesterday for the annual meeting in London of the parent company, International Thomson Organisation.' *Guardian*, 28 June 1979.

Throughout 1979, indeed, Times Newspapers were paralysed as managers and staff failed to agree over the introduction of computerized techniques. *Plate 132* is a rich document. The meeting here between the Managing Director of Times Newspapers and union representatives is entirely fortuitous; the means of communication is a union leaflet. Marmaduke Hussey was a perfect representative of that section of the upper class which had emerged from the nineteenth-century upper-middle class: his grandfather had been an Anglican clergyman. On the occasions when Hussey appeared on television to explain the management case his public-school accent was in sharp contrast with the London working-class accents and grammar of the National Graphical Association representatives.

Against all this, Britain had a fair claim to leadership of the world in the production of decent television programmes. Partly this was because its best-educated young people, whether from the traditional upper class, or upwardly mobile members of the middle or working classes, preferred the arts and entertainment to the world of industry; the truly upper class still drifted towards the City, though they did not need to be particularly well-educated for that. But the book trade, once a genuine source of pride, was in trouble. Book prices shot up; hitherto impregnable firms turned in large trading losses; retrenchment and redundancy struck suddenly and often arbitrarily.

*Plates 133 and 134* give us a sense, even when artistic licence and the necessary exaggeration of caricature are allowed for, of the continuing hold of class stereotypes which would not have been utterly out of place in the 1920s. Mark Boxer, who produced a daily cartoon in *The Times*, was a marvellous portrayer of idiosyncrasies and assumptions which indicate the continued existence of a coherent upper class (one of his characteristic figures has the line: 'I don't believe in class, myself, but fortunately my butler disagrees with me'). Apparently the cartoon in *Plate 133* is about Anthony Wedgwood Benn, the most influential left-wing figure in the then Labour government. This was at the time of the 1975 referendum on membership of the EEC, to which Benn, in contrast with Prime Minister Harold Wilson and his immediate associates, was opposed. One of Benn's arguments was that continued membership of the Common Market would bring further disaster to British industry, involving massive unemployment. Benn, in addition, had sprung from a type of upper-class background not utterly dissimilar to that of Marmaduke Hussey. His grandfather had been a nonconformist minister, and his father W. Wedgwood Benn, a Liberal convert to Labour, had been created Viscount Stansgate in 1941. Marc's two upper-class old duffers (the near one has a hearing aid as well as a stick) have misunderstood. That they should actually be pleased about what they understand to be a promise of unemployment has the exaggeration of satire; but there is no exaggeration in the sense of class solidarity with the son of a viscount.

The manifestly working-class figures in the Giles cartoon are clearly better-off, less down-trodden, than their counterparts of the twenties (*Plate 134*). The *Daily Express*, as we have noted, was a very right-wing newspaper, and Giles himself was notorious for pandering to right-wing prejudices. Here the political point is the absence of any sense of solidarity between the striking power worker and other workers.

Giles' world was a ruthless world of personal hostilities, with little sign of the softening influences of the Welfare State. The original Beveridge notion of flat-rate benefits had been abandoned in 1959, and the new earnings-related principle had been extended by the Labour government in 1966. In the sixties also there had been a retreat from the principle of universality which Conservative and Labour experts both now felt was wasteful of resources in that it spread inadequate benefits too thinly across the entire nation. The major act of the sixties was the 1966 Ministry of Social Security Act which sought, among other things, to remove the stigma which still deterred many deserving individuals from applying for National Assistance by replacing it with Supplementary Benefits.

The major innovation of the 1970s was the Employment Protection Act of 1975, whose provisions covered the right not to be unfairly dismissed, entitlement to a written statement of terms and conditions of employment, guaranteed pay, time off work for trade union duties, and also redundancy pay, minimum periods of notice, and maternity rights. The whole structure of the medical services was reorganized in the early 1970s to meet the criticisms which had been voiced since 1948; but the critics, or most of them, now said that the new structure was even worse. The Labour government did try to reassert universalist principles in education when after 1974 it moved forward with a policy of directly absorbing public-sector grammar schools into comprehensive schools and indirectly exerting pressure on independent schools to join in by withdrawing their direct

"I do beg your pardon, mate—I'd no idea you worked at our local power station."

grants. There was much debate over whether or not the absorption of grammar schools into comprehensive schools meant a lowering of standards.

## Separate Development

The government of the Republic of South Africa – rightly, much criticized – claimed that its apartheid policies offered blacks 'separate development'. By contrast, Roy Jenkins and others who had sponsored the 'civilized society' legislation of the later sixties had hoped to achieve a greater social unity through the closer integration of hitherto persecuted and disadvantaged groups into the community. One of the characteristics of the seventies was the manner in which minorities preferred, very visibly and vociferously, to go their own way and assert their distinctiveness from society as a whole; in an unprecedented way active pressure groups operated on behalf of particular minorities and special interests.

British information services, of course, preferred to present the image of an integrated society. In the caption to *Plate 135*, a photograph of Brixton market, Brixton is described as 'a multi-racial area of South-West London'. The picture supports the caption remarkably well, down to the West Indian to the rear on the right wearing the traditional British working-class cloth cap and the Scottish trader with his tartan tammy. In this picture there is nothing more exotic than breadfruit, aubergine and avocado pears; but even ten years before, such items would have been rare in British markets and shopping streets. The seventies, more than the sixties, saw a true absorption into British society of foreign foods and an amazing range of foreign restaurants. In *Plate 121* in Chapter Eight we saw evidence of the independent religious tradition of the Asian community. *Plate 136* seems to show a blending of cultural traditions: the western film, naturalized in the East, then re-exported to the West; the turbanned head, with the knitted pullover and fashionable trousers. Actually, Southall to the west of London had become very much a separate Asian enclave, peaceful and industrious. However, as we shall see, Southall, and Brixton, were to become

133 Marc cartoon, *The Times*, May 1975.

134 Giles cartoon, *Daily Express*, 4 November 1977.

135 'BRIXTON MARKET, SOUTH-WEST LONDON.
Photograph shows a street market in Brixton,
a multi-racial area of South-West London.'
British Official photograph for British
Information Services, 1973.

136 Outside a cinema at The Green, Southall,
23 September 1976.

scenes of extremely violent confrontation. On 23 April 1979 the National Front deliberately held a meeting in the Town Hall of Southall. 4,000 policemen were drafted in to confront 3,000 anti-National Front demonstrators. A large number of these were Asians, but there were also many whites; and it was a white teacher, Blair Peach, who was killed that day, quite possibly at the hands of a member of the Special Patrol Group. While Notting Hill and Brixton seethed, the big clash which spread shock throughout society came in the poverty-stricken St Paul's district of Bristol. On the late afternoon of Wednesday 2 April and on into the night, a police raid on a club there led to rioting in which nineteen policemen and six other people were taken to hospital, and in which a bank, other buildings, and police cars were burnt out, with at the same time much looting and vandalism.[4]

We have to make a distinction between the first generation of West Indian and Asian immigrants, keen to preserve their culture and traditions, but keen also to blend as unobtrusively as possible, and with as little provocation as possible, into British society, and the younger generation, born in Britain, but only too conscious, particularly as the economic climate worsened, of their deeply underprivileged position. One West Indian school-leaver unable to find employment remonstrated with his father:

> If you don't even read the newspapers to find out what kids like me are going through now I pity you. What the hell you think this is all about, man? You think this is a game I am playing, running all over the city begging people to make up work for me to do? Deliver little parcels for them or wipe up floors? You think it's going to get better, that suddenly the government's going to hand down a million new jobs for people? You know what they got planned? They got this thing so worked out it makes me sick. They got a plan that all the little coloured kids, we are told to leave school and think about jobs and making money. Then you know what happens? A few of us get our little rotten work so we are helping them, right? But the most of us, we don't get anything.[5]

By a not altogether dissimilar process, within the feminist movement there was a change from, as Germaine Greer put it, 'genteel middle-class ladies' clamouring for reform to 'ungenteel middle-class women . . . calling for revolution'.[6] Feminists mounted attacks on spheres of life which men had never really thought of as discriminatory and which women, if they had thought about them, did not question. Women, it had been held for centuries, who wandered alone after dark in dicey areas were at best foolish, and at worst accessories to anything which might happen to them. All this was challenged in the campaigns for 'the right to the night'.

Some commentators spoke of a 'new piety' as if there were some kind of puritan reaction against the permissiveness of the swinging sixties. In reality there was precious little evidence of this, save insofar as feminists were taking a baleful look at the whole concept of sexual liberation. Many did spread the message that sexual involvement with a man, far from being the highest fulfilment for a woman, was rather a dangerous drug to be avoided. When it seemed that the Conservative victory of 1979 and the return of many younger Conservatives of distinctly illiberal convictions might jeopardize the 'right to choose' embodied in the Abortion Act of 1967, feminists mobilized themselves in a particularly dramatic way, reminiscent of the suffragette processions at their peak (*Plate 137*).

Of course, strong hostility to feminist claims remained, some of it of a distinctly shameful character, as in the Emmwood cartoon published in the *Daily*

137 Women's torchlight demonstration against alterations to the 1967 Abortion Law, 8 February 1980.

*Mail* on 16 February 1973 (*Plate 138*). Between militant feminists on the one side, and reactionary male chauvinists on the other, there was a moving middle ground in which a distinctively woman's point of view (too long ignored) could be deployed in rational analysis of the complexities and absurdities of human life and the relations between the sexes. The *Guardian* published the original, and devastatingly accurate, cartoon strips of Posy Simmonds (*Plate 139*). The very title of Margaret Drabble's best novel for many years was *The Middle Ground* (1980). Kate, the central character, reflects that a baby's excrement, over which some feminists made so much fuss, was really nearly all milk, whereas men, including her father, a sewage worker, had to deal with the really disgusting excrement of the world. In the main, British feminist novelists (as distinct from their American counterparts) seemed ready to accept that in the real contemporary world there was no prospect of full women's liberation as extreme feminists envisaged it; the

"YOU'RE ALL FOR WOMENS' LIB - YOU GO AND GET HELP!"

138 Emmwood cartoon, *Daily Mail*, 16 February 1973.

problem being woman's own nature. The vulnerability, more than the unconquerability, of women were major themes in for example, *Sweet William* (1975) by Beryl Bainbridge, and *Praxis* (1978) by Fay Weldon.

Still, the separateness of women's groups was constantly being stressed; the watchword 'men keep out'. Similarly, while Leo Abse had hoped that his piece of sixties legislation would enable homosexuals to play a full part in ordinary society, the separateness of homosexual culture was also being emphasized. Young people, too, had their exclusive groups: mods, rockers, skinheads, punks and variations thereof. It was in the sixties that drug abuse had become a problem of youth, as opposed to one confined to a handful of forlorn adults. Drug abuse continued to be a prime feature of the different youth sub-cultures of the seventies.

Rather than a great cultural revolution, the later seventies underwent fissiparous and centrifugal tendencies. Perhaps for this reason there were no great artistic, dramatic and few filmic successes to rival the sixties. British art merged anonymously into the major international trends; and these trends, incorporating photographic and other technological techniques, stressing literalness and 'superrealism', pushing political messages, and emphasizing feminism and homosexuality, were not themselves of a sort to assist the revelation of distinctively national or personal genius. Stephen Willats wrote a book about *The Lurky Place* (1978), the subject matter also for the painting of that name one of whose panels is reproduced in *Plate 140*. 'The Lurky Place' is actually the name given by local residents to an area of wasteland, bang in the middle of the urban environment, in Hayes, not far from Southall, west of London. Willats' own statement may or may not mean anything, but it is typical of the type of jargon being spouted by certain artists and intellectuals of the time (and beautifully captured, of course, by Posy Simmonds): 'The nature of this

139 Posy Simmonds
strip cartoon, 1979.

My institutionalised past.

Identify the moments of transition.

140 *The Lurky Place* by Stephen Willats, August–September, 1978. One of four panels: photographic prints, gouache, photographic dyes, ink, letraset on card.

place is, of course, a product of the surrounding society. . . . The value it has for residents of surrounding housing estates is as a symbol of a consciousness which is counter to that of the predominant social stereotypes'.[7] *Art and Artists* explained further:

> The Contemporary Art Society's four-panel work *The Lurky Place*, made from August to September 1978, depicts four types of determinism and four freedoms centred on an unemployed girl. In fact the sex of the participant is ambiguous – she was described as a boy by one reviewer. The social situation of the subject is not limited by gender and identification with her as a 'person' by viewers of both sexes is facilitated. The four areas of determinism in the photographs on the top of each panel are the school, the tower block, the car dump ('my role within a planned economy') and the factory ('my generation's outlook for the years ahead' – optimism was still possible in '78). These all lie on the border of the wasteland. From there we are led to four objects found within the wasteland set within a 'concept frame' (Behaviour/Function/Convention/Belief). We are then taken over the centre line of the panel and via the framed head of the girl who is walking in the wasteland to an imperative statement (e.g. 'Restructure the framework of priorities'). From this Lurky Place perspective, the subject's place in society can be re-thought: images from both inside and outside the wasteland are presented in a second 'concept frame' (Reasoning/Response/Understanding/Feeling).[8]

*The Lurky Place*, with its use of photographic prints, gouache, photographic dyes, ink, letraset on card, may or may not be an important work of creative art; taken with the verbal material just quoted, it is certainly an important piece of documentation of one of the sorts of sub-culture manifest in Britain at the end of the seventies. No doubt, British society in earlier times had had just as wide a range of interest groups and esoteric societies; but never before had they been so visible or so clamorous.

Chapter Ten

# Britain Today:
# New Course, Or Same But Worse?

As Britain moved into the eighties (perhaps a more accurate metaphor would be: as the eighties moved away from Britain) certain features, rather at odds with the broad development of society since 1900, stood out. These were: privatization; polarization – or rather polarizations, since along with a growing basic divide in society there was a whole jungle of embattled polemics; unemployment and industrial collapse; and violence on the streets. *Privatization*: the publicly-owned high-technology electronics conglomerate Amersham International was sold off (at a disgraceful loss to the taxpayer), as were, for example, railway hotels and assets in British oil; local authorities turned refuse collecting and hospital cleaning over to private firms. *Polarization*: trade unionists, all who believed in co-operation and community care, the victims of poverty and ill-health, the northern and celtic parts of the nation were all more alienated from authority and the southern parts of the nation than at any time since 1939; in debates between nuclear disarmers and all others the former increasingly implied that all who opposed them were warmongers, while Conservative opponents of CND brought in absurd and malicious charges of communist influence; the women CND supporters camping out at the American airbase at Greenham Common insisted on keeping this impressive demonstration an all-female one; by the summer of 1983 the initially tolerant and even supportive attitudes of the local people at Greenham had turned to an angry hostility; the Labour Party broke up into faction fighting at national and local level, between traditionalists in the Attlee mould and the increasingly dominant Marxist and Trotskyist groups. *Unemployment and industrial collapse*: in December 1982 the numbers claiming Unemployment Insurance reached 3,063,026 – *Plate 148*, when compared with *Plate 49* in Chapter Four hints, on the surface at least, that, even if the country had not recovered the Victorian values urged by Mrs Thatcher, it was returning to the industrial shambles of the 1930s; even the magnificent new aluminium smelter which a dozen years before had given renewed hope of survival to Invergordon, in Scotland, was shut down (*Plate 141* shows the smelter in its heyday – it conveys some of the aura of late-twentieth-century civilization, as does the Loch Long oil terminal (*Plate 127* in Chapter Nine) – would that, too, go the same way when the oil was exhausted?). *Violence on the Streets*: some of the most horrific events yet took place in 1981 and 1982 (*Plates 142, 143 and 144*).

The first blaze of devastating rioting in Brixton took place over the long weekend of 9–13 April 1981: 143 policemen were taken to hospital, one seriously

203

ill with a fractured skull; at least 30 civilians were treated in hospital; 199 people were arrested; 76 shops and homes were seriously damaged, as, in addition, were many police and private motor-vehicles.[1] It was immediately announced that Lord Scarman would conduct a public inquiry. The Scarman Inquiry was still sitting when simultaneously, on Saturday 4 July, there was a violent confrontation between skinheads and Asians in Southall, and clashes between police and young blacks in Toxteth, Liverpool, followed by an orgy of repression and destruction. *Plate 142* provides as graphic an image of the Toxteth riots as one could find. It does not, however, convey the fact that a crippled white man, aged twenty-two, was run down and killed by a police vehicle. In the following week violence again broke out in Brixton, and also in Manchester and Bristol. *Plate 143*, dated 10 July 1981, from the second outbreak of Brixton rioting, clearly shows two police officers attacking a civilian who is attempting to shield his head. Published in December, the Scarman Report indicated the extent to which insensitivity and, indeed, downright provocation on the part of the police had contributed to riots, which, however, were largely born of frustration in an economic recession which weighed most heavily on black youth.[2]

On 20 July 1982 (the same month in which unemployment reached its highest total ever in British history, 3,190,621, or 13.4 per cent) one IRA bomb in the Regent's Park bandstand, and another detonated from a car as the Household Cavalry marched past, killed a total of eleven soldiers, and viciously wounded many others (*Plate 144*). The next day crowds turned out to cheer the Household

141 Aluminium smelter, Invergordon. Record photo by John Dewar Studios, Edinburgh.

142 Toxteth, 6 July 1981. News photo by *Liverpool Daily Post & Echo.*

143 Brixton, 10 July 1981. News photo by John Sturrock of Network.

144 Hyde Park, 20 July 1982. 'IRA bomb attacks kill eight: Police and soldiers help the injured after the car bomb explosion in the South Carriage Drive, Hyde Park.' *The Times*, 21 July, 1982.

145 Lady Diana Spencer on her way to St Paul's Cathedral, *Guardian*, 30 July 1981.

Cavalry on parade: whatever Brixton and Toxteth revealed about the failings of the police and the alienation of black youth (and it was a lot) IRA terrorism only showed that it was still far too early to write off British social cohesion as a thing of the past.

Indeed, much as it might puzzle the rational, and infuriate the revolutionary, from a relatively low point in the austerity years, the popularity of royalty as a focal point for national sentiment had been steadily growing.[3] This was encapsulated in one great piece of pageantry on 29 July 1981, the wedding of Charles, Prince of Wales, to Lady Diana Spencer (*Plate 145*). No doubt there was a touch of *kitsch* in *The Times* account; yet the lighthearted reference to other events of that July was not entirely unjustified:

> Riotous behaviour gripped the heart of London yesterday. More than a million jubilant demonstrators took to the streets, confronting nearly 4,000 police, reinforced by thousands of servicemen, and keeping hundreds of ambulancemen at full stretch. All along the procession route the Royal Wedding proved a riot of colour, good humour, and fun.[4]

But no amount of enthusiasm for royalty could conceal the fact that by early the following year, under the Thatcher government, while inflation had first continued to rise sharply, and even now was very far from being under control,

unemployment had been multiplied by two-and-a-half times since the Conservatives took over from Labour. In its defence cuts, the government had also gravely weakened its ability to defend such remote outposts as the Falkland Islands, and indeed had seemed to imply that it had no will to defend them. On 2 April the Argentines mounted their invasion of the islands, the British marines surrendering after a hopeless three-hour battle. Three days later a task force set sail for the South Atlantic. On 14 June, after feats of great heroism and military skill, the British forces secured the surrender of the occupying Argentinian force. In the succeeding weeks the major ships taking part, including the main troop carrier, *Canberra*, returned to home base, to scenes of great patriotic jubilation and pride (*Plate 146*).

As the victorious warlady, Mrs Thatcher now seemed in an unassailable position. She was greatly helped, of course, by the internal squabbling and poor figure cut by the Labour Party. Duly winning the election of June 1983, though with fewer votes than she had gained in 1979, she was now able to indicate that Britain definitely was embarked on a new course, though whether that course was one destined to produce economic revival and national reconciliation was highly dubious. As a limited war, the Falklands campaign, then, had mainly negative, rather than constructive effects on British society, though clearly it did inspire and canalize sentiments of pride and national unity. While there was an orgy of chauvinism and bloodlust in certain of the tabloids, in society as a whole there were not the bitter divisions of the Suez campaign. It is fairly clear that intelligent opinion in Britain felt that the Falklands episode should have been avoided; at the same time there was a reluctance to do anything which might undercut support for British troops at risk. The Falklands factor did not of itself sweep radical right-wing Conservatism back into power; a less ineffective opposition could well have turned to fruitful account the very grave doubts which lay, and must continue to lie, behind this entire tragedy.

Meantime more mundane, but highly critical, concerns continued. In April 1983 some productivity figures were presented with brutal clarity. In 1982 Ford's Halewood Plant, near Liverpool, had produced 721 Escorts a day with 9,700 workers; Ford's sister plant at Saarlouis in West Germany produced 1,232 a day with only 7,300 workers. In the economy as a whole each British worker each week was creating wealth to the extent of £150: in France, the figure was £330 and in West Germany £390.[5] Some of the reasons might be found in *Plate 131* of Chapter 9. *Plate 147*, however, presents a rather more encouraging vision of high productivity on the new, and successful, Sierra. Socially menacing though the robots, all of American manufacture, appear, the fact was that the introduction of the Sierra actually created new jobs. Britain, alas, had not generally emulated Japan in combining advanced technology with job security. Among those joining the influx into the Ford Motor plant, as was revealed in August 1983, were a number of Socialist Workers Party 'moles'. But the confessions of one mole of older vintage suggest that the damage done to productivity by SWP infiltrators

---

146 'A day to remember: a spectacular welcome from a wildly cheering multitude at Southampton Water yesterday as the Canberra steamed in after its voyage with the victorious Falklands force.' *The Times*, 12 July 1983.

147 'SIERRA BODIES PUT TOGETHER BY ROBOTS: One hundred and twenty robots – the biggest concentration in British industry – have been installed at the Dagenham Body Plant for the construction of the new Sierra. . . . Here the Sierra bodyshells pass along a line of 12 Cincinnati robots for finish welding prior to the fitting of bonnet, doors and tailgate.' Ford publicity photograph, September 1982.

was minimal compared with that done by the rigid structure of British industrial relations:

> At the end of the day the trade union structure was as big a stumbling-block to what we were trying to achieve as the management themselves.
> In fact, I ended up with a far greater loathing for the union than for the management. I thought that as employers they treated us quite well, quite liberally.
> It was the trades unions that used to get up my nose. The full-time officials never used to take the initiative on anything and when we did come to a really important battle over redundancy, they essentially sabotaged our attempt to fight the threat to industry.
> And once you got involved in the union you realised just what an undemocratic organisation it was, how much control the officials had. Probably more of my energy went into trying to democratise the union than in fighting the management.[6]

As suggested above, *Plate 148*, when compared with the photograph of the Jarrow Crusade, hints at the extent to which the country had returned to the crisis of the thirties; but it also indicates the many ways in which Britain in the eighties was very different from Britain in the thirties. Oddly, the background is taken up by that great product of thirties culture, the Hoover factory on Western Avenue. While the Jarrow crusaders, with their worn faces, crumpled suits and sashes, had conveyed deep suffering, resignation, perhaps even deference, as well as nobility and protest, the job marchers, younger, better-fed, have just a whiff of the professional protester about them; and this impression does not derive solely

from the smart yellow and green jackets which were indeed a necessary safety measure on roads crowded beyond anything dreamed of in 1936. Unemployment is a tragedy whatever era it occurs in. But whereas the Jarrow crusade definitely brought a new consciousness of the plight of industrial Britain to the prosperous south, the job marchers had much less impact in the polarized society of 1983: they met, as *The Times* put it, 'the usual mixture of emotional support, antagonism and apathy'. Irrelevant to the main issue though the point may be, there was widespread awareness that unemployment benefits (even though their real value had been reduced by the Thatcher government) remained a genuine barrier against the desperate deprivation which had been so prevalent in the 1930s.

'Emotional support, antagonism and apathy': that phrase goes to the heart of much of what was wrong with British political culture in the 1980s. Where were the required qualities of rationality, co-operation and commitment? Early in 1981 certain figures in the Labour Party, upholders of the moderate Attlee tradition, critics of the stagnation and arthritic social and industrial relations brought about by upper-class complacency and trade-union conservatism, formed the Social Democratic Party. Yet, though many who remained in the Labour Party were very close in outlook to those who had made this bid to 'break the mould of British politics', and vice versa, it was part-and-parcel of the football-fan mentality of British politics that the parties directed some of their bitterest

148 March for jobs, June 1983: 'Marchers crossing Western Avenue, Ealing, yesterday (Photograph: John Voos).' *The Times*, 4 June 1983.

rhetoric against each other. However, an electoral Alliance was formed between the new party and the Liberals to fight the 1983 General Election. In that election the Alliance ran very close to Labour in the total popular vote, though gaining few seats in parliament: Labour's sources of strength were almost exclusively in the old industrial areas, and it decreasingly looked like a party with any appeal in the more prosperous parts of Britain.

I draw this book to a close, not with a whimper, but with a jest, a jest which focuses the attention on the important issue that, while visual evidence can add immensely to our understanding of past and present, it must be approached with all the care that historians lavish on other forms of evidence. *Plate 149* appeared in the north London local newspaper *The Hampstead and Highgate Express* on 23 July 1982. The caption underneath read: 'Police making their first arrest at Parliament Hill fields on Sunday'. Were this photograph to be lodged in the archives, almost certainly this is the caption which would be recorded, together with a brief reference to an anti-nuclear demonstration, originally planned by a group calling themselves 'Nudes Against Nukes'. Provided simply with that information, a historian of the future could quite well put a wrong construction on this photograph. Only if one reads through to the end of the accompanying news story does it emerge that the man arrested had absolutely nothing to do with the demonstration but had in fact been recognized by a policeman as someone who was wanted at that time in connection with a totally different matter.

The vineyard of evidence in which historians daily toil is in fact a minefield. Yet it is from the evidence that I must endeavour to frame my conclusions to this study. On 28 September 1983, Sir John Hoskyns, formerly head of Mrs Thatcher's Policy Unit, in a lecture to the Institute of Directors entitled 'Conservatism is not Enough' gave his explanation of Britain's decline:

> Over the past thirty years, we have suffered the consequences of a massive failure of intelligence and nerve on the part of an inbred political establishment. . . . I do not believe that [the] conventions, culture and machinery which failed us between 1950 and 1980, will somehow succeed between 1980 and 2000.

'For the purposes of government,' he continued, 'a country of 55 million people is forced to depend on a talent pool which could not sustain a single multi-national company'. Conservative politicians saw 'Britain as a canvas on which the young MP . . . can paint his political self-portrait, making his way in the world until he holds one of the great offices of state, finally retiring full of honour and respectability'.[7]

This diagnosis may be set beside a feature on British universities presented a few days earlier in the *Observer Colour Supplement*.[8] One section identified 'the socially smart "Sloane" [cf 'Sloane Rangers', from fashionable Sloane Street in London] universities' and colleges within universities. The upper class which I have introduced from time to time throughout this book lives on, and its younger members can be encountered at Oxford (particularly at New College, Magdalen and Christ Church), Cambridge (particularly Trinity, Magdalene and King's), Exeter, Durham, Bristol, Southampton, St Andrews, Kent, York 'and, marginally, Edinburgh'. Hoskyns' description of the attitudes of the young Conservative MP is brilliant. But the indictment cannot be limited to one alleged political establishment; it must be applied to the entire self-defining upper class

149 Nudes against Nukes, July 1982: 'Police making their first arrest at Parliament Hill fields on Sunday' (John Gogill news photograph, printed in *Hampstead and Highgate Express*, 23 July 1982).

from which all of the different interlocking 'establishments' are drawn. This upper class, though poorly educated compared with its European counterparts, has continuously fostered the notion, unfortunately very readily accepted throughout society, that British ways are not just best, but eternal. In tacit collaboration with the major unions this class has encouraged belief in the divine right of the big battalions, at the expense of genuine innovation and enterprise.

However, this upper class also created and prolonged the anglican compromise, which has ensured that in so many ways, even in 1983, the amenities of British stability and tolerance still compared favourably with the social mores of other developed countries. To blame a class is not to provide a full answer, since from the Second World War onwards there have been powerful figures from outside the upper class in all British governments. Nowhere has there been a clear perception of the interrelationship between educational, economic and political institutions and a determination to attack the roots of the problem: instead the fire of reform has been burnt up uselessly in the irrelevant incantations of the professional left, which, determined either to identify a small *capitalist* class, or to excoriate the entire bourgeoisie, misses the existence of a very real *upper* class.

If we turn purely to the realm of economics, I am not sure that the serious miscalculations and wrong decisions go back as far as some commentators have suggested. The main failing from the late nineteenth century onwards was the neglect of industrial training. On the major economic indicators (and for that matter, most political and social ones as well) Britain, though obviously subjected to an increasing competition which could not just be made to disappear, was not, up till the Second World War, doing all that badly, when worldwide economic circumstances are taken into account. At the end of the Second World War, if anything, Britain had (given the realities of American and Russian power) greater opportunities than any of her direct competitors. It was, decisively, in the middle fifties that governments, civil servants and economic advisors allowed priorities to switch to consumption rather than production, while exaggerating all the other unfortunate features of British economic and political policy which I have already described. The British disease got sharply worse in the 1970s; in the eighties it appeared that the proposed 'cures' were worse than the disease itself.

This chronology does not sit well with the thesis of growing corporatism. Dr Middlemas saw the decisive swing towards corporatism as having been brought about by the circumstances of the First World War without anyone deliberately intending it; after the war, however, he maintained it was deliberate policy to develop the corporativist momentum, though the policy was cloaked in secrecy. To Middlemas, the process was greatly extended during the Second World War when, indeed, Churchill recognized the unions as 'an estate of the realm'. It reached a climax in the postwar years with trade unions and employers' organizations bargaining directly with government, while parliament itself had no real role in the government of the country. Speaking for myself, I have to say that I find this analysis grossly exaggerated. During the evolution of parliamentary government in the nineteenth century, Britain was very much a pluralist society, with many different pressure groups having a direct effect on political decision making. What we have seen during the First World War and after is the rise of new groups, and the decline of old ones. Through the participation dimension of war, trade union bargaining power has certainly increased greatly. But it seems to me perverse to lay so much emphasis on the direct power of employers' organizations, when many of the politicians most continuously in power were themselves drawn from the same social class as the major employers.

From images (as in *Plate 149*) I have, of course, turned back to controversies. The modernization thesis has not offered much help, though it forms a convenient shorthand for making the point that in broad outline the major transformations taking place in Britain were but local manifestations of world-wide trends. This book has sought to get behind the trends to some of the detail; it has been concerned with 'our' Britain as much as 'our' century. Within the limited frame, the significance in social change of two world wars and, perversely, of the tiny Falklands war, have stood out. In no way, of course, does that suggest that wars are necessary for change. That equation is as false as the one which asserts that the virtues of secular anglicanism, of tolerance, of consensus and co-operation, must be replaced by conflict and confrontation to produce economic growth. Britain has suffered from too many of the wrong kind of compromises: nevertheless co-operation builds, conflict destroys.

# Notes

## Chapter One
### Into the Twentieth Century: 1900–1914

1 Peter N. Stearns, *European Society in Upheaval: Social History since 1750* (1975), p. 2.
2 Donald Read, *Edwardian England* (1972), p. 26.
3 *Parliamentary Papers*, 1914, XLI, Cd.7190, pp. 6–8.
4 C. F. G. Masterman, *The Condition of England* (1909), pp. 57–8.
5 L. C. Money, *Riches to Poverty* (1905), 1913 edition, p. 202.
6 *First Annual Report of the Medical Research Committee, 1914–15*, *Parliamentary Papers*, 1914–16, XXXI, Cd.8101, pp. 3–5.
7 Cd.7190, p. 8.
8 R. H. Tawney, 'The Abolition of Economic Controls, 1918–21', in *Economic History Review*, 1943, p. 1.
9 *Birmingham Magazine*, 1898.
10 *Condition of England*, p. 58.
11 A. L. Bowley, *The Division of the Product of Industry* (1919), p. 18.
12 C. S. Peel, *The Eat-Less-Meat Book* (1917), p. 23.
13 *Annual Report of the Local Government Board, 1913–14*, *Parliamentary Papers*, 1914, XXXVIII, Cd.7610, p. xii.
14 George Sims, *Living London. Its work and its play. Its humour and its pathos. Its sights and its scenes*, vol. II (1903), p. 321.
15 Quoted in Catherine Cline, *E. D. Morel, 1873–1924: The Strategies of Protest* (1980), p. 60.
16 Quoted in D. Newsome, *Godliness and Good Learning* (1961), p. 202.

## Chapter Two
### The Great War and its Consequences

1 Paul Thompson, *The Edwardians* (1975), p. 269.
2 Ross McKibbin, *The Evolution of the Labour Party 1910–1924* (1974), p. 239.
3 Martin D. Pugh, 'Politicians and the Woman's Vote 1914–18', in *History*, October 1974; *Politics and the Reform of the Franchise 1880–1920* (1978), and *Votes for Women* (Historical Association pamphlet), 1979.
4 David H. Close, 'The Collapse of Resistance to Democracy: Conservatives, Adult Suffrage, and Second Chamber Reform, 1911–1928', *Historical Journal*, vol. XX no. 4 (1977), p. 898.

5 L. Housman (ed.), *Letters of Fallen Englishmen* (1930), p. 150.
6 *Letters of a Durisdeer Soldier* (no date), p. 84.
7 Alan Bishop (ed.), *Chronicle of Youth: Vera Brittain's War Diary 1913–17* (1981), p. 305.
8 Note by Secretary of the War Babies and Mothers League, 1915. Women's Collection, Imperial War Museum, BO4.
9 *Report of Board of Education 1914–15*, *Parliamentary Papers*, 1916, VIII, Cd.8274, p. 1.
10 *House of Commons Debates*, 10 August 1917.
11 *Ibid.*
12 *Parliamentary Papers*, 1917–18, XIV, Cd.8663, p. 31.
13 *Parliamentary Papers*, 1917–18, XIV, Cmd.8731, and *Parliamentary Papers*, 1918, XXVI, Cmd.9087.
14 P. A. Sorokin, *Man and Society in Calamity* (1943); G. W. Baker and D. D. Chapman (eds), *Man and Society in Disaster* (1962); A. H. Barton, *Social Organization under Stress* (1963); F. C. Iklé, *The Social Impact of Bomb Destruction* (1958).
15 *Parliamentary Papers*, 1914–16, L, Cd.8005.
16 See Arthur Marwick, *The Deluge: British Society and the First World War* (1965), pp. 232–5, and the sources cited there.
17 *The Times*, 1 March 1915.
18 *Parliamentary Papers*, 1917–18, XIV, Cd.8662, p. 2.
19 *Observer*, 21 October 1917.
20 Gail Braybon, *Women Workers in the First World War* (1981), esp. chaps. 6, 7 and 8.
21 *Parliamentary Papers*, 1917–18, XIV, Cd.8570, p. 7.
22 *New Statesman*, 23 June 1917.
23 Robert Roberts, *The Classic Slum* (1971), p. 174.
24 Marion Kozak, 'Women Munition Workers in the First World War', PhD dissertation, University of Hull 1976.
25 R. D. Blumenfeld, *All In A Life Time*, pp. 51 and 9. Sadler is quoted in A. P. Newton (ed.), *The Empire and the Future* (1916), p. 4.
26 W. H. Dawson, *After War Problems* (1917), p. 7.
27 Paul Nash, *Outline, An Autobiography and Other Writings* (1949), pp. 210–11.
28 Leicester Galleries, *Exhibition No. 258, May 1918*, pp. 4–5.
29 P. G. Konody, Introduction to *Modern War: Paintings by C. R. W. Nevinson* (1917).
30 K. L. Nelson, *The Impact of War on American Life* (1971), Introduction.

31 M. G. Fawcett, *The Women's Victory and After: Personal Reminiscences 1911–1918* (1920).

## Chapter Three
## The Twenties

1 See in particular, Keith Burgess, *The Challenge of Labour: The Shaping of British Society 1850–1930* (1980), chapters 5 and 6.
2 James E. Cronin, 'Coping with Labour, 1918–1926', chapter 6 in *Social Conflict and the Political Order in Modern Britain*, (1982) edited by James E. Cronin and Jonathan Schneer.
3 The argument is impressively set out in Keith Middlemas, *Politics in Industrial Society: The Experience of the British System since 1911* (1979).
4 J. A. Dowie, '1919–20 is in Need of Attention', in *English Historical Review* (1975); D. Aldcroft, *The Interwar Economy: Britain 1919–1939* (1970); S. Glynn and J. Oxborrow, *Interwar Britain: A Social and Economic History* (1976).
5 *Nation*, 13 November 1926.
6 R. F. Harrod, *The Life of John Maynard Keynes* (1951) p. 357.
7 P.R.O., CAB23/15, 606 (5 August 1919).
8 Cronin, 'Coping with Labour', pp. 119–120.
9 These quotations are from Cronin pp. 113–116.
10 Cronin, p. 119. W. Kendall, *The Revolutionary Movement in Britain, 1900–1921* (1969), p. 195. Kenneth Morgan, in his elegant analysis of this period, *Consensus and Disunity* (1979), shrewdly notes (p. 53) that reports of revolutionary activity 'were taken less seriously by the leading members of the government than they were by liberal-minded historians of the 1960s'.
11 P.R.O., CAB23/9, 521(2) (28 January 1919).
12 W. Gallacher, *Revolt on the Clyde* (1936), p. 221.
13 *Morning Post*, 4 August 1919.
14 P.R.O., CAB23/21, 26(20) and 27(20).
15 P.R.O., CAB23/22 (10 August 1920).
16 *The Times*, 14 April 1921.
17 *The Times*, 19 April 1926.
18 G. A. Phillips, *The General Strike* (1976), pp. 208–9.
19 Quoted in W. J. Reader, *Imperial Chemical Industries: A History*, vol. 2 (1975), pp. 24–5.
20 Middlemas, *Politics in Industrial Society*, pp. 20–21.
21 L. McNeil Weir, *The Tragedy of Ramsay MacDonald: A Political Biography* (1938); David Marquand, *Ramsay MacDonald* (1977); Robert Skidelsky, *Politicians and the Slump* (1967); and Ross McKibbin, 'The Economic Policy of the Second Labour Government 1929–31', *Past and Present*, 1975, no. 63.

## Chapter Four
## The Thirties

1 See Tony Aldgate, 'Comedy, Class and Containment: The British Domestic Cinema of the 1930s', chapter 15 in *British Cinema History* (1983), edited by James Curran and Vincent Porter.

2 Ben Pimlott, *Labour and the Left in the 1930s* (1977), p. 196.
3 Quoted in Kenneth Harris, *Attlee* (1982), p. 169.
4 Henry Pelling, *The British Communist Party* (1958), p. 192.
5 John Stevenson and Chris Cook, *The Slump: Society and Politics During the Depression* (1977), p. 244.
6 A. Marwick, 'Middle Opinion in the Thirties, Planning, Progress and Political "Agreement"', *English Historical Review*, 1964.
7 Charles Loch Mowat, *Britain Between the Wars* (1955), pp. 495–8.
8 P. Collison, *Cutteslowe Walls: A Study in Social Class* (1963).
9 Philip Corrigan, 'Film Entertainment as Ideology and Pleasure: Towards a History of Audiences', chapter 2 in *British Cinema History* (1983), edited by James Curran and Vincent Porter.

## Chapter Five
## World War Two

1 *Monty Meets the Factory Workers*, Imperial War Museum Film Archives.
2 BBC Written Archives: 'Reconstruction-Political ("Working Man") Talks', Acc.No.1644.
3 M. Cosens, *Evacuation: A Social Revolution* (January 1940); W. Boyd (ed.), *Evacuation in Scotland* (1942); W. Padley and M. Cole, *Evacuation Survey* (1943); R. Titmuss, *Problems of Social Policy* (1950), pp. 122ff, 174ff, 437, 516; Women's Group on Public Welfare, *Our Towns* (1943).
4 *Current Affairs*, 5 December 1942.
5 *Mass Observation*, File 431.
6 *Parliamentary Papers*, 1941–42, IV, Cmd.6394, p. 25.
7 *British Industry*, October 1940.
8 José Harris, *William Beveridge: A Biography* (1977), pp. 380–81.
9 Mass Observation, File No. 2067 and 2149; J. Mackay, 'Archway Letter', 8 April 1942, Mackay Collection, Imperial War Museum.
10 Social Insurance and Allied Services (The Beveridge Report), *Parliamentary Papers*, 1942–43, VI, Cmd.6404.
11 P.R.O., S.I.C. (32), 20 May 1942.
12 *The Times*, 3 December 1942.
13 Arthur Marwick, *The Home Front* (1976), p. 130 (drawing on P. J. Grigg papers, Churchill College, Cambridge); Paul Addison, *The Road to 1945* (1975), p. 217.
14 Beveridge Papers, VII, 36, British Library of Political and Economic Science; Attlee Papers, University College, Oxford – see Kenneth Harris, *Attlee* (1982), pp. 220–21.
15 Quoted by Charles Graves, *The Women in Green* (1948), p. 129.
16 Doris White, *D for Doris V for Victory* (1981), p. 81.
17 Appendix to *Report on Pensionability of Unestablished Civil Service*, *Parliamentary Papers*, 1945–6, XII, Cmd.6942.

**18** Sidney Pollard, *The Wasting of the British Economy* (1982), p. 124.

**19** N. M. Hunnings, *Film Censors and the Law* (1967), p. 114, and Michael Balfour, *Propaganda in War 1939–1945* (1979), pp. 57–60.

**20** See 'Mirror, 1937–1945', in *Paper Voices: The Popular Press and Social Change 1935–1965*, by A. C. H. Smith (1975).

**21** A. Marwick, 'Print, Pictures, and Sound: The Second World War and the British Experience', in *Daedalus* (Fall 1982), p. 150.

**22** José Harris, 'Some Aspects of Social Policy in Britain During the Second World War', in Wolfgang Mommsen, *The Emergence of the Welfare State in Britain and Germany* (1981), p. 249, *Beveridge*, pp. 380–81.

**23** John Macnicol, *The Movement for Family Allowances, 1918–45* (1980), p. 195.

**24** R. Titmuss, *Problems of Social Policy* (1950), p. 508.

**25** Macnicol, pp. 195–6.

**26** *Ibid*, p. 178.

## Chapter Six
### Postwar Britain: 1945–1951

**1** David Butler, *The Electoral System in Britain* (1953), p. 184.

**2** *Ibid*, p. 177; R. McCallum and A. Readman, *The British General Election of 1945* (1947).

**3** J. B. Priestley, *Three Men in New Suits* (1945), p. 168.

**4** Joe Gormley, *Battered Cherub* (1982), p. 28.

**5** J. L. Hodson, *The Way Things Are* (1947), p. 24.

**6** John Braine, *Room at the Top* (1957), p. 153.

**7** House of Commons Debates, vol. 422, col. 43ff.

**8** Pollard, *Wasting of the British Economy*, chapters 4 and 7.

**9** M.R.C. Report, 1945–1948, *Parliamentary Papers*, 1948–49, XVIII, Cmd.7846, p. 13.

**10** Quoted in Mary Banham and Bevis Hillier (eds), *A Tonic to the Nation: The Festival of Britain 1951* (1976), p. 21.

**11** Quoted in *Ibid*, p. 196.

**12** Quoted in *Ibid*, pp. 165–6.

**13** *Ibid*, p. 14.

## Chapter Seven
### The Early and Middle Fifties

**1** Peter Chambers and Amy Landreth (eds), *Called Up* (1955), p. 32, 178.

**2** King George's Jubilee Trust, *Citizens of Tomorrow* (1955).

**3** Basil Spence, *Phoenix at Coventry: The Building of a Cathedral* (1962), pp. 86–7, on which this paragraph is based.

**4** Personal recollection: I was there. Uncorroborated personal testimony, of course, is a dangerous source for the historian.

**5** L. Epstein, *British Politics in the Suez Crisis* (1964), pp. 147ff.

**6** Tom Maschler (ed), *Declaration*( 1957), p. 155.

## Chapter Eight
### The Cultural Revolution: 1959–1973

**1** George Brown, *In My Way* (1971), p. 29.

**2** *Parliamentary Papers*, 1959–60, IX, Cmnd.1191, pp. 3–4.

**3** *Ibid*, p. 7.

**4** Christian Economic and Social Research Foundation, *Sixth Annual Report on Drunkenness Among Persons Under 21 in England and Wales 1950–1958* (1959), p. 5.

**5** This television news film can be viewed in the Open University TV programme, *Images of Violence*, Programme 8 in the series Conflict and Stability in the Development of Modern Europe.

**6** *Ibid*.

**7** Callaghan and Nossiter are quoted in T. A. Critchley, *The Conquest of Violence* (1970), p. 1.

**8** David Lockwood, 'The "New Working Class"', *Archives Européennes de Sociologie* (1960), pp. 248–59; Ferdynand Zweig, *The Worker in an Affluent Society* (1961).

**9** Quoted in R. Fraser (ed), *Work: Twenty Personal Accounts*, vol. 2 (1968), pp. 88–9.

**10** See for example John Hill, 'Working-Class Realism and Sexual Reaction: Some Theses on the British "New Wave"', in James Curran and Vincent Porter (eds) *British Cinema History* (1983), pp. 303–11.

## Chapter Nine
### Recession: 1973–1980

**1** Central Office of Information, *Britain 1981: An Official Handbook* (1981), pp. 303–4.

**2** *Britain 1974: An Official Handbook* (1974), p. 353.

**3** *Royal Commission on the Press: Final Report* (1977), *Parliamentary Papers*, 1976–77, XL, Cmnd.6810.

**4** *The Times*, 3 April 1979.

**5** Thomas J. Cottle, *Black Testimony* (1978), p. 116.

**6** Germaine Greer, *The Female Eunuch* (1970), p. 11.

**7** Stephen Willats, *The Lurky Place* (1978), quoted in *Art and Artists*, October 1982.

**8** Michael Newman in *Art and Artists*, October 1982.

## Chapter Ten
### Britain Today

**1** The accounts given here of these events are drawn from *The Times* and other newspapers.

**2** *The Brixton Disorders 10–12 April 1981 (Scarman Report)*, *Parliamentary Papers*, Cmnd.8427, November 1981.

**3** See Philip Ziegler, *Crown and People* (1978), esp. chapter 9.

**4** *The Times*, 30 July 1981.

**5** *New Society*, 7 April 1983.

**6** Printed in the *Observer*, 21 August 1983.

**7** Reported in *The Times*, 29 September 1983.

**8** *Observer*, 25 September 1983.

# Primary and Secondary Sources: A Brief Note

Any historical account is composed from primary sources (the raw materials of history) and secondary sources (books and articles written by other historians). This brief note merely offers some clues as to the materials I have used, and some hints for further reading.

## I IMAGES

(a) The major repositories from which photographs and other visual materials were obtained are: Imperial War Museum, National Portrait Gallery for the *Daily Herald* photos, now removed to the National Museum of Photography, Film and Television, Bradford; GLC Library; Leeds Public Library; Liverpool Corporation; Mitchell Library, Glasgow; Strathclyde Regional Archives; Fawcett Library; BBC Hulton Picture Library; Popperfoto; Fox Photos (now Keystone); *The Times*; *The Guardian*; National Coal Board; John Topham Picture Library; British Petroleum; Central Office of Information; National Film Archive and the University of Kent Centre for Study of Cartoons and Caricature.

(b) For secondary studies on photography and other visual evidence a good start is provided by the University of Delaware, *Visual History: An Introduction and Selected Bibliography* (1981). *Photography: A Concise History* (1981) by Ian Jeffrey is exactly what it says, and has a useful bibliography. Susan Sontag, *On Photography* (1977) is rather too elaborate for me. Charles Craig's CNAA thesis 'The British Documentary Photograph as a Medium of Information and Propaganda During the Second World War, 1939–1945' (1982) is far and away the best thing yet in the field; it will I hope be published before too long. Another important pioneering work is Eric J. Evans and Jeffrey Richards, *Britain in Postcards 1870–1930* (1980).

## II CONTROVERSIES

(a) Much of the primary material for twentieth-century British social history is available in print, though for studying, for example, the attitudes of politicians towards 'revolution', 'corporatism', or social reform in wartime, the Cabinet and other ministerial papers in the Public Record Office are essential: such papers, at the time of writing, were available up till 1952. Invaluable private collections, helpful for assessing the reactions of those not in the seats of power, are housed in the Imperial War Museum, the Modern Records Centre at the University of Warwick, and at Churchill College, Cambridge. The Mass Observation Archive at the University of Sussex has a special value all of its own. But a fundamental source must always be the government reports, surveys, etc. mainly served up in the form of the Parliamentary Papers to which I refer from time to time in my chapter references. Alongside these must be placed the great social surveys: Hubert Llewellyn Smith, *New Survey of London Life and Labour* (9 vols, 1930–35) and D. Caradog Jones, *Social Survey of Merseyside* (3 vols, 1934). Such works as the decennial *Social Survey of England and Wales*, by A. Carr-Saunders and D. Caradog Jones and the two studies by Margaret Stacey and her associates, *Tradition and Change: A Study of Banbury* (1960) and *Power, Persistence and Change: A Second Study of Banbury* (1975) occupy that no-man's-land between primary and secondary which, for twentieth-century history, is as extensive and fraught with peril as that of the Great War. For the contemporary period the interviews collected by Tony Parker in *The People of Providence* (1983) speak worlds. Published memoirs, diaries and even collections of letters abound: Robert Roberts, *The Classic Slum* (1971) is itself a classic. *Memoirs of the Unemployed* (1934), edited by H. L. Beales and R. S. Lambert is moving; *Nella Last's War* (1982) is almost frightening, for a mere male at least. Students will be able to track down the masses of printed primary material through the bibliographies of the books in Sections (b) and (d) marked with an asterisk. As my text, I hope, has demonstrated, newspapers, periodicals, novels, radio programmes (the BBC Written Archives at Caversham is a wonderful place), films and television, as well as the other visual sources which I have been able to show in this book, are all vital.

(b) **Some standard general histories, covering most, or part of the period.** The Americans have told us a lot about ourselves: for the bonus of a study of the centuries preceding our own turn to Robert K. Webb, *Modern England: From the Eighteenth Century to the Present* (1969), while Alfred Havighurst's platitudinous title covers a sensible book, *Britain in Transition* (1979). The

French are worth listening to also, and I commend François Bédarida, *A Social History of England, 1851–1975* (1979) and Roland Marx, *La Grande-Bretagne Contemporaine 1890–1973* (1973). From among the natives no one has, or could, surpass A. J. P. Taylor's masterpiece, *English History, 1914–1945\** (1965), but, for the shorter period it covers, C. L. Mowat, *Britain Between the Wars\** (1955) remains an outstanding example of the historian's art. Lesser mortals have yielded the following: W. N. Medlicott, *Contemporary England, 1914–74\** (1976), Trevor Lloyd, *Empire to Welfare State: English History, 1906–1976* (1979), L. C. B. Seaman, *Post-Victorian Britain, 1902–1951* (1966), Keith Robbins, *The Eclipse of a Great Power: Modern Britain 1870–1975* (1983), C. J. Bartlett, *A History of Post War Britain, 1945–74* (1977) and my own *Britain in the Century of Total War 1900–67\** (1968). A. H. Halsey, *Trends in British Society Since 1900* (1972) is very useful, particularly for statistical information.

(c) **A few important articles.** To get a really clear insight into how historians work, how they painstakingly build up their representations of the past, how they get involved in controversies, one really has to look at examples of the product which is as characteristic of the ordinary working historian as the steak-and-kidney pie is of the ordinary English pub: the learned article. There was a time when the *English Historical Review* would have considered any article outside of the reign of Queen Victoria as contemptible journalism. Yet as far back as 1964 this august journal published my 'Middle Opinion: Planning, Progress, and Political "Agreement" in the 1930s' which, though I say it myself, is a good example of an article which has been constantly referred to and quoted from ever since; times change, and the volume for 1981 contains a fascinating article by T. J. Hollins, 'The Conservative Party and Film Propaganda Between the Wars'. A most stimulating article which added a new dimension to the argument over the effects of the First World War on the emancipation of women was Martin D. Pugh, 'Politicians and the Woman's Vote 1914–1918', *History* (1974); and an article which reopened what had seemed like the closed subject of government economic policy at the end of the First World War was J. A. Dowie, '1919–20 is in Need of Attention', *Economic History Review* (1975). Finally, two articles to demonstrate the range of important issues to which serious historians are now addressing themselves: E. M. Holtzman, 'The Pursuit of Married Love: Women's Attitudes Towards Sexuality and Marriage in Great Britain, 1918–1939', *Journal of Social History* (1982), and Ross McKibbin, 'Working-Class Gambling in Britain 1880–1939, *Past and Present* (1977).

(d) **Particular periods and topics.**

*1 Edwardian Britain*
There are two particularly excellent general studies: Donald Read, *Edwardian England\** (1972), and Paul

Thompson, *The Edwardians\** (1975), which is distinguished by its effective use of oral evidence; nor should one neglect the final sections of F. M. L. Thompson, *English Landed Society in the Nineteenth Century* (1963). Among the many primary works I would single out Mrs Pember Reeves, *Roundabout a Pound a Week* (1906), L. C. Money, *Riches and Poverty* (1905), and, above all, C. F. G. Masterman, *The Condition of England* (1909). Lastly, three specialist secondary works of great originality: the relevant sections of *Voices Prophesying War 1763–1984* (1966) by I. F. Clarke tell us much about Edwardian attitudes and fears, Richard Price, *An Imperial War and the British Working Class* (1972) illuminates a difficult, but important, area, and P. F. Clarke, *Lancashire and the New Liberalism* (1971) throws light much more widely than the title might suggest.

*2 Modernization, Corporatism and Major Economic Issues*
Reliable general economic histories are: Sidney Pollard, *The Development of the British Economy, 1914–1967* (1969), R. W. Breach and R. M. Hartwell, *British Economy and Society, 1870–1970* (1972), G. A. Phillips and R. T. Maddock, *The Growth of the British Economy 1918–1968* (1973), and S. Glynn and J. Oxborrow, *Inter-War Britain: A Social and Economic History* (1976). Books which engage with the increasingly desperate, and despairing, arguments over Britain's industrial production are: Barry Supple (ed), *Essays in British Business History* (1977), D. H. Aldcroft (ed), *The Development of British Industry and Foreign Competition, 1875–1914* (1968), N. K. Buxton and D. H. Aldcroft (eds), *British Industry Between the Wars* (1979), H. W. Richardson, *Economic Recovery in Britain 1932–39* (1967), B. W. E. Alford, *Depression and Recovery? British Economic Growth, 1918–1939* (1972), and M. W. Kirby, *The Decline of British Economic Power* (1981). Arguments relating to the growth of corporatism in British society will be found in Keith Middlemas, *Politics in Industrial Society* (1979), Michael Moran, *The Politics of Industrial Relations* (1977) and Peter Hennessy and Keith Jeffery, *States of Emergency: British Governments and Strike Breaking Since 1919* (1983). The notion of modernization can be followed through in Peter N. Stearns, *European Society in Upheaval* (1975); the link between modernization and war (subject of my next section) is made by K. L. Nelson, *The Impact of War on American Life* (1971); there have been no British takers. E. J. Hobsbawm, *Industry and Empire* (1968) is a miracle of compression from one of the country's most distinguished living historians.

*3 World Wars I and II: The War and Social Change Debate*
(i) War seen as having little, no, or merely negative effects: Havighurst, Robbins (see Section (b)), H. and M. Wickwar, *The Social Services* (1949), Derek Fraser, *The Evolution of the Welfare State* (1973), Ross McKibbin, *The Evolution of the Labour Party*

1910–1924 (1974), Martin Pugh, *Electoral Reform in War and Peace, 1906–18* (1978), and *Women's Suffrage in Britain, 1867–1928* (1980), Gail Braybon, *Women Workers in the First World War* (1981), Pat Thane (ed) (and many of her contributors), *The Origins of British Social Policy* (1978), John Macnicol, *The Movement for Family Allowances 1918–45* (1980), Angus Calder, *The People's War* (1970), Henry Pelling, *Britain and the Second World War* (1970).

(ii) Seeing a positive interrelationship between war and social change: Taylor, Marwick (see Section (b)), Arthur Marwick, *The Deluge: British Society and the First World War* (1965), *War and Social Change in the Twentieth Century* (1974), *The Home Front: The British and the Second World War* (1976), *Women at War* (1977) and several articles; Maurice Bruce, *The Coming of the Welfare State* (1961), J. M. Winter (ed), *War and Economic Development* (1975), Alan Milward, *The Economic Effects of the World Wars on Britain* (1970), David H. Close, 'The Collapse of Resistance to Democracy: Conservatives, Adult Suffrage, and Second Chamber Reform, 1911–1928', *Historical Journal* (1977), Paul Addison, *The Road to 1945: British Politics in the Second World War* (1975), P. F. Clarke, *Liberals and Social Democrats* (1981), J. M. Winter, *Socialism and the Challenge of War: Ideas and Politics in Britain 1912–1918* (1974), Edward Smithies, *Crime in Wartime* (1982), Marion Kozak, 'Women Munition Workers during the First World War', Hull University PhD thesis (1977), and Bernard Waites, 'Some Aspects of Class and Status in England 1910–1920', Open University PhD thesis (1982).

*4 Revolution, Stability, and the Inter-War Years*
Among those who think that there was revolution around somewhere are: Walter Kendal, *The Revolutionary Movement in Britain, 1900–1921* (1969), James E. Cronin, *Industrial Conflict in Modern Britain* (1979), James E. Cronin and Jonathan Schneer, *Social Conflict and the Political Order in Modern Britain* (1982), and Keith Burgess, *The Challenge of Labour* (1980). Among those who do not are: Kenneth O. Morgan, *Consensus and Disunity: The Lloyd George Coalition Government 1918–1922* (1979), John Stevenson and Chris Cook, *The Slump: Society and Politics During the Depression* (1978), Ben Pimlott, *Labour and the Left in the 1930s* (1977), G. A. Phillips, *The General Strike* (1976), and Stuart MacIntyre, *Little Moscows: Communism and Working-Class Militancy in Inter-War Britain* (1980). For a really clear account of British social policy in the inter-war years Bentley B. Gilbert, *British Social Policy 1914–1939* (1970) cannot be beaten.

*5 Class: Attitudes of the British Élite*
The fundamental problem (purely in my personal view, of course) is that social classes as real phenomena in twentieth-century British society do not conform to the scenario laid down for them by Marx and the Marxists, or even to the slightly different version of Weber and the Weberians. I have endeavoured to open up a more pragmatic and historical approach in my *Class: Image*

and Reality in Britain, France and the USA since 1930 (1980) and 'Images of the Working Class since 1930' in *The Working Class in Modern British History: Essays in Honour of Henry Pelling* (1983), edited by Jay Winter. T. H. Marshall in *Citizenship and Social Class* (1950) tried to preserve the old scenario by bringing in the concept of citizenship as a force modifying class. The full Marxist analysis is persuasively argued in John Westergaard and Henrietta Resler, *Class in a Capitalist Society: A Study of Contemporary Britain* (1975), and John Scott, *The Upper Classes: Property and Privilege in Britain* (1982). However, W. D. Rubinstein in *Wealth and the Wealthy* (1980) and *Men of Property* (1981) shows how difficult it actually is to locate precisely the alleged capitalist class. The literature is immense, but can be followed up in the bibliographies of the few books noted here. The best-known denunciation of the British ruling élite for its neglect of the needs of industrial growth is Martin J. Wiener, *English Culture and the Decline of the Industrial Spirit* (1981).

*6 What Went Wrong After 1945?*
Exciting, if painful, is the relentless pursuit of first causes, causes behind causes, and alternative causes, in Sidney Pollard, *The Wasting of the British Economy* (1982). Michael Stewart, *The Jekyll and Hyde Years* (1974) exposes the futilities of the political system. Other cries of agony, or contempt, can be found in Jeremy Seabrook, *What Went Wrong?: Working People and the Ideas of the Labour Movement* (1978), R. Emmett-Tyrrell, *The Future That Doesn't Work* (1977), Isaac Kramnick (ed), *Is Britain Dying?* (1979), and Samuel H. Beer, *Britain Against Itself* (1982). The condition of British trade unionism is well conveyed by Robert Taylor, *The Fifth Estate: Britain's Unions in the Modern World* (1975).

*7 The Cultural Revolution and Other Aspects of Recent History*
I have dealt with the period more fully in my *British Society since 1945* (1982), and with certain aspects more deeply in my 'Room at the Top, *Saturday Night and Sunday Morning*, and the "Cultural Revolution" in Britain', in *Journal of Contemporary History* (1984). Important features can be studied in Kenneth Leech, *Youthquake: The Growth of a Counter Culture Through Two Decades* (1973) and Dick Hebdige, *Subculture: The Meaning of Style* (1979). Here, or possibly in the previous section, would be the place to note T. A. Critchley, *The Conquest of Violence* (1970) and the book by Hennessy and Jeffrey already mentioned. Very important are Elizabeth Wilson, *Only Halfway to Paradise: Women in Post War Britain, 1945–1968* (1980) and Ruth Adam, *A Woman's Place* (1975). Charlie Gillett's classic history of rock, *The Sound of the City* (new edition 1983) is indispensable.

*8 Literature, Art, and Mass Communications*
British broadcasting has found its Gibbon – Asa Briggs, *History of British Broadcasting* (5 vols 1970–79); British cinema has yet to do so: best bets are Roy Armes, *A*

*Critical History of British Cinema* (1979), James Curran and Vincent Porter (eds), *British Cinema History* (1983), and Jeffrey Richards and Anthony Aldgate, *Best of British: Cinema and Society 1930–1970* (1983). Here now is a rapid assortment of other relevant books: Samuel H. Hynes, *The Edwardian Frame of Mind* (1968), Paul Fussel, *The Great War in Modern Memory* (1975), Richard John Stone, *The Will to Believe: Novelists of the 1930s* (1982), Blake Morrison, *The Movement* (1976), Charles Harrison, *English Art and* *Modernism 1900–1939* (1981), and James Curran, Michael Gurevitch and Janet Woollacott (eds), *Mass Communications and Society* (1979).

The quickest way of amplifying these brief notes is to turn to the standard bibliography, *Modern British Society* (latest edition, 1979) by John Westergaard: this brings in just about everyone except, for some reason, myself.

# Acknowledgments for Illustrations

Associated Newspapers Group 89, 138; courtesy Lord Baldwin 47; City of Birmingham Public Library 5 (Benjamin Stone Collection), 15; Mark Boxer 133; British Aluminium Company 141; BBC Hulton Picture Library 4, 6, 8, 13, 16, 19, 20, 36, 37, 41, 42, 43, 46, 49, 50, 57, 65, 77, 78, 80, 82, 83, 84, 85, 87, 96, 97, 98, 99, 100, 107; British Leyland Cars Ltd 131; BP Oil Ltd 127; copyright of Cadbury Ltd 7; Central Office of Information 95, 121, 135; John Cogill 149; Contemporary Art Society 140; Fawcett Library, City of London Polytechnic 33; by courtesy of the Port of Felixstowe Company 129; Ford Motor Company 147; The Glasgow Herald and Evening News 105; Mitchell Library, Glasgow 34; People's Palace Museum, Glasgow 32; Greater London Council 17; Sally and Richard Greenhill 137; The Guardian 132, 145; Dyfed Cultural Services, Haverfordwest Library 14; courtesy Hoover Ltd 54; ICI PLC 39, 40; Imperial War Museum 21, 22, 24, 25, 26, 27, 28, 30, 31, 64, 66, 70, 73, 76; Centre for the Study of Cartoons and Caricature, University of Kent 138; Keystone 67 (Fox), 68 (Fox), 106 (Fox), 113 (Fox), 118 (Fox), 123 (Fox), 136 (Central Press); Christopher Lee 111; Leeds City Council, courtesy Pickard 101, 102; Leeds City Library 58; Liverpool Corporation, City Engineers Department 10; Liverpool Daily Post and Echo PLC 142; London Express News and Features 74, 93 (cartoon by David Low by arrangement with Trustees and the Evening Standard), 112, 134; Manchester Central Library 1; Manchester City Art Gallery 92; Kunsthalle, Mannheim 91; courtesy Marks and Spencer PLC 60; National Coal Board 86; National Exhibition Centre, Birmingham 120; National Film Archive 109, 110; National Portrait Gallery 52, 56 (Syndication International), 61, 62; John Sturrock, Network 143; Museum of the City of New York 55; City of Norwich Planning Division 124, 125; courtesy Peterlee Development Corporation 103; reprinted by permission of A. D. Peters and Co. Ltd 139; Popperfoto 69, 72, 79, 90, 94; Press Association 144; courtesy Mary Quant 114; Institute of Agricultural History and the Museum of Rural Life, University of Reading 2; courtesy Royal Women's Voluntary Service 75; Owned by Mr and Mrs J. J. Sher, Cape Town 115; reproduced by permission of Strathclyde Regional Council from an original in the Regional Archives 23; Sunday Times 126; Tate Gallery 63; The Times 119, 120, 146, 148; John Topham Picture Library 88, 104, 108, 117, 122, 130; Trades Union Congress Library 51; Victoria and Albert Museum 3, 81; courtesy of the Waddington Galley 116.

# Index

Figures in italics refer to pages on which illustrations appear

All books must be returned within specified
loan period. Charges will be assessed for each
book kept past the due date.

**LUBBOCK CITY-COUNTY LIBRARIES**